THE BUSINESS PLAN WORKBOOK

The Definitive Guide to Researching, Writing up and Presenting a Winning Plan

6th edition

COLIN BARROW, PAUL BARROW AND ROBERT BROWN

KOGAN PAGE

London and Philadelphia

Publisher's note

Every possible effort has been made to ensure that the information contained in this book is accurate at the time of going to press, and the publishers and authors cannot accept responsibility for any errors or omissions, however caused. No responsibility for loss or damage occasioned to any person acting, or refraining from action, as a result of the material in this publication can be accepted by the editor, the publisher or any of the authors.

First published in Great Britain by Kogan Page Limited 1988
Second edition 1992
Reprinted with revisions 1994, 1995 (twice)
Third edition 1998
Fourth edition 2001
Fifth edition 2005
Sixth edition 2008

120 Pentonville Road
London N1 9JN
United Kingdom
www.koganpage.com

525 South 4th Street, #241
Philadelphia PA 19147
USA

© Colin Barrow, Paul Barrow and Robert Brown, 1988, 1992, 1998, 2001, 2005, 2008

ISBN 978 0 7494 5231 5

British Library Cataloguing-in-Publication Data

A CIP record for this book is available from the British Library.

Library of Congress Cataloging-in-Publication Data

Barrow, Colin.
    The business plan workbook : the definitive guide to researching, writing up and presenting a winning plan / Colin Barrow, Paul Barrow and Robert Brown. -- 6th ed.
        p. cm.
    Includes index.
    ISBN 978-0-7494-5231-5
    1. Business planning. 2. Business enterprises--Finance. I. Barrow, Paul, 1948– II. Brown, Robert, 1937– III. Title.
    HD30.28.B3685 2008
    658.4'01--dc22
                                                            2008010356

Typeset by JS Typesetting Ltd, Porthcawl, Mid Glamorgan
Printed and bound in Great Britain by MPG Books Ltd, Bodmin, Cornwall

Contents

THE
BUSINESS
PLAN
WORKBOOK

Preface

In this workbook we have attempted to distil the knowledge and experience of the faculty at Cranfield School of Management gained in teaching the many thousands of students, business executives, entrepreneurs, public sector managers and those charged with running charitable, not-for-profit and social enterprises, who have taken part in our programmes.

Business planning is at the core of organizational and business strategy and is the essential precursor whether you are starting a new business, expanding an existing one, gaining approval for funding for a project, securing a grant or even entering a competition such as *Dragon's Den*. Over the years we have developed and tested this method of helping people to research and validate their proposals, and then to write up a business plan themselves.

Towards the end of each programme we invite a distinguished panel of senior bankers, venture capital providers and others involved in appraising proposal for external support of various kinds to review and criticise each business plan presentation. Their valued comments not only have spurred our programme participants to greater heights, but have given the faculty at Cranfield a privileged insight into the minds and thought processes of the principal providers of capital for new and growing enterprises.

This workbook brings together for the first time the processes and procedures required by the relative novice to write a business plan. Also included throughout are examples from the business plans of entrepreneurs and others who for the most part have gone on to start up successful enterprises.

In addition, we have included criticisms, warnings, and the experiences of backers, investors and of recently successful entrepreneurs when they have a direct bearing on writing and presenting a business plan.

We don't pretend to have made writing up business plans an easy task – but we do think we have made it an understandable one that is within the grasp of everyone with the determination to succeed.

Thousands of students have passed through Cranfield's business planning programmes going on to make their mark in business, charities and the public sector in this country and around the world.

How to use the workbook

The workbook contains 25 assignments that, once completed, should ensure that you have all the information you need to write and present a successful business plan. That is, one that helps to accomplish your objective, whether it is to gain a greater understanding of the venture you are proposing to start and its viability, or to raise outside money or gain support for your proposals from senior levels of management. Throughout the book the term 'entrepreneur' has been used interchangeably with innovator, manager, champion and similar terms used in a wide range of organizations in both the profit and not-for-profit sectors. The definition of entrepreneur used is that of someone who shifts resources from a low to a higher level of value added; this is the defining characteristic of almost everyone who writes a business plan regardless of the nature of their organization, actual or prospective.

The workbook does not set out to be a comprehensive textbook on every business and management subject – finance, marketing, law, etc. Rather, it gives an appreciation as to how these subjects should be used to prepare your business plan. The topics covered under each assignment will often pull together ingredients from different 'academic' disciplines. For example, elements of law and marketing will be assembled in the assignment in which you are asked to describe your service or product and its proprietary position (patents, copyright, design registration, etc).

For some of the assignments you will almost certainly need to research outside the material contained in this workbook. However, 'technical' explanations of such subjects as cash flow, market research questionnaire design and break-even analysis are included.

The assignments are contained in seven phases that, as well as having a practical logic to their sequence, will provide you with manageable 'chunks' either to carry out yourself at different times, or to delegate to partners and professional advisers. While it is useful to make use of as much help as you can get in preparing the groundwork, you should orchestrate the information and write up the business plan yourself. After all, it is your future that is at stake – and every prospective financier will be backing you and your ability to put this plan into action, not your scriptwriter.

The seven phases are:

Phase 1: History and position to date

Here you should describe your organization, innovation or business idea so far as you have already developed it. In particular, explain your aims, objectives and eventual aspirations.

Introduce your management team, yourself included, and show how your skills and experiences relate to this venture.

Describe your product or service, its current state of development or readiness for the market, and whether or not you have any proprietary rights such as a patent, copyright or registered design.

Phase 2: Market research

This involves identifying the data needed both to validate the need for what you are proposing and to decide upon the best start-up or growth strategy. In this phase you will be encouraged to gather market research data from as many sources as possible. Particular emphasis will be laid on researching customer needs, market segments and competitors' strengths and weaknesses. The appropriate research methodology and data sources are also described.

Phase 3: Competitive business strategy

This involves planning how you will operate each element of your business, based upon the information collected and analysed in earlier phases. In relation to your chosen product or service, the market segment(s) you plan to serve and the competitive situation, you will decide on such factors as price, promotion, location, and channels of distribution.

Phase 4: Operations

This involves detailing all the activities required to make your strategy happen. It will include such subjects as manufacturing, purchasing, selling, employing people, legal matters and insurance. Your business plan must demonstrate that you have taken account of all the principal matters that concern the operations of your venture.

Phase 5: Forecasting results

Based on the strategy evolved so far, in this phase you will carry out assignments enabling you to forecast the expected results of your venture. Projections will be made showing likely sales volume and value, pro forma profit and loss, cash-flow forecast and balance sheet, and a break-even analysis.

Although these first five phases are shown in sequence here and in the workbook, in practice you would expect to move backwards and forwards from phase to phase, as a result of new information or a modification of your earlier ideas.

Phase 6: Business controls

Here you must demonstrate how you will keep track of your business, both as a whole and for each individual element. As well as a bookkeeping system you will need sales and marketing planning records, customer record cards, personnel files and production control information.

Phase 7: Writing up and presenting your business plan

The workbook assignments, when completed, are not your business plan. They are intended to help you to assemble the information needed to write up your business plan. The plan will require substantial editing and rewriting; the way in which it is written up will undoubtedly influence the chances of getting a hearing, if you are seeking outside support for your venture.

Finally, you must give some thought as to how you will handle the meeting with your bank, venture capital house, other backers or the boss or organization to whom you have to 'sell' your ideas. Presentation skills and good planning will all help to make for a good 'production', and showbiz counts for a surprising amount when it comes to gaining support for new ideas.

Here are some guidelines to help you and your colleagues complete the business plan assignments:

1. Each assignment will contain:
    (a) An introduction or brief description of the content and purpose of the assignment, usually broken down into two or more stages.
    (b) Examples of how others preparing business plans have answered or commented on parts of the assignment.
    (c) An explanation or amplification of any technical topics that need to be understood immediately.
    At the end there is an assignment worksheet with some specific questions for you to answer concerning your business. On this page you will also find suggestions for further reading on broader aspects of the subject of the assignment.
2. When tackling assignments this work pattern has proved successful:
    (a) Read up on the assignment and draft your own answer to the questions.
    (b) Discuss your answers, and any problems concerning the assignment with your prospective business partner(s), colleagues or some other knowledgeable individual such as an advisor, bank manager or accountant. If you are on, or plan to go on, a business training programme, then your course tutor will also be able to help.
    (c) Revise your own answers in the light of these discussions – and then let your colleagues, and such other people as are involved, know your latest views on the assignment topic (you may need to go back and forth from steps (b) and (c) several times before you are entirely satisfied).
3. The contents of some assignments will suggest where and how to obtain the information needed to complete the assignment. However, don't expect to be told where to find all of the information about your business in these instructions. You will need to do some research yourself.
4. Example assignment completions taken from other business plans will also be presented to you in each assignment. These are presented only to give you a feel for the subject discussed. Your write-up of the assignment may need to be more or less elaborate, depending on your business.
5. The examples have been taken from actual business plans, but some have been changed in name and content, with some of the information

purposely missing. Therefore do not copy a sample, however good it may sound; use it to help you to understand the purpose of the business plan assignment only.

6. Try to write up as much information as possible after reading each assignment. In this way you will know what remains to be researched (and do not wait until your information flows in perfect English before recording it).

7. Try to strike a balance between qualitative and quantitative statements in writing up your assignments. That is, try to back up as many of your statements as possible with numbers and documented sources of information. However, do not include numbers just because you have them; make sure that they really serve a purpose.

8. *Finally*, before attempting to write up your business plan, make sure the answers to all the assignments are internally consistent – and if you have business partners, make sure you are all in substantive agreement both at each stage and with the final outcome.

Believe it or not, the joint founders of one business fell out as they were making their presentation to a venture capital panel. They had divided up the workload of preparing the business plan, and one had not told the other of some fairly major modifications to the product range, provoked as a result of completing the workbook assignments. (There was a happy ending but for a moment it was a close-run thing.)

Why prepare a business plan?

Perhaps the most important step in launching any new venture or expanding an existing one is the construction of a business plan. Such a plan must include your goals for the enterprise, both short and long term; a description of the products or services you will offer and the market opportunities you have anticipated for them; and finally, an explanation of the resources and means you will employ to achieve your goals in the face of likely competition. Time after time, research studies reveal that the absence of a written business plan leads to a higher incidence of failure for new and small businesses, as well as inhibiting growth and development.

Preparing a comprehensive business plan along these lines takes time and effort. In our experience at Cranfield on our programmes, anything between 200 and 400 hours is needed, depending on the nature of your business and what data you have already gathered. Nevertheless, such an effort is essential if you are to crystallise and to focus your ideas, and test your resolve about entering or expanding your business or pursuing a particular course of action. Once completed, your business plan will serve as a blueprint to follow which, like any map, improves the user's chances of reaching his destination.

There are a number of other important benefits you can anticipate arising from preparing a business plan:

- This systematic approach to planning enables you to make your mistakes on paper, rather than in the marketplace. One potential entrepreneur made the discovery while gathering data for his business plan that the local competitor he thought was a one-man band was in fact the pilot operation for a proposed national chain of franchised outlets. This had a profound effect on his market entry strategy!

  Another entrepreneur found out that, at the price he proposed charging, he would never recover his overheads or break even. Indeed, 'overheads' and 'break even' were themselves alien terms before he embarked on preparing a business plan. This naive perspective on costs is by no means unusual.

- Once completed, a business plan will make you feel more confident about your ability to set up and operate the venture. It may even compensate for lack of capital and experience, provided of course that you have other factors in your favour, such as a sound idea and a sizeable market opportunity for your product or service.

- Your business plan will show how much money is needed, what it is needed for and when, and for how long it is required.

  As under-capitalisation and early cash-flow problems are two important reasons why new business activities fail, it follows that those with a soundly prepared business plan can reduce these risks of failure. They can also experiment with a range of alternative viable strategies and so concentrate on options that make the most economic use of scarce financial resources.

  It would be an exaggeration to say that your business plan is the passport to sources of finance. It will, however, help you to display your entrepreneurial flair and managerial talent to the full and to communicate your ideas to others in a way that will be easier for them to understand – and to appreciate the reasoning behind your ideas. These outside parties could be bankers, potential investors, partners or advisory agencies. Once they know what you are trying to do, they will be better able to help you.

- Preparing a business plan will give you an insight into the planning process. It is this process that is important to the long-term health of a business, and not simply the plan that comes out of it. Businesses are dynamic, as are the commercial and competitive environments in which they operate. No one expects every event as recorded on a business plan to occur as predicted, but the understanding and knowledge created by the process of business planning will prepare the business for any changes that it may face, and so enable it to adjust quickly.

The empirical data also strongly supports the value of business planning. Studies consistently show that organizations with a strong planning ethos constantly outperform those who neglect this discipline.

Despite these many valuable benefits, thousands of would-be entrepreneurs still attempt to start without a business plan. The most common among these are businesses that appear to need little or no capital at the outset, or whose founders have funds of their own; in both cases it is believed unnecessary to expose the project to harsh financial appraisal.

The former hypothesis is usually based on the easily exploded myth that customers will all pay cash on the nail and suppliers will wait for months to be paid. In the meantime, the proprietor has the use of these funds to finance the business. Such model customers and suppliers are thinner on the ground than optimistic entrepreneurs think. In any event, two important market rules still apply: either the product or service on offer fails to sell like hot cakes and mountains of unpaid stocks build up, all of which eventually have to be financed; or it does sell like hot cakes and more financially robust entrepreneurs are attracted into the market. Without the staying power that adequate financing provides, these new competitors will rapidly kill off the fledgling business.

Those would-be entrepreneurs with funds of their own, or, worse still, borrowed from 'innocent' friends and relatives, tend to think that the time spent in preparing a business plan could be more usefully (and enjoyably) spent looking for premises, buying a new car or installing a computer. In short, anything that inhibits them from immediate action is viewed as time-wasting.

As most people's perception of their business venture is flawed in some important respect, it follows that jumping in at the deep end is risky – and unnecessarily so. Flaws can often be discovered cheaply and in advance when preparing a business plan; they are always discovered in the marketplace, invariably at a much higher and usually fatal cost.

There was a myth at the start of the internet boom that the pace of development in the sector was too fast for business planning. The first generation of dot.com businesses and their backers seemed happy to pump money into what they called a 'business' or 'revenue' model. These 'models' were simply brief statements of intent supported by little more than wishful thinking. A few months into the new millennium, a sense of realism came to the internet sector. In any business sector only ventures with well-prepared business plans have any chance of getting off the ground or being supported in later-stage financing rounds.

Live4now.com

Serena Doshi was working as an accountant at Schroders until a moment of serendipity changed her life: 'I called out an engineer to fix my printer,' said the 27-year-old from Fulham, London. 'This chap showed up and when we started talking, we just hit it off.' The young chap in question was 21-year-old Ewan MacLeod. Their business Live4now.com, a lifestyle site for 18- to 35-year-olds, raised £250,000 in seed capital, a further £500,000 from the US-based investment arm of Japan's Trans Cosmos, and was valued at £20 million within two years of writing up its first business plan.

But while the founders got on immediately, their business plan took a bit more work. In order to make their idea credible to prospective backers, Doshi spent six months working until 9 pm at Schroders then coming home and working until 3 am on the business plan.

What backers look out for

Business plans are written to be read: that in turn means that the readers' needs, however few or diverse, have to be carefully considered in the preparatory process. Lenders want to be sure their money is safe, investors need to be enticed by the expectation of future profits and managers, be they running a health service, utility company or a charity want to be convinced that the proposal is needed and likely to come in on time and on budget.

Almost every new venture needs finance and if you are in competition with others, say with another division of your company or a bank choosing who to lend to, then as well as the operational benefits of preparing a business plan, it is important to examine what financial backers expect from you, if you are to succeed in raising those funds.

It is often said that there is no shortage of money for new proposals – the only scarce commodities are good ideas and people with the ability to exploit them. From the potential entrepreneur's position this is often hard to believe. One major venture capital firm alone receives several thousand business plans a year. Only 500 or so are examined in any detail, fewer than 25 are pursued to the negotiating stage, and only six of those are invested in.

To a great extent the decision whether to proceed beyond an initial reading of the plan will depend on the quality of the business plan used in supporting the proposal. The business plan is the ticket of admission giving the entrepreneur or proposal champion the first and often only chance to impress prospective backers with the quality of the proposal.

It follows from this that to have any chance at all of getting financial and/or managerial support, your business plan must be the best that can be written and it must be professionally packaged.

In our experience at Cranfield the plans that succeed meet all of the following requirements.

EVIDENCE OF MARKET ORIENTATION AND FOCUS

CASE STUDY

Bookham Technologies

We saw the market opportunity and then went looking for the technology. That is the right way to do it.

Bookham Technologies (www.bookham.com) founded by Andrew Rickman, could well have been an example of a high-technology start-up in search of a market. With an honours degree in mechanical engineering from Imperial College, London and a PhD in integrated optics from the University of Surrey, Rickman certainly had the makings of a boffin. But an MBA from Cranfield changed his fervour for technology to an end in itself.

'Back in 1988 I came across the forerunners of the internet and it struck me at the time that optical fibre was going to become a very important part of the internet because it was the best way of transmitting lots and lots of information,' he says.

Communication via optical fibres rather than copper wires uses light instead of electrical signals to carry and process information and is ideally suited to the heavy data traffic of the internet age. Fibre-optic cables have been used for at least 10 years but the optical components at each end of the cables used to be expensive, involving the hand assembly of tiny lasers, filters and lenses.

This was the problem that Rickman set out to solve. He says, 'Our vision at the beginning of the business was to find a way of integrating all of the functions needed in optical components on to a chip in the same way that the electronics industry has done.' This simplification would allow automated volume manufacture, bringing down cost and encouraging growth in the use of the internet. 'The only thing that is likely to prevent the continued exponential growth in the use of the internet is that cost reduction in use does not come down fast enough.'

The business started in a room above the garage of his home, with his wife as company secretary. But the idea did not stem from academic research work that Rickman had carried out. Rickman designed the business model to meet a market need rather than to exploit an existing technology. He says, 'I had briefly worked in the venture-capital community and, at the outset of Bookham Technologies, formulated a model for the ideal technology company. We saw the market opportunity and then went looking for the technology. That is the right way to do it.'

Once the initial scientific breakthroughs had been made, the company raised private equity finance totalling $110 million over several rounds and had backing from 3i, Cisco, Intel and others. It was a very long road to travel with substantial challenges. Bookham, like Cisco, is a supplier of 'picks and shovels' to the internet market. The company when listed on the London Stock Exchange and the NASDAQ was valued at £5 billion making Rickman a billionaire, on paper at least.

Entrepreneurs must demonstrate that they have recognized the needs of potential customers, rather than simply being infatuated with an innovative idea. Business plans that occupy more space with product descriptions and technical explanations than with explaining how products will be sold and to whom usually get cold-shouldered by financiers. They rightly suspect that these companies are more of an ego trip than an enterprise.

Market orientation is not in itself enough. Backers want to sense that the entrepreneur knows the one or two things their business can do best – and that they are prepared to concentrate on exploiting these opportunities.

Two friends who eventually made it to an enterprise programme – and to founding a successful company – had great difficulty in getting backing at first. They were exceptionally talented designers and makers of clothes. They started out making ballgowns, wedding dresses, children's clothes – anything the market wanted. Only when they focused on designing and marketing clothes for the mother-to-be that allowed her still to feel fashionably dressed was it obvious they had a winning concept. That strategy built on their strength as designers and their experiences as former mothers-to-be, and exploited a clear market opportunity neglected at that time by the main player in the marketplace – Mothercare.

From that point their company made a quantum leap forward from turning over a couple of hundred thousand pounds a year into the several million pounds league in a few years.

EVIDENCE OF CUSTOMER AND USER ACCEPTANCE

Backers like to know that your new product or service will sell and is being used, even if only on a trial or demonstration basis.

The founder of Solicitec, a company selling software to solicitors to enable them to process relatively standard documents such as wills, had little trouble getting support for his house conveyancing package once his product had been tried and approved by a leading building society for its panel of solicitors.

If you are only at the prototype stage, then as well as having to assess your chances of succeeding with technology, financiers have no immediate indication that, once made, your product will appeal to the market. Under these circumstances you have to show that the 'problem' your innovation seeks to solve is a substantial one that a large number of people will pay for.

One inventor from the Royal College of Art came up with a revolutionary toilet system design that, as well as being extremely thin, used 30 per cent less water per flush and had half the number of moving parts of a conventional product, all for no increase in price. Although he had only drawings to show, it was clear that with domestic metered water for all households a distinct possibility and a UK market for half a million new units per annum, a sizeable acceptance was reasonably certain.

As well as evidence of customer acceptance, entrepreneurs need to demonstrate that they know how and to whom their new product or service must be sold, and that they have a financially viable means of doing so.

PROPRIETARY POSITION

Exclusive rights to a product through patents, copyright, trademark protection or a licence helps to reduce the apparent riskiness of a venture in the financier's eyes, as these can limit competition – for a while at least.

One participant on a Cranfield enterprise programme held patents on a revolutionary folding bicycle he had designed at college. While no financial institution was prepared to back him in manufacturing the bicycle, funds were readily available to enable him to make production prototypes and then license manufacture to established bicycle makers throughout the world.

However well protected legally a product is, it is marketability and marketing know-how generally that outweigh 'patentability' in the success equation. A salutary observation made by a US professor of entrepreneurship revealed that fewer than 0.5 per cent of the best ideas contained in the US *Patent Gazette* in the last five years have returned a dime to the inventors.

FINANCIERS' NEEDS

Anyone lending money to or investing in a venture will expect the entrepreneur to have given some thought to his or her needs, and to have explained how these can be accommodated in the business plan. This will apply even if the money is coming from an 'internal' source such as a parent company, a divisional budget or a government department.

Bankers, and indeed any other sources of debt capital, are looking for asset security to back their loan and the near certainty of getting their money back. They will also charge an interest rate that reflects current market conditions and their view of the risk level of the proposal. Depending on the nature of the business in question and the purpose for which the money is being used, bankers will take a 5- to 15-year view.

As with a mortgage repayment, bankers will usually expect a business to start repaying both the loan and the interest on a monthly or quarterly basis immediately the loan has been granted. In some cases a capital 'holiday' for up to two years can be negotiated, but in the early stage of any loan the interest charges make up the lion's share of payments.

Bankers hope the business will succeed so that they can lend more money in the future and provide more banking services such as insurance, tax advice, etc to a loyal customer. It follows from this appreciation of a lender's needs that lenders are less interested in rapid growth and the consequent capital gain than they are in a steady stream of earnings almost from the outset.

As new or fast-growing businesses generally do not make immediate profits, money for such enterprises must come from elsewhere. Risk or equity capital, as other types of funds are called, comes from venture capital houses, as well as being put in by founders, their families and friends.

Because the inherent risks involved in investing in new and young ventures are greater than for investing in established companies, venture capital fund managers have to offer their investors the chance of larger overall returns. To do that, fund managers must not only keep failures to a minimum; they have to pick some big winners too – ventures with annual compound growth rates above 50 per cent – to offset the inevitable mediocre performers.

Typically, a fund manager would expect, from any 10 investments, one star, seven also-rans and two flops. It is important to remember that despite this outcome, venture capital fund managers are only looking for winners, so unless you are projecting high capital growth, the chances of getting venture capital are against you.

Not only are venture capitalists looking for winners, they are also looking for a substantial shareholding in your business. There are no simple rules for what constitutes a fair split, but *Venture Capital Report*, a UK monthly publication of investment opportunities, suggested the following starting point:

- for the idea: 33 per cent;
- for the management: 33 per cent;
- for the money: 34 per cent.

It all comes down to how much you need the money, how risky the venture is, how much money could be made – and your skills as a negotiator. However, it is salutary to remember that 100 per cent of nothing is still nothing. So, all parties to the deal have to be satisfied if it is to succeed.

Venture capital firms may also want to put a non-executive director on the board of your company to look after their interests. You will have at your disposal a talented financial brain, so be prepared to make use of him or her, as these services won't be free – either you'll pay up front in the fee for raising the capital, or you'll pay an annual management charge.

As fast-growing companies typically have no cash available to pay dividends, investors can only profit by selling their holdings. With this in mind, the venture capitalist needs to have an exit route such as the Stock Exchange or a potential corporate buyer in view at the outset.

Unlike many entrepreneurs (and some lending bankers) who see their ventures as lifelong commitments to success and growth, venture capitalists have a relatively short time horizon. Typically, they are looking to liquidate small-company investments within three to seven years, allowing them to pay out to individual investors and to have funds available for tomorrow's winners.

So, to be successful your business must be targeted at the needs of these two sources of finance, and in particular at the balance between the two. Lending bankers ideally look for a ratio of £1 of debt to £1 of equity capital, but have been known to go up to £4–5. Venture capital providers will almost always encourage entrepreneurs to take on new debt capital to match the level of equity funding.

If you plan to raise money from friends and relatives their needs must also be taken into account in your business plan. Their funds can be in the form of debt equity, but they may also seek some management role for themselves. Unless they have an important contribution to make, by virtue of being an accountant or marketing expert or respected public figure, for example, it is always best to confine their role to that of a shareholder. In that capacity they can 'give' you advice or pass on their contacts and so enhance the worth of their (and your) shareholding, but they won't hold down a post that would be better filled by someone else. Alternatively, make them non-executive directors, which may flatter them and can't harm your business. Clearly, you must use common sense in this area.

One final point on the needs of financial institutions: they will expect your business plan to include a description of how performance will be monitored and controlled.

One budding entrepreneur blew an otherwise impeccable performance at a bankers' panel by replying when asked how he would control his venture: 'I'm only concerned with raising finance and getting my business started at the moment – once that's over I'll think about "bean counting".' He had clearly forgotten who owned the beans!

BELIEVABLE FORECASTS

Entrepreneurs are naturally ebullient when explaining the future prospects for their business. They frequently believe that 'the sky's the limit' when it comes to growth, and money (or rather the lack of it) is the only thing that stands between them and their success.

It is true that if you are looking for venture capital, then the providers are also looking for rapid growth. However, it's as well to remember that financiers are dealing with thousands of investment proposals each year, and already have money tied up in hundreds of business sectors. It follows, therefore, that they already have a perception of what the accepted financial results and marketing approaches currently are for any sector. Any new company's business plan showing projections that are outside the ranges perceived as acceptable within an industry will raise questions in the investor's mind.

Make your growth forecasts believable; support them with hard facts where possible. If they are on the low side, then approach the more cautious lending banker, rather than venture capitalists. The former often see a modest forecast as a virtue, lending credibility to the business proposal as a whole. But if you believe in your vision and have patience and resilience take your proposal to institutions that are up for big risks in return for the chance of big rewards.

Hotmail

In September 1988, Sabeer Bhatia arrived at Los Angeles International Airport. He had won a transfer scholarship to Caltech by being the only applicant in the entire world to get a passing score on the notorious Caltech Transfer Exam in 1988 (there are usually about 150 who give it a try). Sabeer had scored a 62 out of 100 – the next highest score was 42.

Sabeer intended to get his degrees and then to go home to work – probably as an engineer for a very large Indian company. He was following a modest path of life like his parents. His mother was an accountant at the Central Bank of India for her entire career and his father spent 10 years as a captain in the Indian Army.

But as a graduate student at Stanford, Sabeer was drawn to the basement of Terman auditorium. There, the speakers were entrepreneurs like Scott McNealy, Steve Wozniak and Marc Andressen. Their fundamental message was always the same: 'You can do it too.' When he graduated, Sabeer did not want to go home. So, along with Jack Smith, he took a job at Apple Computer. Sabeer could have worked at Apple for 20 or 30 years, but he got swept up in the decade's fever: you haven't lived until you've gone solo.

Sabeer met a man named Farouk Arjani. Arjani had been a pioneer in the word-processing business in the 1970s and had since become a special limited partner of Sequoia Ventures. The two hit it off and Arjani became Sabeer's mentor. What really set Sabeer apart for Arjani from the hundreds of entrepreneurs was the size of his dream. Even before he had a product, before he had any money behind him, he was completely convinced that he was going to build a major company that would be worth hundreds of millions of dollars.

In mid-1995, Sabeer began taking around a two-page executive summary business plan for a net-based personal database called JavaSoft. When Jack Smith, by now a partner in the venture – albeit a reluctant one – and Sabeer came up with the Hotmail idea in December, JavaSoft effectively became the front for Hotmail. Sabeer knew that Hotmail was such an explosive concept, he didn't want a less-than-ethical venture capitalist to reject him, then turn around and copy his idea. He kept showing JavaSoft and showed Hotmail only to those venture capitalists for whom he had gained respect. 'It was fine that they were rejecting JavaSoft. But in so doing, I got to see how their mind worked. If they rejected JavaSoft for stupid reasons, then I said thank you and left. If they rejected it for the right reasons, then I showed them Hotmail.'

Sabeer presented his business plan to Steve Jurvetson of Draper Fisher Jurvetson (DFJ). Jurvetson remembers:

> Sabeer's revenue estimates showed that he was going to grow the company faster than any in history. Most entrepreneurs have that trait, but they also are concerned with looking like a fool. Sabeer's projections were dismissed outright, but Sabeer's passionate belief was unchanged and he was right. He grew the subscriber base faster than any company in the history of the world.

One might have presumed that, since Sabeer had been rejected by 20 venture capitalists previously and was virtually a nobody, he would be grateful to accept DFJ's US$300,000 on their terms. The venture capitalists made the perfectly reasonable offer of retaining 30 per cent ownership on a US$1 million valuation. Sabeer held out for double that valuation, with DFJ's cut at 15 per cent. The negotiations got nowhere, so Sabeer shrugged, stood up and walked out of the door. His only other available option was a US$100,000 'friends and family' round that had been arranged as back-up – not nearly enough money. If he had gone that route, Hotmail wouldn't exist today. What actually happened was that DFJ relented; it called back the next day to accept 15 per cent.

It took enormous confidence to do what Sabeer did: first, to hide his real idea, and second, to hold out for the valuation that he thought the company deserved. Both of these actions are extremely rare. But Sabeer gives credit to the culture of Silicon Valley itself:

> Only in Silicon Valley could two 27-year-old guys get US$300,000 from men they had just met. Two 27-year-old guys who had no experience with consumer products, who had never started a company, who had never managed anybody, who had no experience even in software – Jack and I were hardware engineers. All we had was the idea. We didn't demo proof-of-concept software or a prototype or even a graphic printed on a piece of paper. I just sketched on Steve Jurvetson's whiteboard. Nowhere in the world could this happen but here.

On New Year's Eve just two years after writing the first draft of his business plan, Sabeer sold Hotmail to Microsoft in exchange for 2,769,148 of their shares. At that time those shares were worth US$400 million. It was barely nine years since Sabeer had stepped off his flight from Bangalore, India, with US$250 in his pocket – the limit allowed by Indian customs officials.

SUGGESTED FURTHER READING

Arundale, K (2007) *Raising venture capital finance in Europe: a practical guide for business owners, entrepreneurs and investors*, Kogan Page, London

Barrow, P (2004) *Raising finance: a practical guide to starting, expanding and selling your business*, Kogan Page, London

Berkery, D (2007) *Raising venture capital for the serious entrepreneur*, McGraw-Hill Professional, New York

Phase 1

History and position
to date

INTRODUCTION

Starting a new venture, whether it is a for-profit business, a social enterprise or public initiative, may seem a daunting task when you first start to gather ideas together and make tentative plans. Many would-be entrepreneurs (the word is used here in the economic sense as someone who shifts resource from a low to a higher value added task) after putting a toe in the water quickly pull back reckoning that either they don't have the skills, their business concept is not all that compelling or raising the money is going to be challenging, expensive and altogether too risky a proposition.

The first useful fact to know is that the rumour of calamities awaiting most new ventures is just that – an unfounded and incorrect piece of oft-repeated misinformation. An exhaustive study by Bruce A Kirchoff of the eight-year destinations of all 814,000 US firms founded in a particular year revealed that just 18 per cent actually failed, meaning that the entrepreneurs were put out of business by their financial backers, lack of demand or competitive pressures (Kirchoff, 1994). True, some 28 per cent of businesses closed their doors voluntarily, their founders having decided for a variety of reasons that either working for themselves or this particular type of business was just not for them.

But the majority of the businesses studied in Kirchoff's mammoth and representative study survived and in many cases prospered. With a degree of preparation, a fair amount of perspiration and a modicum of luck you can get started and may even, as in the 'Blooming Marvellous' case study in Assignment 1 describes, end up with a substantial, successful and growing enterprise. These first three chapters will help you shape up the framework of your venture. As the saying goes, 'To begin well is to end well.'

REFERENCE

Kirchoff, Bruce A (1994) *Entrepreneurship and dynamic capitalism*, Praeger, New York

Business purpose and aims

In this first assignment you should introduce your 'business' proposition to the future readers of your business plan. Explain something of how you arrived at your business idea, why you think people have a need for your product or service, and what your goals and aspirations for the business are. If your proposition needs financing, you could give some preliminary idea of how much you may need and what you intend to do with those funds. Remember, all these ideas are likely to be significantly modified later on – some more than others – but you need to have some idea at the outset of where you are going if you are to have any chance at all of getting there.

It may be useful to organize your information in this section using the pyramid of goals later in this chapter as a framework.

Mission statements and objectives are important in two main ways:

- to concentrate your own and your employees' efforts (rowing harder does not help if the boat is headed in the wrong direction);

- to concentrate attention on problems to be solved (problem solving is finding ways to get you from where you are to where you want to be).

Large organizations may spend long weekends at country mansions wrestling with the fine print of their mission statements; in principle, given the narrower scope of the new business, the task facing the new business owner should be less daunting.

To take mission statements and objectives first, as they are inevitably intertwined, these are direction statements intended to focus your attention on essentials, to encapsulate your specific competence(s) in relation to the markets/customers you plan to serve.

First, the mission should be narrow enough to give direction and guidance to everyone in the business. This concentration is the key to business success because it is only by focusing on specific needs that a small business can differentiate itself from its larger competitors. Nothing kills off a new business faster than trying to do too many different things at the outset.

Second, the mission should open up a large enough market to allow the business to grow and realize its potential.

Interestingly enough, one of the highest incidences of failure in small businesses is in the building trade. The very nature of this field seems to mitigate against being able to concentrate on any specific type of work, or on customer need. One successful new small builder defined his mission in the following sentence: 'We will concentrate on domestic house repair and renovation work, and as well as doing a good job we will meet the customers' two key needs: a quotation that is accurate, and starting and completion dates that are met.' When told this mission, most small builders laugh. They say it cannot be done, but then most go broke.

Ultimately, there has to be something unique about your business idea or yourself that makes people want to buy from you. That uniqueness may be confined to the fact that you are the only photocopying shop in the area, but that is enough to make you stand out (provided, of course, that the area has potential customers).

Also, within the objectives you need some idea of how big you want the business to be: your share of the market, in other words. It certainly is not easy to forecast sales, especially before you have even started trading, but if you do not set a goal at the start and instead just wait to see how things develop, then one of two problems will occur. Either you will not sell enough to cover your fixed costs and so lose money and perhaps go out of business, or you will sell too much and run out of cash – in other words, overtrade.

Obviously, before you can set a market share and sales objective you need to know the size of your market. We shall consider how to find that out in later assignments.

The 'size' you want your business to be is more a matter of judgement than forecast – a judgement tempered by the resources you have available to achieve those objectives and, of course, some idea of what is reasonable and achievable and what is not. You will find the range of discretion over a size objective seriously constrained by the financial resources at your disposal – or realistically available from investors and lenders – and the scope of the market opportunity.

It will be useful to set near-term objectives covering the next 18 months or so, and a longer-term objective covering up to five or so years.

In summary, the mission statement should explain:

- what business you are in and your purpose;

- what you want to achieve over the next one to three years, ie your strategic goal;

- how, ie your values and standards.

Above all, mission statements must be realistic, achievable and brief.

CASE STUDY

Blooming Marvellous

Judy Lever and Vivienne Pringle started Blooming Marvellous literally on a kitchen table back in 1983. Having attended a business start up course in London's Kensington, they put further flesh onto their big idea. Both were pregnant and after searching for the kind of fashionable clothes they used to wear and drawing a blank, they guessed they had found a gap in the market. They stated their purpose and goals as follows:

> Arising out of our experiences, we intend to design, make and market a range of clothes for mothers-to-be that will make them feel they can still be fashionably dressed. We aim to serve a niche missed out by Mothercare, Marks & Spencer, etc, and so become a significant force in the mail order fashion for the mothers-to-be market. We are aiming for a 5 per cent share of this market in the South-East, and a 25 per cent return on assets employed within three years of starting up. We believe we will need about £25,000 start-up capital to finance stock, a mail order catalogue and an advertising campaign.

They kept on their day jobs and would meet after work every day at Judy's house to answer enquiries, send out leaflets and despatch products in the post every day. They outsourced work to a pattern cutter, a small factory, some fabric suppliers, and eventually to a small distribution centre. After a year or so of modest sales they felt confident enough to set up their first business premises – a 1,200 sq ft warehouse on a business park staffed by four of the women who had been working in their distribution centre.

The company now employs 150 people, has 14 shops and has extended its range to include nursery products, toys, themed bedroom accessories and a separate brand called Mini Marvellous that caters for children aged 2–8 years. Over a third of sales come directly via their website (www. bloomingmarvellous.co.uk).

Contrast the clarity of this mission with the one below, and it is not too hard to see why Blooming Marvellous has succeeded where so many have failed.

CASE STUDY

iSKY

iSKY provides a complete outsourced customer-loyalty management solution to both electronic businesses and traditional companies seeking to enhance their customers' online and offline experiences before, during and after a purchase. Our customer loyalty management services use interactive one-to-one communications, enhanced by real-time, personalized data collection and management, to find, win, keep and enhance profitable customer relationships. We offer our clients a customized, fully integrated, web-enabled solution for interacting with their customers through a variety of media including real-time, text chat, e-mail, voice over internet protocol, telephone and facsimile.

iSKY had to pull its initial public offering (IPO) and rethink its strategy from the bottom up.

In contrast the Blooming Marvellous mission was evolved long before the internet was even thought of, yet its founders had no difficulty absorbing it into the core of what they did by adding just the single word 'internet' alongside 'mail order'. Even though they now derive much of their income from the internet, they still have not used words commonly found in technology-based companies' mission statements.

Many companies separate out their specific objectives, which they wish to keep confidential, from the mission statement, which they realize they must communicate widely, via meetings and company literature, to promote greater company cohesion and concentration.

Thus the first paragraph alone of the Blooming Marvellous statement above could serve as the mission statement, for communication to all employees. Remember also that mission statements will change over time, as the environment and the company progresses. Barrie Haigh, the founder of Innovex (www.innovex.com) revisited his mission statement with his top team for each of the six years after attending the Cranfield Business Growth Programme. Over that six-year period he took his business from £8 million a year turnover to a value of £550 million in a trade sale, netting himself some £350 million in the process.

Mission statements must not become too bland or too general. For example, can you tell what business this company is in, what it aims to achieve in the next three years and how?

> Our key strategy is the aggressive pursuit of quality and performance in providing a wide and comprehensive range of business and consumer services.
>
> Constantly developing these in line with our market driven approach to expanding into new areas of profitable growth, we are ready to meet the challenge of identifying and exploiting new opportunities where they exist.

No wonder that Sketchley plc, soon after the publication of the above in its *Annual Report*, was the subject of hostile takeover bids, ultimately failing and disappearing from the high street.

For the founders of Blooming Marvellous, the advantage of their clear mission statement lay in the fact that they could translate their principal objectives into specific key tasks and action plans. This plan consists of 'how to' statements to achieve specific objectives and goals.

Objectives within three years:

- Achieve 5 per cent market share in south-east England.

- Obtain a 25 per cent return on assets employed.

Tasks:

- Identify mailing lists and promotion media within three months.

- Design 12 items of fashion clothes within six months.

- Produce mail-order catalogue within nine months.

- Locate packaging and distributor organizations within six months.

Action plan:
Monday morning:

- Start design on product.

- Write for mailing-list details.

- Look up trade directories for distributors.

It would also be useful at this stage to explain how you arrived at your business idea, what makes you believe it will succeed, and why you want to go ahead with it now.

Safariquip

Julian McIntosh's business, Safariquip, equips safaris, or anyone else planning long overland travel. The corporate and institutional market – involving expeditions and surveys for oil or minerals, or other projects in the developing world – is just beginning to open up too.

The idea was born out of the difficulties McIntosh experienced when he went exploring Africa by Land Rover and climbing mountains there. It took him two years to prepare for the trip. There was no single source of help, advice or supplies. This gave him the first inkling that there might be a market. Was it, he asked himself, the same for all similar overland travellers, whether going on safari, travelling for fun, mounting geographical expeditions or even prospecting for minerals?

Experience, he was to discover, showed that anyone travelling long distances over rough terrain and living in the bush for long periods while doing so needed much the same sort of equipment and advice. Much of the equipment, though basic, is special enough to be scattered among many different sources and difficult to obtain in total because of the problems involved in tracking down all the individual sources.

His other discoveries during his African safari included the disconcerting fact that roof racks on vehicles destroy the points at which they are anchored during the course of 21,000 miles of driving over rough ground. The solution as he saw it was to find better-designed and more easily stowable items in the first place, as well as redesigning stowage facilities inside the vehicle. He rebuilt his vehicle from the chassis up during two years in South Africa, funding his work by taking a job as a middle manager in a mining company. He then, over a further two-year period, returned home, learning yet more about travelling and rough driving.

It was redundancy, after a variety of jobs, that pushed him finally into making his move. 'I decided to market my skills as a traveller. Many people need to know how to do it. I put an ad in *The Traveller* magazine, offering equipment and advice and started to pick up business very gradually.'

FRANCHISING AND NETWORK MARKETING

Franchising and network marketing are business models used to improve and expand the distribution of a product or service. The franchisor or network marketing company supplies the product or teaches the service to new recruits, who in turn sell it to the public. In return for this you pay a fee and a continuing royalty, based usually on turnover. You may also be required to buy materials or ingredients from the host business, giving it an additional income stream. The advantage to the new recruit is a relatively safe and quick way of getting into business for him or herself, but with the support and advice of an experienced organization close at hand.

The franchise or network marketing chain can expand their distribution with the minimum strain on their own capital and have the services of a highly motivated team of owner-managers. These are not paths to great riches, nor is it for the truly independent spirit, as policy and profits will come from the parent company.

These ways into business usually come with a ready-made business plan provided by the vendor. The trouble is that these plans are selling documents and at best are cast in a favourable light; at worst they are little more than spin. You should never take such plans at face value. Rather you should make your own projections and plan accordingly. Use the document provided as a template, by all means, but put it through the same rigorous analysis as you would if you were starting from scratch. You are heavily dependent on the success of the parent organization. If that fails, so do you. Cabuchon grew spectacularly as a jewellery networking company aimed primarily at women, and failed because of quality problems and the management's inability to control a bigger business. You could even find that a change in philosophy, such as occurred when Dorling Kindersley Family Learning was closed by its new owners Pearson, could pull the rug from under your feet.

Check whether the firm you are considering is a member of British Franchise Association (www.thebfa.org), the Direct Selling Association (www.dsa.org.uk), the Direct Marketing Association (www.dma.org.uk), the Federation of European Direct and Interactive Marketing (www.fedma.

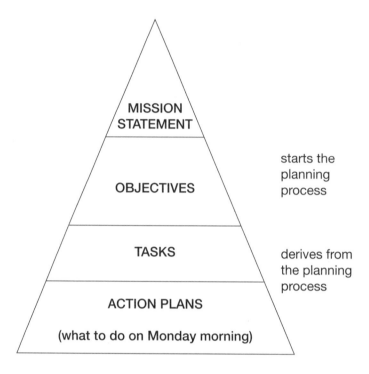

Figure 1.1   The pyramid of goals

org) or the Multi-Level Marketing International Association (www.mlmia.com). These professional associations carry out a level of vetting and as well as directories of members have links on their websites to lawyers, accountants, banks and other advisors who can help with your business plan.

WORKSHEET FOR ASSIGNMENT 1: BUSINESS PURPOSE AND AIMS

1. Explain how you arrived at your proposition.
2. What makes you believe it will succeed?
3. Write a mission statement linking your product or service to the customer needs it is aimed at.
4. What are your principal objectives:
    (a)   short term?
    (b)   long term?

5. List your tasks and action plans as you see them at present.
6. How much money do you think will be needed to get your business started? Provide a short 'shopping list' of major expenses.
7. If you are considering a franchise or network marketing opportunity, have you discussed the projections provided with a professional advisor?

SUGGESTED FURTHER READING

Abrams, J (2007) *101 mission statements from top companies*, Ten Speed Press, USA

Angelica, E (2001) *The Wilder nonprofit field guide to crafting effective mission and vision statements*, Amherst H Wilder Foundation, St Paul, Minn

Talbot, M (2002) *Make your mission statement work: identify your organisation's values and live them every day*, 2nd rev edn, How To Books, Oxford

A description of your business

The two essential ingredients for success in any new venture are a good proposition and the right people to turn that idea into a business. Your business plan must therefore not only include a description of your purpose or mission, but give full details of your and your prospective partners' experience and 'suitability' for this venture.

You also need to explain the name of your business, why you chose it, and under what legal form you propose to trade. If your business has been trading for some time, you should give a brief description of achievements to date and a summary of financial results. Full accounts can be included in an appendix to your business plan. Let's look at each in turn.

YOU AND YOUR TEAM

The right stuff

To launch a new venture successfully, you have to be the right sort of person, your business idea must be right for the market, and your timing must be spot on. The world of business failures is full of products that are ahead of their time.

The entrepreneur is frequently seen as someone who is always bursting with new ideas, is highly enthusiastic, hyperactive and insatiably curious.

But the more you try to create a picture of the typical entrepreneur, the more elusive he or she becomes.

Peter Drucker, the international business guru, captured the problem clearly with this description:

> Some are eccentrics, others painfully correct conformists; some are fat and some are lean; some are worriers, some relaxed; some drink quite heavily, others are total abstainers; some are men of great charm and warmth, some have no more personality than a frozen mackerel.

That said, there are certain characteristics that successful newcomers to business do have in common, and you should emphasize these in respect of yourself in the business plan.

Self-confident all-rounders

Entrepreneurs are rarely geniuses. There are nearly always people in their business who have more competence, in one field, than they could ever aspire to. But they have a wide range of ability and a willingness to turn their hands to anything that has to be done to make the venture succeed. They can usually make the product, market it and count the money, but above all they have self-confidence that lets them move comfortably through uncharted waters.

CASE STUDY

Paul Smith

Paul Smith, who left school at 15, launched his clothing business and within a decade had opened three shops in London – one of which was in Covent Garden – and a further one in Tokyo, and turnover was above £2 million pa. Now 'Paul Smith' is an internationally recognized fashion brand.

Explaining his success, Smith states, 'It's not that I'm a particularly brilliant designer or businessman, but I can run a business and I can design. There are so many excellent designers or excellent people but so often the designers can't run the business and businessmen do not have the right product.'

Resilient

Rising from the ashes of former disasters is also a common feature of many successful entrepreneurs.

Henry Ford had been bankrupted twice before founding the Ford Motor Corporation with a loan of US$28,000 in his fortieth year.

CASE STUDY

Timothy Waterstone

Timothy Waterstone, founder of one of the fastest-growing bookshop chains in the West, was fired from WH Smith's US operation in the most bloodcurdling circumstances. He took the first plane back to the United Kingdom and spent two months wondering what to do.

Until this time Waterstone's career path had been smooth and unmeteoric. After Cambridge he did a spell in the family tea-broking business in Cochin, followed by 10 years as a marketing manager for Allied Breweries. Books had always been his obsession, so he went to work for WH Smith. He was quickly sent to New York, where he remained for four years. His wife was in the United Kingdom for long periods, so he spent his spare time wandering around Manhattan bookshops. They were brilliant places: lively and consumer-led with huge stock, accessible staff and long opening hours. He felt there was a gap for similar bookselling in the United Kingdom , but at the time did nothing about it.

A trip to the dole office acted as a catalyst. It was the most horrific experience of his life. Not waiting for his turn, he rushed out and sat in the car. Instead of trying to get a new job, he formulated the Waterstone's concept. High street banks turned him down. He then went to a finance house and struck lucky. He pledged his house, £6,000 savings, £10,000 borrowed from his father-in-law, and the rest was raised through the government's loan guarantee scheme.

Three months later the first Waterstone's opened, based on a simple store plan an art student sketched out for £25. He filled the shops with the type of books that appeal to book lovers, not best-seller buyers. Midnight hours, Sunday trading (where possible) and bonus schemes for staff led to dazzling sales and the company employed 500 people in 40 branches, with a turnover of £35 million a year. The ultimate achievement was to sell back the company to WH Smith for the modest sum of £50 million. Don't get mad, start your own bookshop!

Innovative skills

Almost by definition, entrepreneurs are innovators who either tackle the unknown, or do old things in new ways. It is this inventive streak that allows them to carve out a new niche, often invisible to others.

Trees Unlimited

Trees Unlimited which passed the £1 million sales mark within three years of being started up, was launched by a nucleus of former managers of Porth Textiles, once the United Kingdom's largest manufacturer of decorations, garlands and plastic trees. Roger Freebody, Trees Unlimited's managing director, saw the writing on the wall before Porth collapsed with debts of £8 million, putting 364 people out of work in the Rhondda Valley.

Freebody and his colleagues saw the key to survival as the ability to escape from old-fashioned manufacturing traditions and the ability to innovate and try new marketing approaches. Trees Unlimited introduced a whole range of coloured trees from brown to pink, thus bucking the tradition that said Christmas trees had to be green. It also introduced a new marketing concept of matching trees and their decorations with home decor. Even the Queen's florist in Berkeley Square has bought its products.

Results oriented

Successful people set themselves goals and get pleasure out of trying to achieve them. Once a goal has been reached, they have to get the next target in view as quickly as possible. This restlessness is very characteristic. Sir James Goldsmith was a classic example, moving the base of his business empire from the United Kingdom to France, then the United States – and finally into pure cash, ahead of a stock market crash.

Professional risk-taker

The high failure rate shows that small businesses are faced with many dangers. An essential characteristic of someone starting a business is a willingness to make decisions and to take risks. This does not mean gambling on hunches. It means carefully calculating the odds and deciding which risks to take and when to take them.

Easy Tele-language

Easy Tele-language is a company which specializes in teaching modern European languages over the phone. It is run by 29-year-old Karine Hetherington, who got the idea for it while she was teaching English in Paris. 'I noticed that a lot of the language schools gave lessons over the telephone. It seemed like such a simple but effective idea, and as it was a proven concept the risks were low. Clients could learn on a one-to-one basis, at a time convenient to them, and also without having to travel to lessons. People are also a lot less self-conscious when there's a telephone between themselves and the teacher.'

When she came back to the United Kingdom she was amazed to find the same technique wasn't used here. Three years later her business was booming. The company employs more than 20 language teachers and is looking to increase that number. 'The demand has been phenomenal, far greater than I ever anticipated,' she says. 'It's been extremely hard work and pretty nerve-racking at times, but definitely worth it.'

Having total commitment

You will need complete faith in your idea. How else will you convince all the doubters you are bound to meet that it is a worthwhile venture? You will also need single-mindedness, energy and a lot of hard work to get things started; working 18-hour days is not uncommon. This can put a strain on other relationships, particularly within your family, so they too have to become involved and committed if you are to succeed.

Cyberquin

At the age of 18, when his contemporaries were off to university, Darren Saunders chose the route of the inventor. In pursuit of his 'mad idea' of the Cyberquin – a highly realistic, moving mannequin for display in shop windows and exhibitions – he spent six months in a fruitless search for development cash. 'I must have spoken to 150 people,' he says. 'They all thought I was trying to achieve the impossible.' Finally, he clinched a government innovation grant; his father agreed to an overdraft with his bank to secure the remainder.

Darren got help with the patents from a local patent agent, and took a short course in exporting at the Cardiff Chamber of Commerce. After three long years of development, Saunders succeeded in creating a mannequin that would work 24 hours a day without a hitch, needed no maintenance, and could be easily shipped and effortlessly set up any-where in the world. It took another 18 months of hard graft to get the product accepted, and it was all funded on a shoestring.

'Everyone advised me to stick to the UK,' says Saunders. 'But, I thought, the British never try anything new.'

He was right to follow his instincts. His budding company concentrated on visiting big shop-fittings exhibitions, including Euroshop in Düsseldorf, the biggest of them all. Here, the sight of a dynamic, lifelike mannequin attracted the crowds. The orders – despite a £5,000 price tag – came flooding in.

The Cyberquin (www.cyberquins.com) has been exported by the dozen to 33 countries, including Japan, Korea, Chile, Australia and Kuwait. Cyberquins have been displayed at Disney World and on Fifth Avenue, New York.

All too often budding entrepreneurs believe themselves to be the right sort of person to set up a business. Unfortunately, the capacity for self-deception is enormous. When a random sample of male adults were asked recently to rank themselves on leadership ability, 70 per cent rated themselves in the top 25 per cent; only 2 per cent felt they were below average as leaders. In an area in which self-deception ought to be difficult, 60 per cent said they were well above average in athletic ability and only 6 per cent said they were below.

A common mistake made in assessing entrepreneurial talent is to assume that success in big business management will automatically guarantee success in a small business.

Checking out your entrepreneurial strengths

You can find out more about your likely strengths and weakness as an entrepreneur by taking one or more of the many online entrepreneurial IQ-type tests. A couple of sources are listed below, but an entry in Google will produce a small torrent!

- Tickle Tests (http://web.tickle.com/tests/entrepreneurialiq/?test= entre preneurialiqogt);

- BusMove (www.busmove.com/other/quiz.htm);

- Community Futures, a Canadian small business help website, has a 50-question online test to help you rate your entrepreneurial abilities as well as checklist of desirable traits. See www.communityfutures.com/ cms/Starting_a_Business.159.0.html.

BUILDING THE TEAM

Not surprisingly, an investor's ideal proposal includes an experienced and balanced management team, who have all worked together for a number of years. That will ensure management in depth, thus providing cover for everything from illness to expansion, and guaranteeing some stability during the turbulent early years. For this reason management buy-outs are a firm favourite.

At the other end of the scale is the lone inventor whose management skills may be in doubt, and who is anyway fully stretched getting his or her product from the drawing board to the production line. This type of proposal is unlikely to attract much investment capital. It has obvious risks beyond those every company expects to experience in the marketplace. In any case, without a management team in place the business is ill-prepared for the rapid growth required to service an investor's funds.

In practice, most business proposals lie somewhere between these extremes. Your business plan should explain clearly what the ideal com-position of key managers should be for your business; who you have identified, or recruited so far; and last but certainly not least, how you will motivate them to remain with you and perform well for at least the first few all-important years.

The Listening Company

When Neville Upton set up The Listening Company (www.listening. co.uk), a call centre business based in Richmond, London, aged just 36, he was reasonably confident of getting a hearing when he started to look for funding. After all he had been operations director at Scoot and had both experience and contacts. A harder task was getting some great people to leave good jobs with established businesses and take a pay cut to work for him. What he could offer was the chance to be in charge of part of a growing business, located in a great place to work and in a business that was setting out to change the way clients and users think of call centres. With Travelodge, NCP and Shell in his client list, Upton now employs 1,700 people and has an annual turnover approaching £30 million. The company works hard at picking the right people to work with it and matching them to their clients, and it pays off.

Certainly investors will look for reassurance in this respect and will expect to see more reference to the steps you will take to encourage loyalty.

YOUR BUSINESS NAME

Your business name is almost always the first way people get to hear about your venture and it needs to convey the essence of the business quickly and clearly. Once you have to start explaining what you do, the job of communicating gets harder. As you are going to have to put some effort into creating this name and that of your web presence (domain name) if you plan to have one, it makes good sense to take some steps to protect your investment.

Your company name can, in effect, be the starting and sustaining point in differentiating you from your competitors, and as such it should be carefully chosen, be protected by trademarks where possible and be written in a distinctive way. It follows therefore that the main consideration in choosing a business name is its commercial usefulness.

When you choose a business name, you are also choosing an identity so it should reflect:

- who you are;

- what you do;

- how you do it.

Given all the marketing investment you will make in your company name, you should check with a trademark agent whether you can protect your chosen name (descriptive words, surnames and place names are not normally allowed except after long use).

First, anyone wanting to use a 'controlled' name will have to get permission. There are some 80 or 90 controlled names, which include words such as 'International', 'Bank' and 'Royal'. This is simply to prevent a business implying that it is something that it is not.

Second, all businesses that intend to trade under names other than those of their owner(s) must state who does own the business and how the owner can be contacted. So if you are a sole trader or partnership and you only use surnames with or without forenames or initials, you are not affected. Companies are also not affected if they simply use their full corporate name.

If any name other than the 'true' name is to be used, then you must disclose the name of the owner(s) and an address in the United Kingdom to which business documents can be sent. This information has to be shown on all business letters, orders for goods and services, invoices and receipts, and statements and demands for business debts. Also, a copy has to be displayed prominently on all business premises. The purpose of the Companies Act requirements is simply to make it easier to 'see' who you are doing business with.

If you are setting up as a limited company you will have to submit your choice of name to the Companies Registration Office along with the other documents required for registration. It will be accepted unless there is another company with that name on the register or the Registrar considers the name to be obscene, offensive or illegal.

Cobra Beer

When Karan Bilimoria, now Lord Bilimoria, started Cobra Beer back in 1990 he operated out of his Fulham flat and with cases of beer in the back of a Citroen 2CV drove around selling beer door-to-door to London's Indian restaurants. Although the beer was actually brewed in Bedford, the recipe and the image he wanted for his business were essentially Indian – hence the name Cobra. Determined to expand the business Bilimoria attended a Business Growth course in 1999. By 2007 Cobra Beer was sold in 9,000 restaurants and pubs, and exported to over 40 countries, with sales of over £80 million a year.

Changing your name

It's not the end of the world if you decide after a year or so that your business name is not quite right, as the case study below shows. But you will have largely wasted any earlier marketing effort in building up awareness.

Bridgewater

Emma Bridgewater set up her business 18 months after completing an English degree at Bedford College, London. At first she wasn't sure what business to start but her boyfriend at the time, with whom she lived in Brixton, wanted to set up a craft studio to teach students how to slip-cast (an ancient method of making pottery with liquid clay poured into a mould). Emma visited factories in Stoke-on-Trent and discovered a number of people with this skill. 'Their mug shapes were revolting, though. So I drew my own. I found, doing so, that all my frustration evaporated just like that. Suddenly I knew what I wanted to do.'

She equipped herself with sponges and colours so that she could apply her designs to her mugs in the factories. 'At first the people in Stoke thought I was mad and were sceptical but helpful.' However, within a few months she won her first order, worth £600, from the General Trading

Company, and in April she joined a lot of 'hysterical stall-holders with lavender bags' at a trade fair in Kensington: Brixton Spongeware was launched.

She has since changed the name: 'I was fed up with jokes about reggae music and sweet potatoes. The name "Bridgewater" is far more appropriate. It sounds like an old, established industry. People often imagine it's a family business that has been going for years. That's exactly the mood I want to create.' Just over two years later she had a file full of orders from top department stores in London and New York. Cheap imitators quickly started copying her designs. Now Bridgewater has an established name and a turnover in the millions.

A good name, in effect, can become a one- or two-word summary of your marketing strategy; Body Shop, Toys'R'Us, Kwik-Fit exhausts are good examples. Many companies add a slogan to explain to customers and employees alike 'how they do it'.

The John Lewis slogan, 'Never knowingly undersold', is almost better known than the company name itself. The name, slogan and logo combine to be the most visible tip of the iceberg in your corporate communications effort, and where possible should be protected by trademarks.

Spending time initially on trying to get your name and slogan right could pay off in the long term.

REGISTER A DOMAIN NAME

If you plan to have an internet presence you will need a domain name. That is the name by which your business is known on the internet, and it lets people find you by entering your name into their browser address box. Ideally you want a domain name that captures the essence of your business neatly so that you will come up readily on search engines, and that is as close as possible to your business name.

If your business name is registered as a trademark you may (as current case law develops) be able to prevent another business from using it as a domain name on the internet.

Registering a domain name is simple, but as hundreds of domain names are registered every day and you must choose a name that has not already been registered, you need to have a selection of domain names to hand in case your first choice is unavailable. These need only be slight variations: for example Cobra Beer, could have been listed as Cobra-Beer, CobraBeer or even Cobra Indian Beer, if the original name was not available. These would all have been more or less equally effective in terms of search engine visibility.

Once you have decided on a selection of domain names your internet service provider (ISP), the organization that you use to link your computer to the internet, can submit a domain name application on your behalf. Alternatively you can:

- Use Nominet UK (www.nic.uk), the registry for British internet domain names, where you will find a list of members that can help you register, though you can do so yourself if you are 'web aware'.

  If you want to operate internationally, for example by using a .com suffix or a country-specific domain, check out with one of the world directories of internet domain registries such as www.internic.net and www.norid.no/domreg.html.

- Use websites such as Own This Domain (www.ownthisdomain.co.uk) and 123 Domain Names (www.123domainnames.co.uk) which provide an online domain-name registration service, usually with a search facility so you can see whether your selected name has already been registered.

- Obtain free domain names along with free web space by registering with an internet community. These organizations offer you web pages within their community space as well as a free domain name, but most communities only offer free domain names that have their own community domain tagged on the end. This can make your domain name rather long and hard to remember.

Help and advice on names and their registration

A guidance note entitled *Choosing a company name* is available from Companies House (www.companieshouse.gov.uk>Guidance Booklets>).

Companies such as Altaire (www.altaire.com/domains/index.html) and Electric Names (www.electricnames.co.uk) have detailed domain name registration on their websites as well as offering a same-day registration service for prices between £10 and £25 per annum.

Business Link (www.businesslink.gov.uk>IT&e-commerce>E-commerce> Web hosting options) has comprehensive up-to-date information on choosing a domain name and registering and protecting that name.

DECIDING THE LEGAL FORM OF YOUR BUSINESS

Before you start trading you will need to consider what legal form your business will take. There are four main forms that a business can take, and the one you choose will depend on a number of factors: commercial needs, financial risk and your tax position. Each of these forms is explained briefly below, together with the procedure to follow on setting them up.

Sole trader

The vast majority of new businesses set up each year in the United Kingdom choose to do so as sole traders. This has the merit of being relatively formality-free, and unless you intend to register for VAT, there are few rules about the records you have to keep. There is no requirement for your accounts to be audited, or for financial information on your business to be filed at Companies House.

As a sole trader there is no legal distinction between you and your business – your business is one of your assets, just as your house or car is. It follows from this that if your business should fail, your creditors have a right not only to the assets of the business, but also to your personal assets, subject only to the provisions of the Bankruptcy Acts (these allow you to keep only a few absolutely basic essentials for yourself and family).

It is possible to avoid the worst of these consequences by ensuring that your private assets are the legal property of your spouse, against whom your creditors have no claim. (You must be solvent when the transfer is made, and that transfer must have been made at least two years prior to your business running into trouble.) However, to be effective such a transfer must be absolute and you can have no say in how your spouse chooses to dispose of his or her new-found wealth!

The capital to get the business going must come from you – or from loans. There is no access to equity capital, which has the attraction of being risk-free. In return for these drawbacks you can have the pleasure of being your own boss immediately, subject only to declaring your profits on your tax return. (In practice you would be wise to take professional advice before doing so.)

Partnerships

Partnerships are effectively collections of sole traders, and as such, share the legal problems attached to personal liability. There are very few restrictions to setting up in business with another person (or persons) in partnership, and several definite advantages. By pooling resources you may have more capital; you should be bringing several sets of skills to the business; and if you are ill the business can still carry on.

There are two serious drawbacks that merit particular attention. First, if your partner makes a business mistake, perhaps by signing a disastrous contract, without your knowledge or consent, every member of the partnership must shoulder the consequences. Under these circumstances your personal assets could be taken to pay the creditors even though the mistake was no fault of your own.

Second, if your partner goes bankrupt in his or her personal capacity, for whatever reason, his or her share of the partnership can be seized by creditors. As a private individual you are not liable for your partner's private debts, but having to buy him or her out of the partnership at short notice could put you and the business in financial jeopardy. Even death may not release you from partnership obligations, and in some circumstances your estate can remain liable. Unless you take 'public' leave of your partnership by notifying your business contacts and legally bringing your partnership to an end, you could remain liable.

The legal regulations governing this field are set out in the Partnership Act 1890, which in essence assumes that competent businesspeople should know what they are doing. The Act merely provides a framework of agreement that applies 'in the absence of agreement to the contrary'. It follows from this that many partnerships are entered into without legal formalities – and sometimes without the parties themselves being aware that they have entered a partnership!

The main provisions of the Partnership Act state that:

- All partners contribute capital equally.

- All partners share profits and losses equally.

- No partner shall have interest paid on his/her capital.

- No partner shall be paid a salary.

- All partners have an equal say in the management of the business.

It is unlikely that all these provisions will suit you, so you would be well advised to get a 'partnership agreement' drawn up in writing by a solicitor at the outset of your venture.

One possibility that can reduce the more painful consequences of entering a partnership as a 'sleeping partner' is to have your involvement registered as a limited partnership. It means you (or your partner) can play no active part in running the business, but your risks are limited to the capital that you put in.

Unless you are a member of certain professions (eg law, accountancy) you are restricted to a maximum of 20 partners in any partnership.

Cooperative

A cooperative is an enterprise owned and controlled by the people working in it. Once in danger of becoming extinct, the workers' cooperative is enjoying something of a comeback, and there are over 4,370 operating in the United Kingdom, employing 195,000 people. They are growing at the rate of 20 per cent per annum.

Cooperatives are governed by the Industrial and Provident Societies Act 1965, whose main provisions state:

- Each member of the cooperative has equal control through the principle of 'one person one vote'.

- Membership must be open to anyone who satisfies the stipulated qualifications.

- Profits can be retained in the business or distributed in proportion to members' involvement, eg hours worked.

- Members must benefit primarily from their participation in the business.

- Interest on loan or share capital is limited in some specific way, even if the profits are high enough to allow a greater payment.

It is certainly not a legal structure designed to give entrepreneurs control of their own destiny and maximum profits. However, if this is to be your chosen legal form you can pay from £90 to register with the Chief Registrar of Friendly Societies, and must have at least seven members at the outset. They do not all have to be full-time workers at first. Like a limited company, a registered cooperative has limited liability (see under 'Limited liability companies') for its members and must file annual accounts, but there is no charge for this. Not all cooperatives bother to register, as it is not mandatory, in which case they are treated in law as a partnership with unlimited liability.

Limited liability companies

In the United Kingdom, before the 1895 Companies Act it was necessary to have an Act of Parliament or a Royal Charter in order to set up a company.

Now, out of the 4.5 million businesses trading in the United Kingdom, over 1.4 million are limited companies. As the name suggests, in this form of business your liability is limited to the amount you state that you will contribute by way of share capital (although you may not actually have to put that money in!).

A limited company has a legal identity of its own, separate from the people who own or run it. This means that, in the event of failure, creditors' claims are restricted to the assets of the company. The shareholders of the business are not liable as individuals for the business debts beyond the paid-up value of their shares. This applies even if the shareholders are working directors, unless of course the company has been trading fraudulently. (In practice, the ability to limit liability is severely restricted these days as most lenders, including the banks, often insist on personal guarantees from the directors – see Chapter 4 for more on this subject.) Other advantages include the freedom to raise capital by selling shares.

Disadvantages include the cost involved in setting up the company and the legal requirement in some cases for the company's accounts to be audited by a chartered or certified accountant. Usually it is only businesses with assets approaching £3 million that have to be audited but if, for example, you have shareholders who own more than 10 per cent of your firm they can ask for the accounts to be audited. You can find out the latest information on auditing small firms either from your accountant or on the Business Link website (www.businesslink.gov.uk>Taxes, returns and payroll>Introduction to business taxes>Accounting and audit exemptions for small companies).

A limited company can be formed by two shareholders, one of whom must be a director. A company secretary must also be appointed, who can be a shareholder, director, or an outside person such as an accountant or lawyer.

The company can be bought 'off the shelf' from a registration agent, then adapted to suit your own purposes. This will involve changing the name, shareholders and articles of association, and will cost about £250 and take a couple of weeks to arrange. Alternatively, you can form your own company, using your solicitor or accountant. This will cost around £500 and take six to eight weeks.

The behaviour of companies and their directors is governed by the various Companies Acts that have come into effect since 1844, the latest of which came into effect in November 2006.

Further information

A Guidance Note entitled *Business ownership* is available from Companies House.(www.companieshouse.gov.uk>Guidance Booklets>).

Business Link (www.businesslink.gov.uk>Taxes, returns and payroll> choosing and setting up a legal structure>Legal structure: the basics) has a guide to putting your business on a proper legal footing explaining the tax and other implications of different ownership structures.

Cooperatives UK (www.cooperatives-uk.coop>Services>Co-operative Development) is the central membership organization for co-operative enterprises throughout the United Kingdom. This link is to the regional network.

Desktop Lawyer (www.desktoplawyer.co.uk>BUSINESS>BUSINESS START-UP>Choosing a business structure>The Partnership) has a summary of the pros and cons of partnerships as well as inexpensive partnership deeds.

PAST ACHIEVEMENTS

If your business has already been trading for some time, your business plan should include a summary of past results and achievements. Annual reports, audited accounts, etc, if voluminous, can be included in an appendix, and referred to in this section of your business plan. Otherwise they can be shown in detail. You should emphasize what you have learnt so far that convinces you that your strategies are soundly based.

CASE STUDY

Notonthehighstreet Enterprises Limited

When Holly Tucker and Sophie Cornish decided that a business selling well-designed, high-quality products that cannot easily be found on the high street choosing a name for their venture was the easy bit. Notonthehighstreet (www.notonthehighstreet.com) was distinct and captured the essence of their proposition. The aim was to bring together businesses that lacked the resources to have an effective presence on the high street and put them all under one roof, spreading the cost base accordingly. The 'one roof' as physical concept was ditched in favour of the internet at the early planning stage.

Their first draft of the business plan called for a £40,000 investment, but within months of starting up that grew to £140,000. After scrabbling around family, loans and bank overdraft to fund the first year's growth they pitched to Spark Ventures (www.sparkventures.com), an early stage venture capital company that includes Brent Hoberman, co-founder of Lastminute.com, in its portfolio.

Spark pumped in a sizeable six-figure sum, taking a minority stake in the business which allowed it to plan to more than double sales in its third year of operations (see Table 2.1).

Table 2.1   Sales history of Notinthehighstreet

Year	Sales (£000)
1	100
2	1,000
3	2,500 (forecast)

For a joining fee of £450 suppliers can promote their products on Notonthehighstreet's website for five years. Notonthehighstreet also takes a 20 per cent slice of any sales generated. It offers a tailored audience and a professional web presence that small firms would find hard if not impossible to emulate without spending tens of thousands of pounds. The site has been voted a top fifty website by the *Independent* magazine.

WORKSHEET FOR ASSIGNMENT 2: A DESCRIPTION OF YOUR BUSINESS

1. How did you arrive at your new idea?
2. What is your business name and why have you chosen it?
3. What experience and skills do you have that are particularly relevant to this venture?
4. Who else will be working with you and what relevant experience and skills do they have?
5. Draw an organization chart showing who is responsible for which functions.
6. What people (or skill) gaps are there in the organization you need to run your business? How do you plan to fill them?

7. How will you ensure that your key staff are motivated and loyal during the start-up period?
8. What professional advisers (accountant, lawyer, patent agent, etc) have you used, or do you plan to use?
9. Under what legal form will you trade and why?
10. If your business is already trading, give a brief summary of financial and marketing results and achievements to date.

SUGGESTED FURTHER READING

Adair, J (2007) *The art of creative thinking: how to be innovative and develop great ideas*, Kogan Page, London

Bridge, R (2006) *My big idea: thirty entrepreneurs reveal how they found inspiration*, Kogan Page, London

Clayton, P (2007) *Law for the small business, an essential guide to all the legal and financial requirements*, Kogan Page, London

Assignment 3

A description of your products and/or services

Here you should describe what products or services you propose to market, what stage of development they are at and why they are competitive with existing sources of supply. Part of the information in this section is for the benefit of outside readers who may not be familiar with your business. It should also be useful to you since the research and analysis required will encourage you to examine your offering compared with your competitors'.

Explore these topics in this section of your business plan.

DESCRIPTION OF PRODUCTS AND/OR SERVICES

Explain what it is you are selling. Be specific and avoid unnecessary jargon. The reader should end up with more than just a vague idea about your products and/or services. Obviously, some products and services will require much more explanation than others. If you have invented a new process for analysing blood, you will need to provide the reader with many details. On the other hand, if you are selling your services as a bookkeeper, you may need to do little more than list the services you will provide. A danger of this section is in assuming that the reader can easily understand your products without your providing sufficient detail and description.

Pnu-clean

Pnu-clean, an industrial cleaner aimed specifically at the metal-machining, wood-working and textile-manufacturing industries, included in its business plan this description of the product:

> The method of producing the suction in the cleaner is via a 'jet-pump', which in effect is a stream of high velocity air passed into a tube. It is a very similar device to the vacuum pumps found on the taps in chemistry laboratories but a 'jet-pump' uses air as the prime mover instead of water (compressed air is readily available in most manufacturing units). The high-speed air, when passing down the tube, will accelerate the surrounding air in the tube and draw air into the tube, similar to the draw of a chimney, causing a 'vacuum' effect, an area of lower than atmospheric pressure.

The air is accelerated by a small annular inlet supplied by a manifold surrounding the inlet. The air is controlled by a simple on/off valve. Incorporated into the valve is another position which allows for the provision of a supply of high speed air to be used to clean out difficult-to-get-at areas and to dislodge swarf from awkward places.

Once the dirt/swarf/chippings have been picked up by the vacuum and passed the position of the inlet of accelerated air the dirt/swarf/ chippings are blown down a flexible pipe. This blowing action is much stronger than the vacuum and means that the flexible pipe will never get blocked. It also means that the pipe can be of considerable length. In practice the length will be limited to between 2 and 3 metres to stop it getting in the way and allow for easy handling.

The tube is clipped over the side of an existing dustbin where the air and dirt/swarf/chippings are separated out using a simple filter in order to stop the dirt/swarf/chippings being blown straight out of the dustbin again. You can find out more about the product at the AB Dust Control website: (www.abdustcontrol.com/products/cartridge.htm).

In addition to listing and describing your products and/or services, you should note any applications or uses of your products that are not readily apparent to the reader. For instance, a photocopier can also produce overhead transparencies, as well as its more mundane output. When you make your list, show the proportion of turnover you expect each product or service to contribute to the whole, as illustrated in Table 3.1.

Table 3.1   Example showing products/services and their applications

Product/service	Description	% of sales
		100%

READINESS FOR MARKET

Are your products and/or services available for sale now? If not, what needs to be done to develop them? If you are selling a product, does it require more design work or research and development? Have you actually produced one or more completed products?

Strida bicycle

When Mark Saunders, Cranfield enterprise programme participant, put his proposal for the Strida (www.strida.co.uk), a revolutionary folding bicycle, before the venture capital panel, the only projections he could include with any degree of certainty were costs.

The business proposal for which he sought backing was to take his brainchild from the drawing board to a properly costed production prototype. For this he needed time (about two years), living expenses for that period, the use of a workshop and a modest amount of materials.

Saunders's business plan detailed how he would develop the product over this period, and as a result the concept was backed by James Marshall, one-time manager of golfer Greg Norman. Marshall put together the manufacturing and marketing elements of the business plan, and within 18 months the Strida was in full-scale production and on sale through stores such as Harrods, Next Essentials, John Lewis, House of Fraser, Kelvin Hughes and many others.

Table 3.2 Example showing products/services and additional inputs to be made

Product/service	State of development	Tasks to be done	Completion date

If you are selling a service, do you presently have the skills and technical capability to provide it? If not, what needs to be done?

If additional inputs are required before your products or services are ready to be sold, state both the tasks to be done and time required, as shown in Table 3.2.

PROPRIETARY POSITION

Do your products or services have any special competitive advantage? If so, explain the advantages and state how long this proprietary position is likely to last. You should state any other factors that give you a competitive advantage, even though the advantage is not protected by contractual agreements of the law. Examples could include a special skill or talent not easily obtainable by others. (If you have none of these, and many businesses do not, do not just make something up!)

Getting inventions to market can be an expensive and time-consuming business, as James Dyson is only too eager to confirm. It took five years and 5,127 prototypes before the world's first bagless vacuum cleaner arrived on the scene. It's hardly surprising then that the Dyson (www.dyson.co.uk/about) story includes a legendary but victorious 18-month battle with Hoover, based in the United Kingdom, over patent infringement.

If, like Dyson, you have a unique business idea, you should investigate the four categories of protection: *patenting*, which protects 'how something works'; *trademark registration*, which protects 'what something's called';

design registration, which protects 'how something looks'; and *copyright*, which protects 'work on paper, film and CD'. Some products may be covered by two or more categories, eg the mechanism of a clock may be patented while its appearance may be design-registered.

Each category requires a different set of procedures, offers a different level of protection and extends for a different period of time. They all have one thing in common, though: in the event of any infringement your only redress is through the courts, and going to law can be wasteful of time and money, whether you win or lose.

CASE STUDY

Facebook

When Mark Zuckerberg, then aged 20, started Facebook from his college dorm back in 2004 with two fellow students he could hardly have been aware of how the business would pan out. Facebook is a social networking website on which users have to put their real names and e-mail addresses in order to register, then they can contact current and past friends and colleagues to swap photos, news and gossip. Within three years the company was on track to make US$100 million sales, partly on the back of a big order from Microsoft that appears to have its sights on Facebook as either a partner or an acquisition target.

Zuckerberg, wearing jeans, Adidas sandals and a fleece, looks a bit like a latter-day Steve Jobs, Apple's founder. He also shares something else in common with Jobs. He has a gigantic intellectual property legal dispute on his hands. For three years he has been dealing with a lawsuit brought by three fellow Harvard students who claim, in effect, that he stole the Facebook concept from them.

PATENTS PROTECT 'HOW SOMETHING WORKS'

A patent can be regarded as a contract between an inventor and the state. The state agrees with the inventor that if he or she is prepared to publish details of the invention in a set form and if it appears that he or she has made a real advance, the state will then grant the inventor a 'monopoly' on the invention for 20 years: 'protection in return for disclosure'. The inventor uses the monopoly period to manufacture and sell his or her innovation;

competitors can read the published specifications and glean ideas for their research, or they can approach the inventor and offer to help to develop the idea under licence.

However, the granting of a patent does not mean the proprietor is automatically free to make, use or sell the invention him- or herself, since to do so might involve infringing an earlier patent that has not yet expired. A patent really only allows the inventor to stop another person using the particular device that forms the subject of the patent. The state does not guarantee validity of a patent either, so it is not uncommon for patents to be challenged through the courts.

What inventions can you patent? The basic rules are that an invention must be new, must involve an *inventive* step and must be capable of *industrial exploitation*. You cannot patent scientific/mathematical theories or mental processes, computer programs or ideas that might encourage offensive, immoral or anti-social behaviour. New medicines are patentable but not medical methods of treatment. Neither can you have just rediscovered a long-forgotten idea (knowingly or unknowingly).

If you want to apply for a patent, it is essential not to disclose your idea in non-confidential circumstances. If you do, your invention is already 'published' in the eyes of the law, and this could well invalidate your application.

There are two distinct stages in the patenting process:

- from filing an application up to publication of the patent;
- from publication to grant of the patent.

Two fees are payable for the first part of the process and a further fee for the second part. The whole process takes some two and a half years. Forms and details of how to patent are available free from the Patent Office.

It is possible – and cheaper – to make your own patent application, but this is not really recommended. Drafting a specification to give you as wide a monopoly as you think you can get away with is the essence of patenting and this is the skill of professional patent agents. They also know the tricks of the trade for each stage of the patenting procedure. A list of patent agents is available from the Chartered Institute of Patent Agents.

What can you do with your idea? If you have dreamt up an inspired invention but don't have the resources, skill, time or inclination to produce it yourself, you can take one of three courses once the idea is patented:

- *Outright sale*. You can sell the rights and title of your patent to an individual or company. The payment you ask should be based on a sound evaluation of the market.

- *Sale and royalty.* You can enter into an agreement whereby you assign the title and rights to produce to another party for cash but under which you get a royalty on each unit sold.

- *Licensing.* You keep the rights and title but sell a licence for manufacturing and marketing the product to someone else. The contract between you and the licensee should contain a performance clause requiring the licensee to sell a minimum number of units each year or the licence will be revoked.

Whichever option you select, you need a good patent agent/lawyer on your side.

CASE STUDY

Holomedia

Anthony Robinson, the inventor of Holomedia, a novel hologram display system, decided while on a Cranfield enterprise programme not to make and market his product himself. Instead, he sold the patented product to a large, established company in a complementary field for a substantial six-figure sum, a £20,000 pa retainer and continuing royalties. His business subsequently concentrated exclusively on developing innovative products for other companies to make and sell.

TRADEMARKS PROTECT 'WHAT SOMETHING'S CALLED'

A trademark is the symbol by which the goods or services of a particular manufacturer or trader can be identified. It can be a word, a signature, a monogram, a picture, a logo or a combination of these.

To qualify for registration the trademark must be distinctive, must not be deceptive and must not be capable of confusion with marks already registered. Excluded are misleading marks, national flags, royal crests and insignia of the armed forces. A trademark can only apply to tangible goods, not services (although pressure is mounting for this to be changed).

The Trade Marks Act of 1938 and the Copyright, Designs and Patents Act of 1988 and subsequent amendments offer protection of great commercial value since, unlike other forms of protection, your sole rights to use the trademark continue indefinitely.

To register a trademark you or your agent should first conduct preliminary searches at the trade marks branch of the Patent Office to check there are no conflicting marks already in existence. You then apply for registration on the official trademark form and pay a fee (currently £200 for one class of goods or services, then £50 for each additional class). Your application is then advertised in the weekly *Trade Marks Journal* to allow any objections to be raised. Registration is initially for 10 years. After this, it can be renewed for periods of 10 years at a time, with no upper time limit.

It is not mandatory to register a trademark. If an unregistered trademark has been used for some time and could be construed as closely associated with a product by customers, it will have acquired a 'reputation', which will give it some protection legally, but registration makes it much simpler for the owners to have recourse against any person who infringes the mark.

DESIGN REGISTRATION PROTECTS 'HOW SOMETHING LOOKS'

You can register the shape, design or decorative features of a commercial product if it is new, original, never published before or – if already known – never before applied to the product you have in mind. Protection is intended to apply to industrial articles to be produced in quantities of more than 50. Design registration applies only to features that appeal to the eye – not to the way the article functions.

To register a design, you should apply to the Design Registry and send a specimen or photograph of the design plus a registration fee (currently £90). The specimen or photograph is examined to see whether it is new or original and complies with other requirements of the Registered Designs Act 1949 and the Copyright, Designs and Patents Act 1988 and subsequent amendments to the Act. If it does, a certification of registration is issued which gives you, the proprietor, the sole right to manufacture, sell or use in business articles of that design.

Protection lasts for a maximum of 25 years. You can handle the design registration yourself, but, again, it might be preferable to let a specialist do it for you. There is no register of design agents but most patent agents are well versed in design law.

Wagamama

This small London-based restaurant chain, which has prospered by selling Japanese noodles to city trendies, sees the need to protect its idea as the main plank of its business strategy. Alan Yau, who founded the business, came to the United Kingdom as an 11-year-old economic immigrant from Hong Kong. He joined his father running a Chinese takeaway in King's Lynn, Norfolk. Within 10 years he was running two Chinese restaurants of his own, one of which is close to the British Museum. From the outset he had plans to run a large international chain of restaurants.

Yau's food style is healthy, distinctive and contemporary. The name 'Wagamama' conjures up someone who is a bit of a spoilt brat in Japanese, and the word lodged in Yau's mind. His informal communal dining room, opened under the Wagamama banner, received favourable reviews and the queues, which have become an essential part of the Wagamama experience, started forming. Realising he had an idea with global potential, Yau took the unusual step of registering his trademark worldwide. It cost £60,000, but within two years that investment began to pay off. A large listed company opened an Indian version of Wagamama. The concepts looked similar enough to have led ordinary people to think the two businesses were related. As Yau felt he could lose out, he decided to sue. The case was heard quickly, and within three months Yau had won and his business idea was safe – at least for the five years his trademark protection runs.

In the 15 years since he started up, Yau has opened more than 80 restaurants in the United Kingdom, Europe, the Pacific Rim, the Middle East and the United States. Wagamama (www.wagamama.com) has been shortlisted by *Time Out* magazine for the award of 'best family restaurant' as well as also being recognised as an official 'cool brand' by the CoolBrands council for each of the past four years.

COPYRIGHT PROTECTS 'WORK ON PAPER, FILM AND CD'

Copyright is a complex field and since it is unlikely to be relevant to most business start-ups we only touch on it lightly here. Basically, the Copyright,

Designs and Patents Act 1988 gives protection against the unlicensed copying of original artistic and creative works – articles, books, paintings, films, plays, songs, music, engineering drawings. To claim copyright the item in question should carry this symbol: © (author's name) (date). At a diplomatic conference in Geneva in December 1996, new international copyright and performances and phonograms treaties, which govern the protection of databases, were agreed on and came into force in January 1998.

You can take the further step of recording the date on which the work was completed for a moderate fee with the Registrar at Stationers' Hall. This, though, is an unusual precaution to take and probably only necessary if you anticipate an infringement.

Copyright protection in the UK lasts for 70 years after the death of the person who holds the copyright, or 50 years after publication if this is the later. Copyright is infringed only if more than a 'substantial' part of your work is reproduced (ie issued for sale to the public) without your permission, but since there is no formal registration of copyright the question of whether or not your work is protected usually has to be decided in a court of law.

PROTECTING INTERNET ASSETS

Now that you have gone to so much trouble to develop a business model incorporating your mission, vision, objectives and culture so that you are all set for meteoric growth, it would be an awful pity if someone were to come along and steal it.

Even when times are hard, this is probably not an area to include in any cost-cutting exercise. In the internet world, where all the value is placed in the anticipation of profits from day one, intellectual property may be all that's really worth saving.

It was a fact of life for Edward the Confessor, Julius Caesar and Napoleon that sending or receiving a message at a distance of 100 miles took at least a day, the time it took a messenger on horseback or in a boat to cover the distance. Ideas, information, knowledge and images can now be transmitted globally with an ease that makes it potentially much easier technically to violate businesses' intellectual property rights. In a sense the internet age is just an extension of the problems created by the first printing press and the ensuing early law, the Statute of Anne (1610) to protect authors.

The advent of softer terms, such as 'sharing' music, rather than stealing it, doesn't alter the fact that all the usual intellectual property laws apply to the internet, it is just harder to enforce them. You can find out more about protecting internet assets in the output of the Trust in Digital Repositories website (http://trustdr.ulster.ac.uk) where the practical issues in setting up digital rights management systems (DRM) are examined.

Further information on protecting your products

The UK Intellectual Property Office (www.ipo.gov.uk) has all the information needed to patent, trademark, copyright or register a design.

For information on international intellectual property see these organisations: European Patent Office (www.epo.org), US Patent and Trade Mark Office (www.uspto.gov) and the World Intellectual Property Association (www.wipo.int).

The Chartered Institute of Patents and Attorneys (www.cipa.org.uk) and the Institute of Trade Mark Attorneys (www.itma.org.uk) despite their specialized-sounding names can help with every aspect of intellectual property, including finding you a local advisor.

The British Library (www.bl.uk>Collections>Patents, trade marks & designs> Key patent databases) links to free databases for patent searching to see whether someone else has registered your innovation. The library is willing to offer limited advice to enquirers.

The Institute of Patentees and Inventors (www.invent.org.uk) is a self help and networking association for inventors, with annual membership costing £70 a year, with a one-off joining fee of £15.

COMPARISON WITH COMPETITIVE PRODUCTS AND SERVICES

Identify those products and/or services that you think will be competing with yours. They may be similar products/services or they may be quite different, but could be substituted for yours. An example of the latter is a business that sells copying machines, which competes not only against other copying machines, but also against carbon paper and copy shops.

Once you have identified the major competing products, compare yours with them. List the advantages and disadvantages of yours compared with the competition. Later on, when you do your market research, you will probably want to address this question again and revise this section.

After making the comparison draw your conclusions. If your products/ services will compete effectively, explain why. If not, explain what you plan to do to make them compete.

Pnu-clean

To return to Pnu-Clean Ltd, its business plan presented to the Cranfield enterprise panel included the following statement explaining its competitive advantage:

> As such there is no direct competition for the cleaner. This must be qualified by saying that there are some designs of vacuum cleaner that offer some but not all of the benefits that this design offers. The closest is a product made by Alpha Components Limited but it is based on a very small bore, almost unworkable.

There is considerable indirect competition from electrically powered vacuum cleaners, pneumatic vacuum cleaners and the dustpan and brush. Overcoming this indirect competition should be achieved by making the customer aware that this cleaner is designed especially for use alongside a machine or workstation and offers the most convenient method at a low cost of keeping a high standard of cleanliness.

Remember also that some products differentiate themselves from competitors by their service terms, while some services compete by the physical facilities offered, eg most makes of white goods are similar, but Philips Whirlpool seeks to differentiate its products by offering customers:

- replacement in its first year of any machine that cannot be repaired;
- guarantees on all parts for 10 years;
- payment of £12.50 if the repair engineer does not arrive within two days of call;
- a 24-hour call care line.

Additionally, all retailers in the distribution network are offered extended payment terms, finance for display stock and inventory as well as dealer support for advertising.

Similarly, most management consultants in the 'service' sector ensure that their 'products', their final reports, are faultless and immaculately presented, as are the premises and facilities of the best restaurants and fast food chains.

Guarantees and warranties

Will you be providing either of these with your product or service? Describe the scope of the warranty or guarantee, what it may cost, the benefits you expect from providing it, and how it will work in practice.

Possible future developments

If your product or service lends itself to other opportunities, with relatively minor alteration, which can be achieved quickly and will enhance your business, briefly describe these ideas.

SOME PRODUCT TURN-OFFS

Is one product enough?

One-product businesses are the natural output of the inventor, but they are extremely vulnerable to competition, changes in fashion and to technological obsolescence. Having only one product can also limit the growth potential of the enterprise. A question mark must inevitably hang over such ventures until they can broaden out their product base into, preferably, a 'family' of related products or services.

CASE STUDY

Cobra beer

Cambridge-educated and recently qualified accountant Karan Bilimoria started importing and distributing standard-size 660-millilitre bottles of Cobra beer, specifically brewed to complement Indian restaurant food in the United Kingdom. Soon it became 'the beer from Bangalore, brewed in Bedford'; it became available in 330-millilitre bottles and subsequently on draught. A low-alcohol version was then planned, followed by the addition of 'General Billy's Wine' as Karan widened the product range to meet Indian restaurant demand. Sales grew to over £100 million.

Single-sale products

Medsoft was a business founded to sell a microcomputer and a tailor-made software package to hospital doctors. Unfortunately, the management had no idea of the cost and effort required to sell each unit. Worse still, there were no repeat sales. It was not that customers did not like the products: they did, but each user needed only one product. This meant that all the money and time spent on building up a 'loyal' customer were largely wasted.

In another type of venture, for example selling company cars, you could reasonably expect a satisfied customer to come back every two or three years. In the restaurant business the repeat purchase cycle might be every two to three months.

Non-essential products

Entrepreneurs tend to be attracted to fad, fashion and luxury items because of the short response time associated with their promotion and sale. Companies producing for these markets frequently run into financial difficulties arising out of sudden market shifts. Market security is more readily gained by having products that are viewed as 'essential'.

CASE STUDY

Worlds of Wonder

This toymaker was an immediate success, and sales boomed. Sales in its second full year increased by 252 per cent to US$327 million, and profits by 130 per cent, on the back of two blockbuster products – Teddy Ruxpin, a talking bear, and Lazer Tag, a game of catch using laser beams and sensors.

Worlds of Wonder's mistake was in failing to shield itself against the fickleness of blockbusters. Its choice for its second trading year was Julie, a hi-tech doll that responded to a child's voice, a genus known in the trade as 'interactive plush'. Technically imperfect and costing a high US$100, Julie was an interactive flop with parents whose pockets proved less malleable than children's desires. WOW had nothing else to fall back on, and so – like other and earlier toymakers – it just fell.

The toy business has always been wickedly competitive. There is no shortage of entrepreneurs developing the greatest game since Scrabble and the best doll since Barbie (or, more recently, robot dogs). Margins are thin and entry costs low.

Diversification can be the best course for a firm with a blockbuster, rather than betting that its designers will have another winner next year. Coleco put US$60 million of its earnings from Cabbage Patch Dolls into buying the US makers of Trivial Pursuit, Scrabble and Talking Wrinkles, an electronic puppy. That revived Coleco's sales. More diversified still, Fisher-Price, a wizard with pre-school toys, is owned by Quaker Oats. In such a group the toymaker becomes a high-risk fling with part of group profits. If children turn away, the company can survive.

Too simple a product

Simplicity, usually a desirable feature, can be a drawback. If a business idea is so basic that little management or marketing expertise is required for success, this is likely to make the cost of entry low and the value added minimal. This makes it easy for every Tom, Dick or Harry to duplicate the product idea, and impossible for the original company to defend its market, except by lowering the price.

The video rental business was a classic example of the 'too simple product' phenomenon. Too many people jumped on the bandwagon as virtually anyone with a couple of thousand pounds could set themselves up. Rental prices fell from pounds to pence in a year or so, and hundreds of businesses folded.

CASE STUDY

Character Ltd

The founder of Character (Self-Assembly Furniture) Ltd included this product description in his business plan:

> The system at present allows the construction of chairs, tables, cupboards, chests of drawers, wardrobes, beds, a cot, climbing frame etc, in fact conceivably any item of furniture that a strong box-frame structure can be, or is required to be, an essential part of.

The crux of the system is an easily screwed together (by hand, no tools required) joining method, that imparts rigidity and strength while being only hand tight. An aim of the design was to keep as many components as possible common to each item of furniture, so that certain ideas could evolve by additional follow-up purchases. An example of this idea would be the progression from cot through to playpen, then to climbing frame, some components of the latter being usable in other items such as shelves or chairs. Another aim was to enable the transformation from one item to another to be very simply and very rapidly achieved.

The system will be available in a variety of solid woods or, where appropriate, veneered or laminated synthetic boards like medium density fibreboard (MDF). Metal fittings, where required, eg hinges, clips and holders, will be sturdy but discreet and, where possible, not visible externally.

The appearance is modern, though not avant-garde, with a style expected to be favoured by the groups identified as being the most likely purchasers. The natural style, as a consequence of the method of construction, would not be out of place in a Habitat store.

To summarise, the major features of this system which help to distinguish it are:

1. speed of assembly.
2. simplicity of assembly: no tools are required in the assembly of any piece – tools are only required for wall mounting of shelves or units and in these instances the design minimises the number of drilled holes required and maximises the simplicity of hanging.
3. attractive 'up-market' appearance of the assembled item.
4. consumer choice in the overall dimensions of the piece where possible, eg height of chairs, size and design of climbing frames, size and spacing of shelves in shelf system and room dividers.
5. sturdiness – something missing from much self-assembly furniture (SAF).
6. the buy as you go along feature, especially of the shelf systems and climbing frames.
7. ease and standardisation of manufacture – this should minimise manufacturing costs and offer the option of passing on the consequential benefit to the consumer.

I am at present investigating the possibility of patenting certain aspects of the way in which the elements of this furniture system are put together. A preliminary search at the Patent Office produced an optimistic result and a subsequent discussion with a Patent Agent confirmed that this is a real possibility. To get satisfactory protection for the product in the major European markets will cost around £20,000.

ONE PRODUCT MUST: QUALITY

One of the biggest problems for a new company is creating in the customer's mind an image of product quality. Once there was an almost faddish belief in 'dynamic obsolescence', implying that low quality would mean frequent and additional replacement sales. The inroads that the Japanese car makers have made on western car manufacturers through improving quality, reliability and value for money have clearly demonstrated the fallacy of this proposition.

You cannot sell a product you do not believe in and as James Knock, founder president of a beer company, explained, 'In cold calling the only thing standing between you and the customers' scorn is the integrity of your product.'

The Cranfield entrepreneurs that we have seen prosper have all learnt to fight the cost, quality and service trade-off: 'We are only interested in making the best quality and freshest pasta around,' explained Farshad Rouhani in describing how Pasta Masters had grown to become the leading supplier of fresh pasta to retailers and restaurants in London. Equally, David Sinclair and his team at Bagel Express were at work at 4 am each day to ensure that only freshly baked bagels were on sale each morning. To show the freshness of the product, the bagels were baked each day in open kitchens in front of the customers.

Quality is not just what you do, but also how you do it; each contact point between the customer and company is vital, be it on the telephone, at the counter, at the till. The customer who complains is probably your best friend. Julian Richer, the founder of Richer Sounds© maintains one of his key tasks is to maximize his customers opportunities to complain. By that he certainly doesn't mean giving them cause to be dissatisfied; just the chance to give feedback. Everything from having a bell at the door of each shop to ring if you have enjoyed your shopping experience, to a personally assigned response card in each packaged product is a step aimed at maintaining a direct link with the customer. Getting your customers to help you maintain your quality and standards is perhaps one of the keys to business success. And it isn't easy. It is believed that 96 per cent of complaints don't happen. In other words the customer can't or can't be bothered to complain. The quality obsession is clear; if you do not catch it, you will not survive, and unless you get regular feedback from your customers you will never know.

WORKSHEET FOR ASSIGNMENT 3: A DESCRIPTION OF YOUR PRODUCTS AND/OR SERVICES

1.   Describe your product or service, as if explaining it to a novice.
2.   Is it currently available for sale? If not, what needs to be done, how much will that work cost and how long will it take?
3.   Do you have, or plan to have, any legal protection such as patents? If so, explain what you have done so far to establish your rights.
4.   How is your product or service different from those already on the market?
5.   Will you be providing any warranties, guarantees or after-sales service?
6.   Are there any possibilities of developing new products or services complementary to the one(s) described above?

SUGGESTED FURTHER READING

Barrett, W, Price, C and Hunt, T (2008) *iProperty: profiting from ideas in an age of global innovation*, Wiley, New York
Cornish, W and Llewelyn, D (2007) *Intellectual property: patents, copyrights, trademarks and allied rights*, Sweet & Maxwell, London
Singleton, S (2005) *Internet and the law,* Tolley's Business, London

Phase 2

Market research

INTRODUCTION

Assignments 4–6 are intended to help you to bring your customers, competitors and the marketplace more sharply into focus, and to identify areas you have yet to research. The research should be done before the business is started or a new strategy is pursued, so saving the time and cost incurred if expensive mistakes are made. Obviously, the amount of research undertaken has to be related to the sums at risk. If a venture calls for a start-up investment of £1,000, spending £5,000 on market research would be a bad investment. However, new and small businesses that do not want to join the catastrophically high first-year failure statistics would be prudent to carry out some elementary market research, whatever level their start-up capital is to be.

As the President of the Harvard Business School said: 'If you think knowledge is expensive, try ignorance.'

The starting point in any market research has to be a definition of the scope of the market you are aiming for. A small general shop may only service the needs of a few dozen streets. A specialist restaurant may have to call on a much larger catchment area to be viable.

You may eventually decide to sell to different markets. For example, a retail business can serve a local area through the shop and a national area by mail order. A small manufacturing business could branch out into exporting.

People all too often flounder in their initial market research by describing their markets too broadly: for example, saying that they are in the motor industry when they really mean they sell second-hand cars in Perth; or saying they are in health foods, when they are selling wholemeal bread from a village shop. While it is important to be aware of trends in the wider market, this must not obscure the need to focus on the precise area that you have to serve.

The purpose of gathering the market research data is to help you decide on the right marketing strategy when it comes to such factors as setting your price, deciding on service and quality levels and choosing where and how much to advertise. Assignments 4 and 5 pose the main questions you need to answer concerning your customers and competitors, and Assignment 6 covers the principal ways in which basic market research can be conducted, and where such data can be found.

Assignment 4

Customers

Without customers no business can get off the ground, let alone survive. Some people believe that customers arrive after the firm 'opens its doors'. This is nonsense. You need a clear idea in advance of who your customers will be, as they are a vital component of a successful business strategy, not simply the passive recipients of new products or services.

Knowing something about your customers and what you plan to sell to them seems so elementary it is hard to believe that any potential business-person could start a business without doing so. But it is all too common, and one of the reasons many new businesses fail.

Here's a story that illustrates the pitfalls.

CASE STUDY

Tim Johnston

Tim took voluntary redundancy and decided to start his own business. His redundancy money combined with his savings gave him a total of £15,000, which he put into a vending machine business. He chose vending since he thought that with the demise of the tea lady it must be a growth market.

He surveyed the vending machine manufacturers and selected three machines that were easy to maintain and simple to fill and clean. He bought demonstration models at a discount, and installed them in his newly acquired office-cum-storeroom. He then looked for suppliers of ingredients, paying particular attention to the flavours, since he believed that vended drinks had a poor reputation.

Next he arranged with two leasing companies a deal by which they would finance the machines he sold to satisfactory customers.

All this took Tim four months and, by the autumn, he felt certain that he had a good product to offer. He then started to sell. First he called on established medium-sized local companies. It quickly became clear that they already had either a vending machine or well-rehearsed reasons for not wanting one. So Tim moved downmarket and went to see small and new companies, and immediately hit a new problem. The leasing companies he had lined up would only take on clients with a good financial track record. Otherwise they required the directors of the company to provide personal guarantees in case the company defaulted. Now Tim had to persuade customers not only to buy a vending machine but to abandon the shelter of limited liability to do so!

By the end of the first month of his sales campaign, Tim had called on 250 people, seen 28 and given two quotes for machines. His next task was to identify likely prospects via the telephone, but the closest he got to an order was from a firm that wanted a vending machine to provide refreshments for night-shift workers. The firm didn't care twopence about the quality of the ingredients; its only concern was that the machine could dispense all night on a single fill of drinks.

After six months 'in business' Tim closed down. Nearly half his cash was gone and he hadn't taken a single order.

RECOGNIZING CUSTOMER NEEDS

The founder of a successful cosmetics firm, when asked what he did, replied, 'In the factories we make perfume, in the shops we sell dreams.'

Those of us in business usually start out defining our business in physical terms. Customers on the other hand see businesses having as their primary value the ability to satisfy their needs. Even firms that adopt customer satisfaction, or even delight, as their maxim often find it a more complex goal than it at first appears. Take Blooming Marvellous, a case study in Assignment 1, by way of an example. It made clothes for the mother-to-be, sure enough: but the primary customer need it was aiming to satisfy was not either to preserve their modesty or to keep them warm. The need it was aiming for was much higher: it was ensuring its customers would feel fashionably dressed, which is about the way people interact with each other and how they feel about themselves. Just splashing a tog rating showing the thermal properties of the fabric, as you would with a duvet, would cut no ice with the Blooming Marvellous potential market.

Until you have clearly defined the needs of your market(s) you cannot begin to assemble a product or service to satisfy them.

CASE STUDY

Dockspeed Ltd

Andy Ingleston, a business studies graduate from Dover with a family transport background, noticed the increasing congestion at the United Kingdom's largest roll-on, roll-off port. Dover was the biggest port with the biggest problems: delays in clearing customs averaged 12 hours and could be three days! This was unproductive time for both the driver and the traction unit. Under the UK regulations, drivers were effectively counted as being 'on duty' while actually resting on board a ferry or awaiting clearance at a port. As a result, sailings could be missed during enforced rest periods, creating further expensive 'down time' while the vehicle was earning nothing. Andy identified five target customers – small northern hauliers with under 50 vehicles – who were suffering with this delay problem. By offering empty trailer units to these customers, clearing customs and transporting the original trailers across the Channel himself, he could turn idle time for the northern hauliers into work time for himself. One contract alone enabled him to break even in year 1. Within six years Dockspeed Ltd (http://dockspeed.co.uk), Andy's company, operated 43 vehicles, with a £9 million turnover, and had won many transport industry 'small business of the year' awards.

Extra profitable growth had come from responding to new customer needs as port conditions at Dover improved; in particular, this involved importing refrigerated products for Gervais Danone and exporting cut bread and sandwiches for Marks & Spencer and German Railways. The bulk of Andy's fleet were state-of-the-art refrigerated vehicles. Andy was able to sell the business to a major Danish transport conglomerate and take early retirement at 35! He is one of many Graduate Enterprise Programme millionaires!

Fortunately help is at hand when it comes to getting an inside track on your customers thought process. The US psychologist Abraham Maslow demonstrated in his research that 'all customers are goal seekers who gratify their needs by purchase and consumption'. He then went a bit further and classified consumer needs into a five-stage pyramid he called the hierarchy of needs:

- *Self-actualization.* This is the summit of Maslow's hierarchy in which people are looking for truth, wisdom, justice and purpose. It's a need that is never fully satisfied, and according to Maslow only a very small percentage of people ever reach the point where they are prepared to pay much money to satisfy such needs. It is left to the like of Bill Gates and Sir Tom Hunter to give away billions to form foundations to dispose of their wealth on worthy causes. The rest of us scrabble around further down the hierarchy.

- *Esteem.* Here people are concerned with such matters as self-respect, achievement, attention, recognition and reputation. The benefits customers are looking for include the feeling that others will think better of them if they have a particular product. Much of brand marketing is aimed at making consumers believe that conspicuously wearing the maker's label or logo so that others can see it will earn them 'respect'. Understanding how this part of Maslow's hierarchy works was vital to the founders of Responsibletravel.com (www.responsibletravel. com). Founded six years ago with backing from Anita Roddick (Body Shop) in Justin Francis's front room in Brighton, with his partner Harold Goodwin he set out to create the world's first company to offer environmentally responsible travel and holidays. It was one of the first companies to offer carbon offset schemes for travellers, and Responsibletravel.com boast that they turn away more tour companies trying to list on their site than they accept. They appeal to consumers who want to be recognized in their communities as being socially responsible.

- *Social needs.* The need for friends, belonging to associations, clubs or other groups and the need to give and get love are all social needs. After 'lower' needs have been met, these needs that relate to interacting with other people come to the fore. Hotel Chocolat (www.hotelchocolat. co.uk), founded by Angus Thirlwell and Peter Harris in their kitchen, is a good example of a business based on meeting social needs. They market home-delivered luxury chocolates but generate sales by having 'tasting clubs' to check out products each month. The concept of the club is that you invite friends round and using the firm's scoring system, rate and give feedback on the chocolates.

- *Safety.* The second most basic need of consumers is to feel safe and secure. People who feel they are in harm's way either through their general environment or because of the product or service on offer will not be over interested in having their higher needs met. When Charles Rigby set up World Challenge (www.world-challenge.co.uk) to market challenging expeditions to exotic locations around the world with the aim of taking young people up to around 19 years old out of their comfort zones and teaching them how to overcome adversity, he knew he had a challenge of his own on his hands: how to make an activity simultaneously exciting and apparently dangerous to teenagers, while being safe enough for the parents writing the cheques to feel comfortable. Six full sections on the website are devoted to explaining the safety measures the company takes to ensure that unacceptable risks are eliminated as far as is humanly possible.

- *Physiological needs.* Air, water, sleep and food are all absolutely essential to sustain life. Until these basic needs are satisfied higher needs such as self- esteem will not be considered.

You can read more about Maslow's needs hierarchy and how to take it into account in understanding customers on the MBA website (www.netmba. com>Management>Maslow's Hierarchy of Needs).

Segmenting the market

That customers have different needs means that we need to organize our marketing effort so as to address those individually. However, trying to satisfy everyone may mean that we end up satisfying no one fully. The marketing process that helps us deal with this seemingly impossible task is market segmentation. This is the name given to the process whereby customers and potential customers are organized into clusters or groups of 'similar' types. For example, a carpet/upholstery cleaning business has private individuals and business clients running restaurants and guest houses as its clients. These two segments are fundamentally different, with one segment being more focused on cost and the other more concerned that the work is carried out with the least disruption to the business. Also, each of these customer groups is motivated to buy for different reasons, and the selling message has to be modified accordingly.

These are some of the ways by which markets can be segmented:

- *Psychographic segmentation* divides individual consumers into social groups such as 'Yuppies' (young, upwardly mobile professionals), 'Bumps' (borrowed-to-the-hilt, upwardly mobile, professional show-offs) and 'Jollies' (jet-setting oldies with lots of loot). These categories try to show how social behaviour influences buyer behaviour. Forrester Research, an internet research house, claims when it comes to determining whether consumers will or will not go on the internet, how much they will spend and what they will buy, demographic factors such as age, race, and gender don't matter anywhere near as much as the consumers' *attitudes towards technology*. Forrester uses this concept, together with its research, to produce Technographics® market segments as an aid to understanding people's behaviour as digital consumers (http://www.forrester.com/rb/AllRoleTopics.jsp).

  Forrester has used two categories: technology optimists and technology pessimists, and has used these alongside income and what it calls 'primary motivation' – career, family and entertainment – to divide up the whole market. Each segment is given a new name – 'Techno-strivers', 'Digital Hopefuls' and so forth – followed by a chapter explaining how to identify them, how to tell whether they are likely to be right for your product or service and providing some pointers as to what marketing strategies might get favourable responses from each group.

- *Benefit segmentation* recognizes that different people can get different satisfaction from the same product or service. Lastminute.com claims two quite distinctive benefits for its users. First, it aims to offer people bargains that appeal because of price and value. Second, the company has recently been laying more emphasis on the benefit of immediacy. This idea is rather akin to the impulse-buy products placed at checkout tills, which you never thought of buying until you bumped into them on your way out. Whether 10 days on a beach in Goa or a trip to Istanbul are the types of things people 'pop in their baskets' before turning off their computers, time will tell.

- *Geographic segmentation* arises when different locations have different needs. For example, an inner-city location may be a heavy user of motorcycle dispatch services, but a light user of gardening products. However, locations can 'consume' both products if they are properly presented. An inner-city store might sell potatoes in 1 kg bags, recognizing that its customers are likely to be on foot. An out-of-town shopping centre may sell the same product in 20 kg sacks, knowing its customers will have cars. Internet companies have been slow to extend their reach beyond their own backyard, which is surprising considering the supposed global reach of the service. Microsoft exports only 20 per cent of its total sales beyond US borders, and fewer than 16 per cent of AOL's subscribers live outside the United States. However, the figure for AOL greatly overstates the company's true export performance. In reality, AOL does virtually no business with overseas subscribers, but instead serves them through affiliate relationships. Few of the recent batch of internet initial public offerings (IPOs) have registered much overseas activity in their filing details. By way of contrast, the Japanese liquid crystal display industry exports more than 70 per cent of its entire output.

- *Industrial segmentation* groups together commercial customers according to a combination of their geographic location, principal business activity, relative size, frequency of product use, buying policies and a range of other factors. Logical Holdings is an e-business solutions and service company that floated for over £1 billion on the London Stock Exchange and TechMark index, making it one of the UK's biggest IT companies. It was formed from about 30 acquisitions, with sales of over £800 million, employing 2,000 people wordwide. The company was founded by Rikke Helms, formerly head of IBM's E-Commerce Solutions portfolio. Her company split the market into three: 'small, medium-sized and big', tailoring its services specifically for each.

- *Multivariant segmentation* is where more than one variable is used. This can give a more precise picture of a market than using just one factor.

These are some useful rules to help decide whether a market segment is worth trying to sell into:

- *Measurability.* Can you estimate how many customers are in the segment? Are there enough to make it worth offering something 'different'?

- *Accessibility.* Can you communicate with these customers, preferably in a way that reaches them on an individual basis? For example, you could reach the over-50s by advertising in a specialist 'older people's' magazine with reasonable confidence that young people will not read it. So if you were trying to promote Scrabble with tiles 50 per cent larger, you might prefer that young people did not hear about it. If they did, it might give the product an old-fashioned image.

- *Open to profitable development.* The customers must have money to spend on the benefits that you propose to offer.

● *Size*. A segment has to be large enough to be worth your exploiting it, but perhaps not so large as to attract larger competitors.

One example of a market segment that has not been open to development for hundreds of years is the sale of goods and services to retired people. Several factors made this a particularly unappealing segment. First, retired people were perceived as 'old' and less adventurous; second, they had a short life expectancy; and finally, the knockout blow was that they had no money. In the last decade or so that has all changed: people retire early, live longer and many have relatively large pensions. The result is that travel firms, house builders, magazine publishers and insurance companies have rushed out a stream of products and services aimed particularly at this market segment.

Segmentation is an important marketing process, as it helps to bring customers more sharply into focus, and it classifies them into manageable groups. It has wide-ranging implications for other marketing decisions. For example, the same product can be priced differently according to the intensity of customers' needs. The first- and second-class post is one example, off-peak rail travel another. It is also a continuous process that needs to be carried out periodically, for example when strategies are being reviewed.

CASE STUDY

Flowcrete

In just 18 years, Dawn Gibbons MBE, co-founder of Flowcrete (www. flowcrete.com), took the company from a 400 sq ft unit (the size of a double garage) with £2,000 capital to a plc with a turnover of €52 million in the field of floor screeding technology, and clients including household names such as Cadbury, Sainsbury's, Unilever, Marks & Spencer, Barclays and Ford. Part of Flowcrete's success was down to a continuing focus on technical superiority. This attribute was engendered by Dawn's father, a well-respected industrial chemist with an interest in resin technology.

But arguably Dawn's skills contributed as much if not more to the firm's success. 'We want to be champions of change,' Gibbons claims. 'We have restructured a dozen times, focusing on new trends.' Markets and market segmentation are a vital part of any restructuring process – indeed, the best companies restructure around their customers' changing needs.

The first reappraisal came after seven years in business when Flowcrete realized that its market was no longer those firms that laid floors; it now had to become an installer itself. Changes in the market meant that to maintain growth Flowcrete had to appoint proven specialist contractors, train their staff, write specifications and carry out audits to ensure quality.

DEFINING THE PRODUCT IN THE CUSTOMERS' TERMS

Once you know what you are selling and to whom, you can match the features of the product (or service) to the benefits customers will get when they purchase. *Features* are what a product has or is, and *benefits* are what the product does for the customer. For example, cameras, SLR or lens shutters, even film are not the end product that customers want; they are looking for good pictures. Finally, as in Table 4.1, include 'proof' that these benefits can be delivered.

Remember, the customer pays for the benefits and the seller for the features. So the benefits will provide the 'copy' for most of your future advertising and promotional efforts.

WHO WILL BUY FIRST?

Customers do not sit and wait for a new business to open its doors. Word spreads slowly as the message is diffused throughout the various customer groups. Even then it is noticeable that generally it is the more adventurous types who first buy from a new business. Only after these people have given their seal of approval do the 'followers' come along. Research shows that this adoption process, as it is known, moves through five distinct customer characteristics, from 'innovators' to 'laggards', with the overall population being different for each group (see Table 4.2).

Let's suppose you have identified the market for your internet gift service. Initially your market has been constrained to affluent professionals within 5 miles of your home to keep delivery costs low. So if market research shows that there are 100,000 people that meet the profile of your ideal customer and they have regular access to the internet, the market open for exploitation at the outset may be as low as 2,500, which is the 2.5 per cent of innovators.

Table 4.1   Example showing product features, benefits and proof

Features	Benefits	Proof
We use a unique hardening process for our machine	Our tools last longer and that saves you money	– We have a patent on the process – Independent tests carried out by the Cambridge Institute of Technology show our product lasts longest
Our shops stay open later than others in the area	You get more choice when to shop	– Come and see
Our computer system is fault tolerant using parallel processing	You have no down time for either defects or system expansion	– Our written specification guarantees this – Come and talk to satisfied customers operating in your field

which means that   *you can see this is true because*

Table 4.2   The product/service adoption cycle

Innovators	2.5% of the overall market
Early adopters	13.5% of the overall market
Early majority	34.0% of the overall market
Late majority	34.0% of the overall market
Laggards	16.0% of the overall market
Total market	100%

This adoption process, from the 2.5 per cent of innovators who make up a new business's first customers, through to the laggards who won't buy from anyone until they have been in business for 20 years, is most noticeable with truly innovative and relatively costly goods and services, but the general trend is true for all businesses. Until you have sold to the innovators, significant sales cannot be achieved, so an important first task is to identify these customers. The moral is: the more you know about your potential customers at the outset, the better your chances of success.

One further issue to keep in mind when shaping your marketing strategy is that innovators, early adopters and all the other sub-segments don't necessarily use the same media, websites, magazines and newspapers, or respond to the same images and messages. So they need to be marketed to in very different ways.

CASE STUDY

William Alexander

Kentish hop farmer William Alexander first decided that there must be a market other than breweries for his flowering hop bines when he noticed that some of his bines were actually being stolen from the fields! Drying hop bines over his farmhouse Aga and trying to sell them for decoration purposes to local public houses drew no response. However, while standing in an early-morning flower-market queue at New Covent Garden, he was approached by buyers from the Sloane Street General Trading Company who offered to buy all the bines he was carrying and could produce.

Now equipped with his own drying kilns and a specialist dried-flower shop on his farm, he has daily contact with customers from all over south-east England. An article on the Hop Shop in the Saturday *Times* supplement produced orders from Hong Kong and Singapore. With an expanded dried-flower market range to meet customers' demands, production on 12 hectares of his farm now yields as much revenue as the traditional crops on the remaining 390 hectares.

The winning of a gold medal at the Chelsea Flower Show for dried flowers by his wife, Caroline, added to their growing customer network and reputation.

At the minimum, your business plan should include information on:

● Who your principal customers are or, if you are launching into new areas, who they are likely to be. Determine in as much detail as you think appropriate the income, age, sex, education, interests, occupation and marital status of your potential customers, and name names if at all possible.

McEvoy Wreford

Anthony Wreford was 35 when he started his PR company. He and partner Michael McAvoy invested £5,000 each, hired a secretary and rented three rooms in Mayfair. For the next two years they spent every waking moment getting McAvoy Wreford off the ground. 'We went through our complete list of contacts and invited anyone relevant over for lunch. To avoid wasting time, it became a standing joke to only deal with a MAN, which is shorthand for clients who have the Money, Authority and Need.'

After four years they were approached with a brilliant buy-out offer. Two years and a performance-related contract later, Wreford and McAvoy knew that they were millionaires. Their business is now part of GCI London (www.gciuk.com), which in turn is part of one of the world's biggest advertising agencies, WPP.

● What factors are important in the customer's decision to buy or not to buy your product and/or service, how much they should buy and how frequently?

Kwik-Fit

When Tom Farmer, the son of a Leith shipping clerk who earned £5 a week, launched Kwik-Fit (www.kwik-fit.com/history.asp), he had no idea how successful he would become, but he always knew it would have satisfied customers. The company has grown into a £418 million public company with almost 1,000 outlets. In his own words, the enduring philosophy behind his business, to which he ascribes its success, is '100 per cent customer satisfaction. Just giving service – phoning back in half an hour if you say you will, standing by promises – puts you miles ahead of anyone else in the field.' Knowing that service is as important as the exhaust pipes themselves is what has provided Kwik-Fit with a lasting competitive advantage.

- Many factors probably have an influence, and it is often not easy to identify all of them. These are some of the common ones that you should consider investigating:
  - (a) Product considerations
    - (i)   price
    - (ii)   quality
    - (iii)   appearance (colour, texture, shape, materials, etc)
    - (iv)   packaging
    - (v)   size
    - (vi)   fragility, ease of handling, transportability
    - (vii)   servicing, warranty, durability
    - (viii)   operating characteristics (efficiency, economy, adaptability, etc).

  - (b) Business considerations
    - (i)   location and facilities
    - (ii)   reputation
    - (iii)   method(s) of selling
    - (iv)   opening hours, delivery times, etc
    - (v)   credit terms
    - (vi)   advertising and promotion
    - (vii)   variety of goods and/or services on offer
    - (viii)   Appearance and/or attitude of company's property and/or employees
    - (ix)   Capability of employees.

  - (c) Other considerations
    - (i)   weather, seasonality, cyclicality
    - (ii)   changes in the economy – recession, depression, boom.

- Since many of these factors relate to the attitudes and opinions of the potential customers, it is likely that answers to these questions will only be found through interviews with customers. It is also important to note that many factors that affect buying are not easily researched and are even less easy to act upon. For example, the amount of light in a shop or the position of a product on the shelves can influence buying decisions.

You could perhaps best use the above list to rate what potential customers see as your strengths and weaknesses. Then see if you can use that information to make your offering more appealing to them.

● As well as knowing something of the characteristics of the likely buyers of your product or service, you also need to know how many of them there are, and whether their ranks are swelling or contracting. Overall market size, history and forecasts are important market research data that you need to assemble – particularly data that refer to your chosen market segments, rather than just to the market as a whole.

CASE STUDY

The Oriental martial arts and fitness centre

The Oriental, a martial arts and fitness centre situated in the city of Cambridge, aimed to provide specialized facilities for martial arts clubs, not then available in Cambridge. According to a publication at the time, *Sport in Cambridge*, sports and leisure generated £4.4 billion of consumer spending per annum and accounted for 376,000 jobs. Growth in indoor sports was linked with the growth in facilities. There were already 1,500 public sports centres and halls in the United Kingdom.

The Martial Arts Commission membership figures showed a growth in membership from 28,000 to 106,000 members in the five years prior to Oriental being started up. These figures do not include members of the British Judo Association (BJA), which had 41,700, an increase of 5 per cent over the previous year, or most self-defence classes, which have no governing body. Of martial arts instructors questioned, 77 per cent reported increasing interest in their martial art; none reported decreasing interest.

Fitness and exercise participation has been the fastest growing area for women's activities alongside sports in the past 20 years, with the popularity of jogging, fun-running, weight training and aerobics. A Sports Council survey suggests that 2.4 million women take part regularly in movement and dance, and that 10 per cent of women take part in aerobics and keep fit.

Customer benefits

The benefits offered by the centre were those of a well-equipped training area, large enough comfortably to hold courses and competitions for at least 200 people. The centre specialized in martial arts, but was also suitable for dance and keep fit.

For the primary customer, ie martial arts clubs, the centre offered the highest-quality training facilities for their needs in the area at affordable rates, and promoted their martial art, thus increasing participation levels.

For the secondary customer, ie the student of martial arts and participants in the other classes, the centre offered training in a pleasant atmosphere with good changing and showering facilities, a bar for relaxing in after training and a handy shop where equipment and books could be purchased.

Selected market segments

Two areas of the leisure market were selected for this venture: first, the martial arts sector, and second, the fitness (especially women's) sector.

The martial arts sector (including self-defence) covers the spectrum of income/occupation groups, drawing from all walks of life. Judo has the highest proportion of junior participants (three-quarters of the members of the BJA), whereas the other martial arts show participants mainly in the 25–35 age range.

Students mainly practise twice weekly (50 per cent), with 30 per cent training three or four times weekly and a further 16 per cent training in excess of four times per week; 47 per cent of students attend courses at least twice in a year, most travelling to those close to home, with a few (27 per cent) prepared to travel further than 300 miles, including going overseas.

The keep-fit market was fairly well served in the evenings in Cambridge by the community colleges and sports hall. There was a gap in women's weight training and in daytime classes for the unemployed or for mothers of younger children. This could be filled by offering crèche facilities during daytime classes.

WORKSHEET FOR ASSIGNMENT 4: CUSTOMERS

1. What is the geographic scope of the market you intend to serve and why have you so chosen?
2. What customer needs will your product or service satisfy?
3. List and describe the main different types of customer for your product/service.
4. Which of these market segments will you concentrate on and why?
5. Match the features of your product/service to the benefits on offer to customers in each of your chosen market segments. Provide proof, where possible.
6. Who are the innovators in each of your market segments?
7. What factors are important in the customer's decision to buy or not to buy your product/service?
8. Is the market you are aiming at currently rising or falling? What is the trend over the past few years?
9. What share of this market are you aiming for initially?

SUGGESTED FURTHER READING

Dockspeed Ltd, case history, parts A, B & C, Start-up and growth, teaching note (Reference: 595-004-1) and *The Hop Shop, case history, parts A, B & C,* Start-up and growth, teaching note (Reference: 595-009-1), both available from the European Case Clearing House, Cranfield, Beds MK43 0AL; tel: 01234 750903; fax: 01234 751125; website: www.ecch.cranfield.ac.uk; e-mail: ecch@cranfield.ac.uk

Hill, N, Roache, G and Allen, R (2007) *Customer satisfaction: the customer experience through the customer's eyes,* Cogent Publishing, London (you can download a sample chapter at www.customersatisfactionbook.com)

Stinnett, B (2004) *Think like your customers: a winning strategy to maximize sales by understanding and influencing how and why your customers buy,* McGraw-Hill Professional, USA

Yang, K (2007) *Voice of the customer: capture and analysis,* McGraw-Hill Professional, USA

Competitors

Researching the competition is often a time-consuming and frustrating job, but there are important lessons to be learnt from it. Some of the information that would be of most value to you will not be available. Particularly hard to find is information relating to the size and profitability of your competitors. Businesses, and particularly smaller businesses, are very secretive about their finances. Because of this, you may have to make estimates of the size and profitability of various firms.

RESEARCH ON COMPETITORS

When you begin your research, it is crucial that you make an accurate determination of your competitors. Remember, just because someone sells a similar product or service, that does not necessarily make him or her a competitor. Perhaps he or she makes the same product but sells it in an entirely different market. (By different market, we mean that it could be sold in a different geographical market, or to a different demographic market, etc.) Conversely, just because someone sells a product or service that is different from yours does not mean that he or she is *not* a competitor. Completely dissimilar products are often substitutable for each other.

Once you have identified your competitors, you need to classify them further as to 'primary', 'secondary', 'potential', etc. There are two reasons for doing this. First, you need to limit the number of firms that you will do your research on to a workable number. If you try to research 25 firms in depth, you won't have time to do anything else. If you end up with more than 10 or 12 primary competitors, you should probably do your research on only a sample. Second, you may want to classify competitors into primary and secondary because your marketing strategy may be different for each group.

As mentioned previously, finding out the size and profitability of your competitors may be difficult. You may be able to get some valuable information from the annual accounts that each company has to file at Companies House. However, you should be aware that these are often not filed when required, or they may be incomplete, or contain information of no value.

A second source of information is local business directories, such as *Keynote* and *Kelly's*. In addition to other types of information, these books list the category in which a particular company's sales volume falls. For instance, while they will not tell you the company's exact sales volume, they may tell you whether the company does less than £500,000–£1,000,000, etc.

Another way to find out size and profitability totals is to read the publications that cover the business scene. The financial section of your newspaper and trade magazine often contains stories that can be used for research.

If you have been unable to get the necessary information from published sources, try doing some primary research. Contact the company directly and ask them your questions. Usually you will not get the information that you want, but occasionally this approach does work. Next, contact the firm's suppliers, or other individuals who are in a position to know or estimate the information. Sometimes you can get a ballpark figure, if not an exact one, from a wholesaler or other supplier.

CASE STUDY

David Sinclair

Before starting his own bagel retail operation, David Sinclair studied a number of competitive bagel and croissant outlets. By counting the number of customers at peak hours and on different days, knowing what average purchase amounts were by his own personal visits (£2 per head), David was able to establish what the likely level of turnover would be for his competitors and hence his own future outlet. His first year's sales estimate of £216,000 was within 95 per cent of the actual figure.

Finally, you may be able to make a reasonable estimate from the bits and pieces of information that you were able to collect. This is commonly done with the use of operating ratios. To illustrate, let us assume that you are researching a large restaurant. You are unable to find out its annual sales volume but after striking up a conversation with one of the employees you find out that the restaurant employs 40 full-time people. Because of your knowledge of the restaurant industry, you feel confident in estimating the restaurant's payroll at £240,000 a year. From a book that lists operating ratios for the restaurant industry (published by the trade association) you find that payroll expenses, as a percentage of sales, average 40 per cent. With these facts you are able to estimate the annual sales volume of the restaurant at £600,000.

Several points should be noted here. First, operating ratios are published by a variety of trade associations and businesses. For most types of business they are not that difficult to obtain. Second, this approach is not limited to employment ratios. You can make estimates based upon inventory levels, rent or other expenses. Third, learning to use this technique is not difficult. Once you understand the use and logic of ratio analysis, you should be able to make estimates like the above. These estimates are derived by doing the ratio analysis in reverse. Instead of taking figures and working out the ratio, you start with the ratio and work out the figures. Fourth, the use of estimates resulting from this technique should be only a last resort, or used in conjunction with estimates derived in some other way. The reason for this is not that the ratio you found in the books may be 'average' but that the particular business may, for a variety of reasons, be far from average. (See Assignment 22, 'Financial controls', for a description of the key operating and financial ratios.)

ANALYSING THE COMPETITION

The following are some of the areas that you should cover in this section of your business plan.

Description of competitors

Identify those businesses that are or will be competing with you. If the number is few, list them by name. If there are many, then describe the group without naming them individually ('47 charter fishing boat operators'). List any expected or potential competitors.

Mainframe

Jonathon Woodrow, a 25-year-old fine arts graduate who took part in a Cranfield enterprise programme, prepared the following preliminary analysis of the likely competitors to his company, Mainframe:

- *Framing outlets (franchised).* A company called Fastframe operates in the Newcastle area. They have adapted a US approach to the system, which incorporates the latest picture-framing machinery in workshops attached to the picture shops. They have now established nearly 50 outlets across the country, through a franchise operation which has a combined turnover of £4 million a year. None is based in the Greater London area.

- *The Frame Factory* operates in North London. Within five years of starting up they established 10 shops in Cambridge, Nottingham and secondary locations in Islington, Hampstead and London suburbs such as Streatham and Hornsey. Some of these were set up under a recent franchise operation.

- *Framing outlets (multi-location).* Frame Express was set up in Wimbledon, London. This company closely followed the Fastframe approach (they were originally registered as Fastaframe). They have now established eight shops in central and south-east London.

    A slightly different approach to fast framing has been introduced recently by a company called Fix-A-Frame. They operate two shops, in Old Brompton Road, Kensington and Swiss Cottage in north-west London. Here, customers are invited to do part of the work on their frames themselves, under supervision. This obviously cuts costs, and may appeal to certain customers, but for many people cost is acceptable if the service is good, and very often time is the important factor.

- *Independent shops.* By far the majority of picture framing outlets in London are operated as independent shops providing a local service on a small scale. They offer diverse services which frequently take weeks to achieve, and are considerably more expensive than most fast-framing shops. This is because they incur greater labour charges and do not enjoy the benefits of bulk purchase, due to their comparatively low volume of trade.

- *Local competition.* A survey of the area around Holborn confirms that there are no frame shops comparable to the Mainframe operation for at least a one-mile radius. There are three shops offering a framing service within a short walking distance of the site, of which only one treats framing as the primary activity. These are not seen as direct competition, as they appear to be aiming at a local domestic market, which is not the principal Mainframe target.

Size of competitors

Determine the assets and sales volume of the major competitors. Will you be competing against firms whose size is similar to yours or will you be competing against giant corporations? If assets and sales volume cannot be determined, try to find other indications of size, such as number of employees, number of branches, etc.

CASE STUDY

Scoops

The proprietor of 'Scoops', a proposed pick'n'mix sweet shop, got something of a shock researching his market while on an enterprise programme at Cranfield. He found out from Companies House that the small shop in Bath he proposed to emulate was owned by a multinational food company, and was not a one-man band as he thought. Further research revealed that this multinational planned a chain of franchised outlets if the Bath shop was a success.

His original strategy was to open a similar shop in another town and then perhaps grow slowly over five more years. This new information on his competitive environment confirmed that the market was very attractive, but forced him to adopt a different strategy on premises. He couldn't hope to match a franchisee-resourced chain head on, so he went for a shop-in-shop approach. This meant he could open new outlets at least as fast as his competitor, but use even less capital. His first concession in Hamley's in Birmingham was successful, leading to three more outlets in his first year of operation – a rate of growth he could not have sustained adopting his original strategy. Subsequently, however, when all 'out of London' Hamley's stores were sold, he found himself in difficulties with the new store owners.

Profitability of competitors

Try to determine how profitable the business is for those companies already in the field. Which firms are making money? Losing money? How much?

Operating methods

For each of the major competitors, try to determine the relevant operating methods. For example, what pricing strategy does each firm use? Other issues, besides price, that you may consider are:

- quality of product and/or service;
- hours of operation;
- ability of personnel;
- servicing, warranties and packaging;
- methods of selling: distribution channels;
- credit terms: volume discounts;
- location: advertising and promotion;
- reputation of company and/or principals;
- inventory levels.

Many of the above items will not be relevant to all businesses. Location will not be relevant, perhaps, to a telephone-answering service. On the other hand, there are many items that are not listed above that may be very relevant to your business. In the motor trade, trade-in value and styling may be as relevant as the price. So it is very important for you to determine the relevant characteristics on which you will do your research.

Summary of analysis of competitors

After you have completed your research it is useful to summarize your findings in tabular form, such as shown in Table 5.1. Keep in mind that the characteristics listed are for illustration only. You must decide the relevant characteristics that will go into your own table.

When the table is complete, analyse the information contained in it to reach your conclusions. Is there a correlation between the methods of

Table 5.1 Example showing an analysis of the competition

Name	Assets	Profits	Sales	Quality	Credit terms	Location	Price	Customer service	Inventory levels	Direct sale or wholesale

Conclusions – Key factors for success in your industry are:

operation and other characteristics, and the size and/or profitability of the competitors? A thoughtful analysis is essential because there may be many patterns shown. For instance, you may find that all the profitable companies are large, and all the unprofitable companies are small. That would be an easy pattern to spot (and an important one, as well) because it involves only two factors, profitability and size. However, it is more common that success and failure correlate with a number of factors that are not always so easy to discern, even when your findings are summarized on one page.

Looking for patterns is not the only type of analysis that is needed. You may find that a company is very successful, even though its characteristics are completely different from those of the other profitable firms. What factors apparently contribute to its success? Or you may find that a company is failing despite the fact that its operational characteristics are similar to those of the profitable firms. Can you identify the reason?

Once you have reached conclusions about the competition, relate them to your business. What is the competitive situation in the market? Is everyone making money and expanding, or is it a dog-eat-dog situation? Are your competitors likely to be much larger than you? If so, what effect will this have? Are there some operating methods that appear critical to success in this market? If so, will you be able to operate in the necessary fashion? Are there operating methods or characteristics not being widely used in the market which you think have merit? If so, why are they not found at present? Is it because they have been overlooked, or because they have problems that you have not foreseen?

The above are some of the questions you will want to address. You will probably have many others. The important thing, though, is for you to decide the general outlook for your business. At this point in your research, does it appear that you will be able to compete successfully in this market? Do you now feel that you know what it will take in order to compete successfully? If you can answer these two questions to your satisfaction, you have probably done an adequate job of research, like the Brighton Furniture Co Ltd researcher looking into bulk furniture sales, whose results are shown in the case study.

Brighton Furniture Co Ltd

Despite the fact that there are over 100 furniture dealers in Brighton, the bulk of the new flats and town house developments get their furniture packages from only six firms. In my market research I found that from 80 to 99 per cent (depending on who you talk to) of the 'packages' were sold by those six firms. The firms are identified by name in Table 5.2.

Product characteristics

To get information on the products sold by each of the firms, I talked to eight developers who had selected one or more of the six firms to provide a furniture package for their units; I also talked to 23 individuals who had purchased a package for their premises from one of the six firms. In general, the purchasers felt that their furniture was performing about as they had expected. The one exception was that buyers of the Apartment Furniture Co products all felt that the quality was not as good as they had been led to believe.

A summary of other characteristics for each company is presented in Table 5.2. Based upon these findings, I have divided the six into three groups, and labelled them as follows:

- *High quality, high price.* The only firm in this category is Rattan Imports, which sells only rattan furniture. As one would expect, its sales are to the more expensive developments.

- *Moderate price, high quality.* Again, only one firm, Georgian Furniture, is in this category. The bulk of its sales were made in developments where one-bedroom units cost from £75,000 to £100,000, although it did get the contract for one more expensive building.

- *Low price, varying quality.* Four of the six firms appear to be competing in the lower end of the package-deal market. Three of the four sell 'casual' furniture, and the fourth sells bamboo furniture. Overall, there is not much difference in warranty and delivery service, but there is some variation in price (from a low of £4,200 to a high of £5,100) and upkeep (Apartment Furniture Co and Bamboo Things Ltd products appear to require less maintenance than the other two). There is, however, a wide disparity between the firms in trade-in value.

Table 5.2 Example showing company characteristics

Competitors' names	Sales (£)	Profits (£)	Year started	Credit terms	Salespeople/ Reps	Manufacturer
Condo Supplies Co	750,000	125,000	1993	50% deposit	Salespeople	No
Georgian Furniture	300,000	60,000	1997	50% deposit	Salespeople	No
AAA Furniture Inc	1,250,000	75,000	2000	COD	Salespeople	Yes
Rattan Imports Inc	500,000	125,000	1999	COD	Salespeople	No
Bamboo Things Ltd	600,000	150,000	1998	50% deposit	Salespeople	No
Apartment Furniture Co	400,000	10,000	1999	COD	Salespeople	Yes

Bamboo Things furniture holds its value much better than the other firms' products, being almost 2.5 times better than the products of AAA and Apartment Furniture.

Company characteristics

By talking to four of the six firms (the other two refused) and by researching various published sources, I was able to prepare Table 5.2. Some characteristics that bear mentioning are:

- All six firms use in-house salespeople rather than manufacturers' representatives.

- There does not seem to be any particular correlation between performance and the number of years in business.

- Although the sales of the two firms that concentrate on the higher-price furniture are relatively small, their profits as a percentage of sales are very high.

- The two firms that manufacture their own furniture have the lowest profits as a percentage of sales.

Analysis of competition

Based upon the data gathered, the following analysis of the competition seems reasonable:

- The high-price, high-quality segment of market seems the most profitable. There is only one competitor; the firm has been in existence only a few years and sales are already over £500,000 a year; profit/sales is running at 25 per cent; and the firm is not quite as aggressive as it could be since it requires full payment on delivery.

- The moderate-price, high-quality segment of the market also seems to have good potential since there is only one firm presently in the market. On the negative side, this firm has been operating a year longer than Rattan Imports and seems to be more aggressive than Rattan (as shown by its lower profit/sales ratio and its more liberal credit policy), yet its total sales ratio may be low because of some inefficiencies on the company's part.

- The lower-price segment of the market seems to be very competitive. Of particular concern is the fact that two of the firms manufacture their own furniture. AAA Furniture is the leader in terms of both price and sales, and yet its profits and those of the other manufacturer, Apartment Furniture, seem very low.

It seems likely that both these companies are willing to accept low profits because they are making the bulk of their money from manufacturing. This fact is important because it means that they could even afford to sell at a cheaper price and make money, whereas I have to make a profit on the retail sales.

The fact that Condo Supplies is able to remain profitable in the face of this competition is due to the company's years in business, and the reputation for quality and service that it has cultivated with the big developers. A new firm, such as mine, would be at the mercy of the manufacturers since I do not have the reputation of Condo Supplies, nor a unique product such as Bamboo Things Ltd.

Based on this, I conclude that I have neither the unique line nor the reputation to compete successfully in the lower-priced end of the market. However, I feel that I can upgrade sufficiently to enter the moderate-price, high-quality or the high-price, high-quality segment. Of the two, the high-price segment seems most likely since Rattan Imports is not as aggressive as Georgian Furniture; also, the high-price segment seems to be larger and faster growing than the moderate-price segment.

The purpose of your competitive analysis is twofold:

- to determine where your competitor is weak and how he or she might retaliate to your activity;

- to help you define what should be your product's point of difference, based on your understanding of the key factors for success in your industry sector. (See outline example, Table 5.1, p97.)

DECIDING ON ADVANTAGE

The outcome of your research into customers and competitors is a clear idea of the market niche you are going to sell into first, and what will be different or better about your product or service. For a business planning to offer a local gardening service, the outcome of its research should allow it to make the following kind of analysis.

We have two local competitors:

- Thompson's with six employees has been around for 10 years and has a small number of larger domestic clients but mostly does work for schools and business premises. It charges £20 an hour, for a minimum of 4 hours a week, and doesn't take away garden refuse from homes. It covers the whole county.

- Brown is a one-man band that been operating for three years but he offers a limited service – he doesn't do hedge trimming, tree pruning or take away garden refuse, and charges out at £12 an hour, with no minimum. He claims to cover a radius of 20 miles, but doesn't seem to want to go more than 5 miles.

My initial strategy will be to concentrate on larger domestic clients within 5 miles who need hedges trimmed and trees pruned and would appreciate having their garden refuse removed for them. I will set out to make these clients feel important in a way that Thompson's does not, as they appear to only take on domestic customers as a 'favour'. I will charge out at £15 an hour with a minimum of 2 hours a week per client, and will target a limited number of quality areas with high-value houses. My goal will be to get at least two clients in an area, and stick to areas that are easily accessible from my home.

The easiest way to find out what your competitors are doing right or wrong is to try them out. Even if you don't actually buy or even need what they sell, there is nothing in the rules that says you can't enquire. Suppose for example you intend to set up a bookkeeping service. First search out local small businesses, using if necessary one of the sources described above. Then 'enquire' about their services with a list of questions, some of which you may find answers to in their leaflet or on their website.

WORKSHEET FOR ASSIGNMENT 5: COMPETITORS

1. List and briefly describe the businesses with which you will be competing directly.
2. Analyse their size, profitability and operating methods, as far as you can.
3. What are their relative strengths and weaknesses compared both with each other and with your business?
4. What, in the light of this competitive analysis, do you believe to be the critical factors for success in your business sector?
5. What is unique about your proposition that makes it stand out from the competition?

SUGGESTED FURTHER READING

Bagel express, case history, parts A, B & C, Start-up and growth, video and teaching note (Reference: 595-032-1), available from the European Case Clearing House, Cranfield, Beds MK43 0AL; tel: 01234 750903; fax: 01234 751125; website: www.ecch.cranfield.ac.uk; email: ecch@cranfield.ac.uk

Fleisher, C and Bensoussan, B (2007) *Business and competitive analysis: effective application of new and classic methods*, Financial Times/Prentice Hall, London

Porter, M E (2004) *Competitive strategy: techniques for analyzing industries and competitors*, Free Press, New York

Assignment 6

A plan for market research

It is unlikely that you will already have the answers to all the important questions concerning your marketplace. The purpose of the market research element of the workbook is to ensure you have sufficient information on customers, competitors and markets so that your market entry or expansion strategy is at least on the target, if not the bullseye itself. In other words, enough people want to buy what you want to sell at a price that will give you a viable business. If you miss the target completely, you may not have the resources for a second shot.

One of the sad aspects of new business starts is that often the one-in-three failure rate for businesses in the first three years of life involves someone investing a lump-sum payment received from a previous redundancy, through taking early retirement, or from an inheritance. It is one of the paradoxes of small businesses that whereas you cannot start without investing some time and money, it may be safer to have more time than money. Those with their own money frequently have less pressure from banks or financial investors to research their ideas thoroughly first, simply because they do not have to go to see the bank manager in the early stages to obtain support before starting. Those with time but inadequate resources always have to seek advice before starting, and inevitably this will include researching the market as widely as possible before commencing. You do not have to open a shop to prove there are no customers for your goods or services; frequently some modest DIY market research beforehand can give clear guidance as to whether your venture will succeed or not.

The purpose of practical DIY market research for entrepreneurs investigating or seeking to start a new business is, therefore, twofold:

- To build *credibility* for the business idea; the entrepreneur must demonstrate first to his or her own satisfaction, and later to outside financiers, a thorough understanding of the marketplace for the new product or service. This will be vital if resources are to be attracted to build the new venture.

- To develop a *realistic* market entry strategy for the new business, based on a clear understanding of genuine customer needs and ensuring that product quality, price, promotional methods and the distribution chain are mutually supportive and clearly focused on target customers.

Otherwise, 'fools rush in, where angels fear to tread'; or, as they say in the army, 'time spent in reconnaissance is rarely time wasted'. The same is certainly true in starting a business, where you will need to research in particular:

- *Your customers*: who will buy your goods and services? What particular customer needs will your business meet? How many of them are there?

- *Your competitors*: which established companies are already meeting the needs of your potential customers? What are their strengths and weaknesses?

- *Your product or service*: how should it be tailored to meet customer needs?

- *What price* should you charge to be perceived as giving value for money?

- *What promotional material* is needed to reach customers; which newspapers, journals do they read and which websites and blogs are they likely to visit?

- *Where should you locate* to reach your customers most easily, at minimum cost?

Research, above all else, is not just essential in starting a business, but once it is launched, must become an integral part in the ongoing life of the company. Customers and competitors change; products have life cycles. Once started, however, ongoing market research becomes easier, as you will have existing customers (and staff) to question. It is important that you monitor regularly their views on your business (as the sign in the barber shop stated: 'We need your head to run our business') and develop simple techniques for this purpose (eg touch screens, questionnaires for customers beside the till, suggestion boxes with rewards for employees).

THE SEVEN STEPS TO EFFECTIVE MARKET RESEARCH

Researching the market need not be a complex process, nor need it be very expensive. The amount of effort and expenditure needs to be related in some way to the costs and risks associated with the business. If all that is involved with your business is simply getting a handful of customers for products and services that cost little to put together, then you may spend less effort on market research than you would for, say, launching a completely new product or service into an unproven market that requires a large sum of money to be spent up front.

However much or little market research you plan to carry out, the process needs to be conducted systematically. These are the seven stages you need to go through to make sure you have properly sized up your business sector.

Step 1: Formulate the problem

Before embarking on your market research you should first set clear and precise objectives, rather than just setting out to find interesting general information about the market. The starting point for a business idea may be to sell clothes, but that is too large and diverse a market to get a handle on. So, that market needs to be divided into, say, clothes for men, women and children, then further divided into clothes for working, leisure, sport and social occasions. This process is known as segmenting the market. A further segment could cover special occasions such as weddings. Even once you have narrowed your idea down to, say, smart clothes for women, the definition of what is smart will differ for each age group. Most businesses end up selling to several different market segments, but when it comes to detailed market research you need to examine each of your main segments separately.

So, for example, if you are planning to open a shop selling to young fashion-conscious women, among others, your research objective could be: to find out how many women aged 18 to 28, with an income of over £25,000 a year, live or work within 2 miles of your chosen shop position. That would give you some idea whether the market could support a venture such as this.

Step 2: Determine the information needs

Knowing the size of the market, in the example given above, may require several different pieces of information. For example, you would need to know the size of the resident population, which might be fairly easy to find out, but you might also want to know something about people who come into the catchment area to work, for leisure purposes, on holiday or for any other major purpose. There might, for example, be a hospital, library, railway station or school nearby that also pulls potential customers to that particular area.

Step 3: Where you can get the information

This will involve either desk research in libraries or on the internet, or field research, which you can do yourself or get help in doing. Some of the most important of these areas were covered earlier in this chapter.

Field research – that is, getting out and asking questions yourself – is the most fruitful way of gathering information for a home-based business.

Step 4: Decide the budget

Market research will not be free even if you do it yourself. At the very least there will be your time. There may well be the cost of journals, phonecalls, letters and field visits to plan for. At the top of the scale could be the costs of employing a professional market research firm.

Starting at this end of the scale, a business-to-business survey comprising 200 interviews with executives responsible for office equipment purchasing decisions cost one company £12,000. Twenty in-depth interviews with consumers who are regular users of certain banking services cost £8,000. Using the internet for web surveys is another possibility, but that can impose too much of your agenda onto the recipients and turn them away from you.

Check out companies such as Free Online Surveys (http://free-online-surveys.co.uk) and Zoomerang (www.zoomerang.com/web/signup/Basic.aspx) which provide software that lets you carry out online surveys and analyse the data quickly. Many such organizations offer free trials.

Doing the research yourself may save costs but may limit the objectivity of the research. If time is your scarcest commodity, it may make more sense to get an outside agency to do the work. Using a reference librarian or university student to do some of the spadework need not be prohibitively expensive. Another argument for getting professional research is that it may carry more clout with investors.

Whatever the cost of research, you need to assess its value to you when you are setting your budget. If getting it wrong would cost £100,000, then £5,000 spent on market research might be a good investment.

Step 5: Select the research technique

If you cannot find the data you require from desk research, you will need to go out and find the data yourself. The options for such research are described in the next section, under 'Field research'.

Step 6: Construct the research sample population

It is rarely possible or even desirable to include every possible customer or competitor in your research. So you have to decide how big a sample you need to give you a reliable indication how the whole population will behave.

Step 7: Process and analyse the data

The raw market research data needs to be analysed and turned into information to guide your decisions on price, promotion and location, and the shape, design and scope of the product or service itself.

FIRST STEPS

There are two main types of research in starting a business:

- *desk research*, or the study of published information;
- *field research*, involving fieldwork in collecting specific information for the market.

Both activities are vital for the starter business.

Desk research

There is increasingly a great deal of secondary data available in published form, and accessible either online or via business sections of public libraries throughout the United Kingdom to enable new home-business starters to quantify the size of market sectors they are entering and to determine trends in those markets. In addition to populations of cities and towns (helping to start quantification of markets), libraries frequently purchase Mintel reports, involving studies of growth in different business sectors. Government statistics, showing trends in the economy, are also held (*Annual Abstracts* for the economy as a whole, *Business Monitor* for individual sectors).

If you plan to sell to companies or shops, *Kompass* and *Kelly's* directories list all company names and addresses (including buyers' telephone numbers). Many industrial sectors are represented by trade associations, which can provide information.

Sources of desk research information

If your market is very confined, the local telephone directory may have all the information you need to list your competitors. If you have to look further to cover a wider geography, including overseas, there are numerous directories that list businesses by trade, area and size.

Aside from the names and basic contact details you will need to find out some facts about your competitors, what they do, how they are organized, what their turnover, profit and financial structure are and whether or not they are privately owned or part of a larger group of businesses. You need this information to see how to compete and decide whether or not the business area looks profitable.

These sources will provide much of the background data on the businesses and customers in your market:

- Applegate (www.applegate.co.uk) has information on 237,165 companies cross-referenced to 57,089 products in the United Kingdom and Ireland. It has a neat facility that allows you to search out the top businesses and people in any industry.

- The British Franchise Association (www.thebfa.org>INTERNATIONAL> WORLD FRANCHISE COUNCIL MEMBERS) is a directory of country franchise associations from which you can find information about franchising in each country.

- Business.com (www.business.com): contains some 400,000 listings in 25,000 industry, product, and service subcategories. Useful for general industry background or details about a particular product line.

- Chambers of Commerce (www.chamberonline.co.uk>International Trade> International Chambers) run import/export clubs, provide international trade contacts, and provide market research and online intelligence through a 150-country local network of chambers. Their Link2Exports (www.link2exports.co.uk) website provides specific information on export markets by industry sector and by country.

- Companies House (www.companieshouse.gov.uk) is the official repository of all company information in the United Kingdom. Its WebCHeck service offers a free of charge searchable company names and address index which covers 2 million companies. You can search by either name or the company's unique company registration number. You can use WebCHeck to purchase a company's latest accounts giving details of sales, profits, margins, directors, shareholders and bank borrowings at a cost of £1 per company.

- Corporate Information (www.corporateinformation.com > TOOLS > Research Links) is a business information site covering the main world economies, offering plenty of free information. This link takes you to sources of business information in over 100 countries.

- Easy Searcher 2 (www.easysearcher.com) is a collection of 400 search engines, both general and specialist, available on drop-down menus, listed by category.

- Euro Info Centres (www.euro-info.org.uk) is a network of 250 centres across Europe providing local access to a range of specialist information and advisory services to help business owners expand. Its services include advice on funding as well as help with market information through its network contacts and specialist information services.

- Europages (www.europages.com) provides 900,000 company addresses from over 35 European countries, hundreds of company brochures, access to key business information and links throughout Europe. The directory can be searched by product, service, name or country.

- Kelly's (www.kellysearch.co.uk) lists information on 200,000 product and service categories across 200 countries. Business contact details, basic product and service details and online catalogues are provided.

- Keynote (www.keynote.co.uk), part of the Bisnode Group, currently operates in 18 countries providing business ratios and trends for 140 industry sectors, which give you information to assess accurately the financial health of each industry sector. Using this service you can find out how profitable a business sector is and how successful the main companies operating in each sector are. Executive summaries are free, but expect to pay between £250 and £500 for most reports.

- Online Newspapers (www.onlinenewspapers.com). Newspapers and magazines are a source of considerable information on companies, markets and products in that sphere of interest. Virtually every online newspaper in the world is listed here. You can search straight from the homepage, either by continent or country. You can also find the 50 most popular online newspapers from a link in the top centre of the homepage. There is also a separate site for online magazines (www.onlinenewspapers.com/SiteMap/magazines-sitemap.htm).

- Research and Markets (www.researchandmarkets.co.uk) is a one-stop shop that holds nearly 400,000 market research reports listed in a hundred or so categories and across over 70 countries. Reports are priced from €20 upwards.

- Thomas Global Register (www.thomasglobal.com) is an online directory in 11 languages with details of over 700,000 suppliers in 28 countries. It can be searched by industry subsector or name either for the world or by country.

- The Wholesaler UK (www.thewholesaler.co.uk) is a directory for a wide range of products. It is intended for businesses looking for additional suppliers, but as such provides a valuable first sift to see who is in the market.

- The World Intellectual Property Organization (www.wipo.org> Resources>Directory of IP Offices) provides a country-by-country directory of the organizations responsible for intellectual property (IP) (patents, trademarks, logos, designs and copyright) around the world. From there you can find the rules and procedures for protecting IP.

- World Market Research Associations (www.mrweb.com), while it does not quite cover the world, does have web addresses for over 65 national market research associations and a hundred or so other bodies such as the Mystery Shopping Providers Association, which in turn has over 150 member companies worldwide.

- Yellow Pages World (www.yellowpagesworld.com>Yellow Pages International) is an international directory of online yellow pages and white pages whose goal is to make it easy to find an online yellow pages or white pages provider in the country you want to search in. Currently 31 countries are covered. Select the country you want, and you will be taken to a link showing the nearest equivalent the country has to a 'yellow pages'. Usually the directory will be in English. For example choosing Brazil takes you to BrazilBiz where you have a choice of English or Portuguese as languages to search with.

Using the internet

The internet is a rich source of market data, much of it free and immediately available. But you can't always be certain that the information is reliable or free of bias, as it can be difficult if not impossible to always work out who exactly is providing it. That being said, you can get some valuable pointers to whether or not what you plan to sell has a market, how big that market is and who else trades in that space. The following sources should be your starting point:

- Blogs are sites where people, informed and ignorant, converse about a particular topic. The information on blogs is more straw in the wind than fact. Globe of Blogs (www.globeofblogs.com), launched in 2002, claims to be the first comprehensive world weblog directory. It links up to over 58,100 blogs, searchable by country, topic and about any other criteria you care to name. Google (http://blogsearch.google.com) is also a search engine to the world's blogs.

- Find Articles.com (www.findarticles.com) aims to provide credible, freely available information you can trust. It has over 10 million articles from thousands of resources, archived dating back to 1984 on its website. You can see a summary of all articles and most are free, though in some cases you may need a modest subscription (rarely costing more than a few pounds). You can restrict your search to those articles that are free by selecting 'free articles only' from the right-hand pull-down menu.

- Google News (www.google.com), which you can tap into by selecting 'News' on the horizontal menu at the top of the page under the Google banner. Here you will find links to any newspaper article anywhere in the world covering a particular topic. Asking for information on baby clothes will reveal recent articles on how much the average family spends on baby clothes, the launch of a thrift store specializing in secondhand baby clothes and the launch of an organic baby clothes catalogue.

- Google Trends (www.google.co.uk>Labs>Google Trends) provides a snapshot on what the world is most interested in at any one moment. For example if you are thinking of starting a bookkeeping service, entering that into the search pane produces a snazzy graph showing how interest measured by the number of searches is growing (or contracting) since January 2004 when Google stared collecting the data. You can also see that South Africa has the greatest interest and the Netherlands the lowest. You can tweak the graph to show seasonality, thus showing that Croydon registers the greatest interest in the United Kingdom overall and 'demand' peaks in September and bottoms out in November.

- The Internet Public Library (www.ipl.org) is run by a consortium of US universities whose aim is to provide internet users with ways of finding information online. There are extensive sections on business, computers, education, leisure and health.

- Inventory Overture (http://inventory.overture.com/d/searchinventory/ suggestion/) is a search tool showing how many people searched Yahoo! for a particular item. So for example while 10,837 looked for either baby or baby and toddler clothing, only 927 searched for organic baby clothing, 167 for used baby clothing and 141 for cheap baby clothing: facts that give useful pointers as to the likely price sensitivity in this market.

- Microsoft (http://adlab.microsoft.com) is testing a product that can give you mass of data on market demographics (age, sex, income etc), purchase intentions and a search funnel tool that helps you understand how your market searches the internet. Using the demographics tool you can find that 76 per cent of people showing an interest in baby clothes are female and 24 per cent are male. The peak age group is the 25–34 year olds, and the lowest is the under 18s followed by the over 50s.

- Trade Association Forum (www.taforum.org>Directories>Association Directory) provides a directory of trade associations on whose websites are links to industry-relevant online research sources. For example you will find the Baby Products Association listed, at whose website you can find details of the 238 companies operating in the sector with their contact details.

Field research

If you are contemplating opening a classical music shop in Exeter focused on the young, while desk research might reveal that out of a total population of 250,000 there are 25 per cent of under 30-year-olds, it will not state what percentage are interested in classical music or how much they might spend on classical CDs. Field research (questionnaire in street) provided the answer of 1 per cent and £2 a week spend, suggesting a potential market of only £65,000 a year (250,000 × 25 per cent × 1 per cent × £2 × 52). The entrepreneurs decided to investigate Birmingham and London instead! But at least the cost had only been two damp afternoons spent in Exeter, rather than the horrors of having to dispose of the lease of an unsuccessful shop.

Fieldwork is big business in the United Kingdom, where market research companies pull in around £1 billion a year from survey work. Most field-work carried out consists of interviews, with the interviewer putting questions to a respondent. We are all becoming accustomed to it, whether being interviewed while travelling on a train, or resisting the attempts of enthusiastic salespeople posing as market researchers on doorsteps ('sugging', as this is known, is illegal, though you might be forgiven for believing otherwise). The more popular forms of interview are currently:

- personal (face-to-face) interview: 55 per cent (especially for the consumer markets);

- telephone and e-mail: 32 per cent (especially for surveying companies);

- post: 6 per cent (especially for industrial markets);

- test and discussion group: 7 per cent.

Personal interviews and postal surveys are clearly less expensive than getting together panels of interested parties or using expensive telephone time. Telephone interviewing requires a very positive attitude, courtesy, and an ability to not talk too quickly and listen while sticking to a rigid questionnaire. Low response rates on postal services (less than 10 per cent is normal) can be improved by including accompanying letters explaining the questionnaire's purpose and why respondents should reply, by offering rewards for completed questionnaires (a small gift), by sending reminder letters and, of course, by providing prepaid reply envelopes. Personally addressed e-mail questionnaires have secured higher response rates – as high as 10–15 per cent – as recipients have a greater tendency to read and respond to e-mail received in their private e-mail boxes.

However, unsolicited e-mails ('spam') can cause vehement reactions. The key to success is the same as with postal surveys – the mailing should feature an explanatory letter and incentives for the recipient to 'open' the questionnaire.

All methods of approach require considered questions. In drawing up the questionnaire attention must be paid first to these issues:

- Define your research objectives; what exactly is it that you need vitally to know (eg how often do people buy, how much)?

- Who are the customers to sample for this information (eg for DIY products, an Ideal Home Exhibition crowd might be best)?

- How are you going to undertake the research (eg face-to-face in the street)?

When you are sure of the above, and only then, you are ready to design the questionnaire. There are six simple rules to guide this process:

- Keep the number of questions to a minimum.

- Keep the questions simple! Answers should be either 'Yes/No/Don't know' or offer at least four alternatives.

- Avoid ambiguity – make sure the respondent really understands the question (avoid 'generally', 'usually', 'regularly').

- Seek factual answers, avoid opinions.

- Make sure at the beginning you have a cut-out question to eliminate unsuitable respondents (eg those who never use the product/service).

- At the end, make sure you have an identifying question to show the cross-section of respondents.

The introduction to a face-to-face interview is important; make sure you are prepared, either carrying an identifying card (eg student card, Association of Market Researchers watchdog card) or have a rehearsed introduction (eg 'Good morning, I'm from Manchester University [show card] and we are conducting a survey and would be grateful for your help'). You may also need visuals of the product you are investigating (samples, photographs), to ensure the respondent understands. Make sure these are neat and accessible. Finally, try out the questionnaire and your technique on your friends, prior to using them in the street. You will be surprised at how questions that seem simple to you are incomprehensible at first to respondents!

The size of the survey undertaken is also important. You frequently hear of political opinion polls taken on samples of 1,500–2,000 voters. This is because the accuracy of your survey clearly increases with the size of sample, as Table 6.1 shows:

Table 6.1

Size of random sample	95 per cent of surveys are right within ... percentage points
250	6.2
500	4.4
750	3.6
1,000	3.1
2,000	2.2
6,000	1.2

So if on a sample size of 600, your survey showed that 40 per cent of women in the town drove cars, the true proportion would probably lie between 36 and 44 per cent. For small businesses, we usually recommend a minimum sample of 250 completed replies.

Remember above all, however, that questioning is by no means the only or most important form of fieldwork. Sir Terence Conran, when questioned on a radio programme, implied that he undertook no market research fieldwork (ie formal interviews) at all. Later in the programme he confessed, nonetheless, to spending nearly 'half of his time visiting competitors, inspecting new and rival products, etc'. Visiting exhibitions and buying and examining competitors' products (as the Japanese have so painfully done, in disassembling piece-by-piece competitor cars, deciding in the process where cost-effective improvements could be made) are clearly important fieldwork processes.

Andrews University in the United States has a free set of lecture notes explaining the subject of sample size comprehensively (www.andrews. edu/~calkins/math/webtexts/prod12.htm). At www.auditnet.org/docs/stats amp.xls you can find some great Excel spreadsheets that do the boring maths of calculating sample size and accuracy for you. ResearchInfo.com (www.researchinfo.com/docs/websurveys/index.cfm) gives the basics of writing a program for you to use your own questionnaire on the internet.

Testing the market

The ultimate form of market research is to find some real customers to buy and use your product or service before you spend too much time and money in setting up. The ideal way to do this is to sell into a limited area or small section of your market. In that way if things don't quite work out as you expect you won't have upset too many people.

This may involve buying in as small a quantity of the product as you need to fulfil the order so that you can fully test your ideas. Once you have found a small number of people who are happy with your product, price, delivery/execution and have paid up, then you can proceed with a bit more confidence than if all your ideas are just on paper.

Pick potential customers whose demand is likely to be small and easy to meet. For example if you are going to run a bookkeeping business, select five to 10 small businesses from an area reasonably close to home and make your pitch. The same approach would work with a gardening, babysitting or any other service-related venture. It is a little more difficult with products, but you could buy a small quantity of similar items in from a competitor or make up a trial batch yourself.

Selling from stalls on a Saturday, or taking part in an exhibition, gives an opportunity to question interested customers and can be the most valuable fieldwork of all. All methods are equally valid, and the results of each should be carefully recorded for subsequent use in presentation and business plans.

Quantum Cars

Mark and Harvey Wooldridge exhibited their prototype fibreglass sports car at the Stoneleigh Kit Car Show, where the previous year they had conducted detailed market research among the kit car crowd enthusiasts. Not only were orders received, but the kit car was favourably reviewed by the top four kit car magazines, enabling the brothers to begin commercial production. Soon their business, Quantum Cars (www.quantumcars. co.uk), was producing two cars a week and had won the confidence-building East Midlands Small Business of the Year Award.

A saloon version and a Mark 2 sports model have subsequently been added to the range, necessitating a move to larger premises as Quantum continues to prosper.

Once the primary market research (desk and field research) and market testing (stalls and exhibitions) are complete, pilot testing of the business should be undertaken in one location or customer segment, prior to setting targets and subsequently measuring the impact of a full regional launch.

Example questionnaire

Back in 1983 Chantal Coady was seeking to open a continental chocolate shop in the lower King's Road, London. Hesitating, because of the size of the annual rent (£27,850 pa at 2008 prices) and premium sought for the premises (£150,000 at 2008 prices), Chantal decided to carry out some market research to see whether there would be enough interested passing customers to carry these heavy costs. The questionnaire used, together with results and comments on this useful exercise, is shown below. Chantal's business, Rococo (www.rococochocolates.com) is still based in the same area of London. She opened a second shop in Marylebone High Street (London), has a thriving mail order business with a turnover of over £3 million a year, and runs workshops in chocolate making at the Rococo factory in Dulwich, south-east London.

Date: Location: Time:

1.   I am interested in people buying chocolate – can you tell me how often you buy the following:

	Every day	Every week	Once a month	Special occasions
Bars				
Boxes				
Loose chocs				

2.   Where do you buy these chocolates?

Supermarket	[ ]
Sweet shop	[ ]
Woolworths	[ ]
Specialist shop	[ ]
Other	[ ]

3.   When was the last time you were given chocs as a present? Some people enjoy receiving chocs as a gift – where would you put yourself on this scale?

Overjoyed   Very pleased   Pleased   Indifferent   Ungrateful
4.   Do you ever buy chocs as a present for anyone?
     The last time you bought chocs for someone, who were they for?
5.   Where did you buy them from?
6.   How much did you spend? Up to £1 [ ] Up to £5 [ ] Over £5 [ ]
7.   Were they wrapped in the shop? (as a gift)
8.   Do you have a favourite chocolate bar or box?
9.   Any preferences for Dark [ ] Milk [ ] White [ ]
10. Do you have a favourite from any particular country?
     English   French   German   Belgian   Swiss   Other
11. Some people say that the existing chocolates on the market are rather boring – would you agree?
12. If there were a shop which sold a unique range of gifts in chocolate, and high-quality loose and boxed chocs, how interested would you be in buying them?
     Extremely   Very   Moderately   Indifferent   Not interested
13. Age group
     Up to 20   [ ]
     21–25   [ ]
     26–30   [ ]
     31–40   [ ]
     41–50   [ ]
     Over 50   [ ]
14. Profession
15. Income bracket
     Up to £5,000   [ ]
     Up to £10,000   [ ]
     Up to £15,000   [ ]
     Over £15,000   [ ]
     Any other comments

Figure 6.1   Questionnnaire for Chantal Coady's 'Rococo' chocolate shop

Objectives and results of the questionnaire

The purpose of the questionnaire was:

● to quantify positive response to a chocolate shop at this location as a percentage of total population;

- to establish the 'character' of the positive respondent in terms of socio-economic grading, ie profession/income bracket, their buying habits and their unfulfilled requirements (ie customer needs);
- to clarify the problem gift area (ie product types).

The character of the target market can be split into two main parts:

- the passing trade, of which the weekday and Saturday influx constitute different subdivisions;
- the genuine residents, many of whom have lived in the area for generations.

Chantal explained:

I have decided to poll the residents in their own right by direct leafleting. There will be an incentive to reply (such as a reduction in the price of a box of chocolates). At the same time I shall be sampling the passing trade, by means of the questionnaire. Thus I expect to obtain information about these different market sectors.

The sample

The figures below represent the first 100 questionnaires. Early results bore out expectations that the Saturday afternoon shoppers on the King's Road were made up of a large number of under-20-year-olds, groups D and E (up to £10,000 pa).

Total sample to date: 100 (50 male, 50 female).

Table 6.2   Results of the first 100 questionnaires

No.	Age		Socio-economic grading	%
30	up to 20	which		
20	21–25	converts	E up to £5,000	42
20	26–30	to:	D £5,001–10,000	28
10	31–40		C £10,001–15,000	11
10	41–50		B £15,001–20,000	8
10	over 50		A over £20,000	11
100				100

General information drawn from the sample

Customers

Ninety per cent of this sample buy chocolate bars more than once a week. Sixty per cent bought boxes of chocolates for special occasions such as birthdays, Christmas, Easter, Mother's Day, or for a thank-you present. Only 10 per cent said that they never bought boxed chocolate.

When asked if they had ever bought chocolate as a gift for a particular person, 86 per cent responded positively, and the categories of people for whom the gift was bought are as follows:

Table 6.3

Category	%
friends	44
mothers	26
relations	15
grandparents	8
wives	4
lovers	3
	100

Price

When asked how much they had spent on the last box of chocolates bought as a gift:

15 per cent spent under £1
75 per cent spent up to £5
10 per cent spent over £5

Ninety-six per cent responded positively when asked if they had ever been given chocolates as a gift. Their reactions to receiving chocolates as a gift were:

- 45 per cent were very pleased or overjoyed.

- Only 3 per cent were ungrateful: one suffered from migraine, one preferred scotch, one was on a diet.

- 20 per cent of the sample bought chocolates from specialist shops, the rest were bought in sweet shops, garages or supermarkets.

Product

Chocolate preferred (by nationality type):

Table 6.4

Chocolate nationality	Preferred by %
Swiss	37
English	25
Belgian	16
French	7
German	3
US	1
Italian	1

Trades and professions in the sample were widely varied, including the titles:

- student;
- secretary;
- civil servant;
- teacher;
- financier;
- hotelier;
- roof tiler;
- jelly-baby maker.

The diversity of favourites showed no clear pattern, and ranged through specialist Belgian fresh-cream chocolates such as Godiva and Leonidas, standard boxes like Lindt and Bendicks, to Mars bars and Double Deckers.

When asked if they thought the existing chocolates on the market were boring (and this was evidently a question that they had not considered):

- 43 per cent said that they found them boring;
- 57 per cent were negative.

An attempt was made to test the response to the 'Rococo' concept of fanciful product lines, without leading the respondent:

- 18 per cent were extremely interested;
- 16 per cent were very interested;
- 21 per cent were moderately interested;
- 20 per cent were indifferent;
- 25 per cent were not interested.

These figures show that 55 per cent responded to 'Rococo' positively.

When examined in terms of age groups and income brackets a pattern quickly became evident: the A/Bs showed a high degree of awareness, and an established buying pattern of high-quality chocolates. They were also interested in a shop which offered a service superior to that otherwise available.

Examination of the lower income brackets showed less awareness of available products and less readiness to spend money on them.

In the age groupings, the over-50s showed little desire to buy novelty chocolates, though the As, Bs and Cs aged 26–50 seemed to have a definite appetite for high-class, well-presented chocolates.

Of the positive respondents only 12 per cent had been offered a gift-wrapping service in the shop where they had bought the chocolate.

Summary of findings so far

The overall habits of the chocolate-buying public (which is the majority of the population) were supported by the early findings, which were that the average Briton eats 8 oz of chocolate per head/per week. I will carry a wide range of chocolate bars for everyday consumption.

It also appears that at some time in the year, most people will buy chocolate as a gift. When chocolate is purchased, in the normal way, it would not come with a gift presentation.

The awareness of certain 'Rococo' product lines will have to be heightened by advertising in the appropriate media; for example: Chocolate Cameras in the *British Journal of Photography*.

Competition

Other chocolate shops in London:

- Charbonnel and Walker, Bond Street;
- Prestats, South Molten Street;
- Thornton, Covent Garden;

- Elena, Hampstead, Edgware and St John's Road;

- Harrods and Selfridges;

- Clare's, Regent's Park;

- Ackermans, Smithfield and NW6;

- Bendicks, Sloane Street and Mayfair;

- Richoux, Knightsbridge;

- Newmans, City and Shaftesbury Avenue.

None of these shops offer the kind of service I am proposing.

Following two further Saturdays of market research, Chantal was able to tabulate the largely positive results and make successful representations to her bank for finance to lease the shop. Rococo has subsequently been a happy 'success story' in the King's Road.

DOING ONLINE QUESTIONNAIRES

Get online user feedback

To get the best out of an online presence you should use your site to learn more about your customers; this will help you to tailor your offerings to their needs. You need to get information about your customers and store it in a way that allows you to use it when they visit your site again. Below are some of the ways in which you can get this user feedback.

Cookies

These are small files deposited on the hard disk of anyone visiting your site. If you have cookies set up on your site, your server will be able to read visitors' cookie files on their hard drives. The information contained in them can be related back to any information on your customer database. A cookie might contain a customer's name, the type of computer they use, their password for accessing your site and any other routine information that would otherwise have to be re-entered every time they returned to your site.

Executable programs

Inviting customers to install an 'executable program' is another means of getting online feedback. This will allow you to get a lot more information about the user, but is seen as intrusive by most people. In all probability, fewer than one in five users will let you install such a program, but in some circumstances it may work well.

Personalization

You could go a stage further and offer an intelligent internet tool such as My Web, which reacts to customers' shopping habits and suggests different sites related to subjects or products in which they are interested. You can then monitor customers' reactions to these suggestions and use the information to refine your own offerings in a highly sophisticated manner.

Questionnaires

Web questionnaires can help by getting very detailed user feedback. They are similar to paper-based questionnaires, but with a few major advantages. As there are no paper or postage costs, you can 'mail' as many users as you like as often as you like. Questionnaire distribution and feedback can be very quick. Also, rudimentary analysis of feedback can be done automatically by inserting links between the questionnaire and some spreadsheets.

CASE STUDY

Julian Talbot-Brady

Julian Talbot-Brady, Cranfield MBA and qualified architect, investigated launching 'EU-architect.com', an internet-based start-up company tar-geted at the United Kingdom's 30,000 registered architects. The aim was to provide a 'one-stop', all-in-one service to meet the needs of busy architects by providing easily accessible online sources for all their information needs. He designed a questionnaire to be e-mailed directly to the top 100 architectural practices in the United Kingdom, as well as to the leading 500 construction product suppliers. He chose to use Zoomerang.com, which at the time provided a free 30-day trial. Despite an accompanying letter (offering possible equity sharing), the resulting response rate of only 12 per cent made him realize that the potential for his service was much smaller than he had anticipated, leading him to accept a post with an industry supplier to develop a similar site for its own products.

Remember, if you are storing personal data about your customers on your site, they have a right to know what is going to happen to those data. In Europe and elsewhere, there are laws on data protection with which you will have to comply.

WORKSHEET FOR ASSIGNMENT 6: A PLAN FOR MARKET RESEARCH

1. What information do you currently have on customers, competitors, markets, etc?
2. What information do you still need to find, and why specifically do you need it?
3. What desk research will you have to carry out to answer this question?
4. What field research will you have to carry out?
5. How much time and money will be needed to carry out this market research?
6. Who will be responsible for each element of the research?
7. When will all the key market research information be available?

SUGGESTED FURTHER READING

Quantum cars, case history, parts 1, 2 & 3, Start-up and Growing the business, teaching note (Reference: 397-115-1), available from the European Case Clearing House, Cranfield, Beds MK43 0AL; tel: 01234 750903; fax: 01234 751125; website: www.ecch.cranfield.ac.uk; e-mail: ecch@cranfield.ac.uk

Adams, K and Brace, I (2006) *An introduction to market and social research*, Kogan Page, London

Barrow, C (2006) *The complete small business guide*, 6th edn, Capstone Reference, Oxford

Kaden, R (2007) *Guerilla marketing research*, Kogan Page, London

Sue, V and Ritter, L (2007) *Conduction of online surveys*, Sage, Calif, USA

Phase 3

Competitive business strategy

INTRODUCTION

The data you have begun to collect should enable you to formulate a competitive business strategy. This will involve explaining exactly how you intend to satisfy your target customers, with the products or service you will provide, in the face of competition.

Musto Ltd

Keith Musto, a round-the-world yachtsman, explains how he developed a winning strategy for Musto Ltd, his sailmaking business.

> We recognized that the boat clothing market was wide open. Most of it was being made by clothing manufacturers who were not sailors. We felt we could turn our sewing machines from making sails to making clothes, faster than they could learn to sail. We knew what was needed to improve clothing design to make sailors perform better. A warm, dry sailor is a safer sailor.

Musto developed a range of designs to keep storms out, from windsurfer to round-the-world yachtspeople. He used the best synthetic materials to keep the wearer comfortable in a three-layer system, which consists of 'good underwear that sucks the moisture from the skin like blotting paper; then a middle layer using fibres to trap as much warm air as possible; and a protective outer layer to keep the storms out'.

His clothing has been endorsed by leading sailors. But the biggest accolade came when the company won a Duke of Edinburgh's Design Award for its latest outfit. The British and Spanish lifeboatmen wore jackets and trousers based on this design, which was rigorously tested by the RAF's Medical Research Centre at Farnborough.

'We were a long way ahead of our competitors in those tests,' says Musto. 'The Spaniards knew the RNLI and the RAF were very thorough and were happy to follow on.'

You have at your disposal a 'mix' of ingredients which, according to how they are used, can produce different end results. There will obviously have to be an internal consistency in your actions. For example, a high-quality image, supported by a prestige location and sophisticated advertising, is hardly consistent with a very low price and untidy staff.

The principal elements of this 'marketing mix', as it is frequently called, are the product or service you have to sell, the price you propose to charge, the promotion you will use to communicate your message, and the place you will operate from or the distribution channels you will use (ie where do your customers have to be for you to get at them?).

You may find when you come to tackle the assignments in this phase that you have to collect more data. This is not unusual – indeed, gathering information is a continuous activity in a healthy business. Unfortunately, this healthy search for additional data can lead to some confusion as to how eventually to formulate strategy.

The strategic framework shown in Figure P3.1 should put the whole strategic process clearly in view and help you to formulate a clear course of action.

STRATEGIC FRAMEWORK

The foundation of this process is a clear statement of the mission of your venture, your objectives and the geographic limits you have set yourself, at least for the time being. These issues were addressed in the first assignment and until they are satisfactorily resolved, no meaningful strategy can be evolved.

Market research data are then gathered on customers, competitors and the business environment, for example, to confirm that your original perception of your product or service is valid. More than likely this research will lead you to modify your product in line with this more comprehensive appreciation of customer needs. You may also decide to concentrate on certain specific customer groups. Information on competitors' prices, promotional methods and location/distribution channels should then be available to help you to decide how to compete.

No business can operate without paying some regard to the wider economic environment in which it operates. So a business plan must pay attention to factors such as:

●   The state of the economy and how growth and recession are likely to affect such areas as sales, for example. During a time of economic recession, start-ups sometimes benefit from increased availability of premises, second-hand equipment etc, and find they develop sales strongly as the economy and markets recover. For example, Cranfield MBA Robert Wright developed ConnectAir at the end of one recession

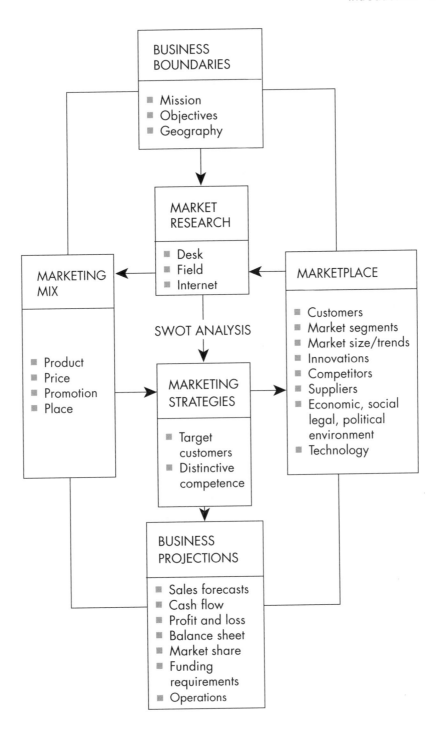

Figure P3.1   Elements of a business strategy

and was able to sell to Air Europe at the height of the Lawson boom – a trick that he subsequently repeated for 10 times that value (£75 million) a decade later!

- Any legislative constraints or opportunities. One Cranfield enterprise programme participant's entire business was founded solely to exploit recent laws requiring builders and developers to eliminate asbestos from existing properties. His business was to advise them how to do so.

- Any changes in technology or social trends that may have an impact on market size or consumer choice. For example, the increasing number of single-parent families may be bad news at one level, but it's an opportunity for builders of starter unit housing. And the increasing trend of wives returning to work is good news for convenience food sales and restaurants.

- Any political pressures, either domestic or pan-European, that are likely to affect your business. An example was New Labour's law against late payment of bills. The government's aim was to help small firms get paid more quickly by large firms. However, experience elsewhere, where such legislation is in force, showed clearly that large firms simply alter their terms of trade. In that way many small firms actually ended up taking longer to collect money owed them, rather than just the unlucky or the inefficient ones.

If you sell on credit to larger firms, debtors will be an important element of your business capital base, in which case this particular political pressure could be an issue for your business. If you run a shop selling for cash to private customers this issue will be of little interest.

The process by which all these data are examined is called the SWOT analysis: your company's strengths and weaknesses are analysed and compared with the perceived environment, opportunities and threats. Its purpose is to allow you to develop a strategy using areas in which you are more able than the competition to meet the needs of particular target customer groups.

Harvard's Professor Michael Porter has concluded that there are three distinctive marketing strategies for a company to pursue:

- *Overall cost leadership,* characteristic of large companies, which are able to achieve economies of scale by major capital investment, to operate on low margins by virtue of efficient control systems and to create barriers of entry through low pricing. The major car manufacturers exemplify these traits; although Henry Ford lost money in his first year of operation with the Model T, he raised his prices considerably above those of Buick in his second year of trading and was subsequently able to trim prices, from a profitable basis, in a growing market.

- *Differentiation*, characterized by quality, good design and image, with high margins, based on achieving brand loyalty and unique products. If you think this is not possible for your company, just remember how Perrier managed to sell a basic commodity, water, in the United Kingdom, at a price that rivals Coca-Cola in the shops and when sold in a pub is on a par with gin and tonic!

- *Focus*, whereby a company serves one particular target market well, with low costs and high margins, creating barriers to entry by the very narrowness of the market and raising distribution barriers. For example, Autoglass Ltd focused simply on the replacement windscreen market in the United Kingdom (the average motorist would suffer only one broken windscreen every 20 years), too small to attract the attention of the major glass manufacturers, and by establishing a depot network was able to build a strong windscreen distribution network, able to supply garages and support a fleet of mobile fitters.

Our experience with new starters at Cranfield has emphasized the importance for the small company of the second and third of these strategies, sometimes judiciously mixed, particularly bringing into play the four major elements of the marketing mix (product, price, promotion and place) to emphasize your differentiation and focus.

Many new start-ups at the turn of the millennium sought to benefit from the newly available internet technology and vigorously pursued a cost leadership strategy. The low margins often implicit in this strategy left little room for manoeuvre when things went awry. For example, Cranfield MBA Dexter Kirk, with 12 traditional clothing stores, noted: 'My heart is only gladdened by the final reality that has set in on dot.com apparel marketing. Funny, we old lags called it "mail order" and knew that you should allow for 30 per cent returns. When I told Boo.com that at a meeting before Christmas, they thought I was mad. I also warned my daughter who is in dot.com PR that "brown boxes" would be the problem, ie fulfilment is the most unsexy part of the job. Sure enough, one of her B2C clients delivered all their Christmas trees on January 5th!'

Needless to say, neither company survived. Hence the need to emphasize differentiation and focus with better margins in the early learning phase of start-up and business growth.

Rex Online

After his success with Goldsmiths Fine Foods, Simon Hersch was called in to help loss-making Rex Online. Its innovative website was designed to link recruitment agencies with job-seeking IT staff. He realized that to be successful, the company had to differentiate itself from other online recruitment companies like Stepstone and Monster.com. To this end, Rex Online was developed to include:

- broadened multi-channel access for employers and job seekers (internet, phone and face-to-face);

- a more personalized service for employers, offering pre-screening and psychometric testing of applicants;

- a device enabling companies to buy direct links on Rex to their own websites;

- the creation of different internet brands – Jobtrack.co.uk, Jobmagic. net and Gimmejobs.com – allowing specialization through target marketing to create industry-specific databases for candidates.

Simon was able to raise £1 million from capital markets to build this differentiated strategy for a predicated higher-margin company.

The final element in this strategic framework is the business projection of the likely financial outcome of your strategic decisions. The outcome should, of course, coincide with your starting objectives.

An example of a competitive business strategy for a Cranfield enterprise programme participant is set out below.

Competitive business strategy for the Total Yoghurt Company

We plan to specialize in retailing frozen yoghurt, a product similar in appearance and consistency to ice cream. There all similarities end as our product is far lower in terms of calories, and is designed as a healthy and delicious snack that can be eaten throughout the year. There will be a variety of flavours, ranging from cappuccino to mandarin orange, complemented by a choice of optional toppings from fresh fruit to chocolate chip – the yoghurt and topping combined will be known as 'Frogurt'.

We are aiming at three primary segments:

- The youth market, aged 6–18, who will make up a small portion of our customer base. They will prefer simple flavours with sweet toppings.

- The 18 to 35 range, who, as Euromonitor's *Healthy Food and Healthy Eating Report* provides irrefutable evidence, combine a rapidly increasing health awareness level with a growing demand for convenience foods and confectionery items. This segment will be the most adventurous, preferring fruity flavours with fresh fruit toppings.

- The 35+ age range, who, although even more health-conscious than the earlier groups and with the highest disposable income, are less likely to be product innovators than either of the previous groups.

There is strong evidence that all three of these segments are already 'heavy' yoghurt users and the overall market has grown from £900 million to £2,800 million in the seven years prior to start-up.

There is also evidence that much of this rapid growth can be attributed to new product innovations such as Frogurt. Over the past six years the sales of fruit yoghurt have shrunk from 93 per cent of the market to 50 per cent, with children's natural, whole milk, set type, long-life and very low-fat yoghurt claiming the balance.

Our objectives are:

Short term: 6 months to 2 years

- To have our first frozen yoghurt outlet up and running successfully.

- To have developed a sound base of expertise upon which to build a substantial enterprise.

Long term: 2 to 7 years

- To have 3–6 retail outlets up and running, owned and managed by the Total Yoghurt Company Ltd.
- To have 15 franchised outlets opened up.
- To make Frogurt a household name.

There are currently six retailers of frozen yoghurt in London:

- The Garden Store, Holborn – health food/fruit shop;
- Natural Dividends, Trocadero – healthy fast foods;
- Onion, Holborn – sandwich bar;
- Selfridges, Oxford Street – food hall;
- Harrods, Knightsbridge – food hall;
- Healthy Eats, Victoria Station – healthy fast foods.

The above outlets exist only as indirect competition to the Frogurt outlet for two reasons:

- Frogurt will specialize in frozen yoghurt, whereas the above treat it as an additional product.
- Frogurt will be started in catchment areas largely unaffected by the above outlets' marketplace.

Competition will arise in the form of ice cream outlets and vans, although Frogurt is not to be seen as an ice cream substitute but rather as a completely different concept of a soft-serve, low-calorie, healthy and original snack.

Marketing strategy (product, price, promotion and place)

One of our policies is to use yoghurt with natural ingredients. The frozen yoghurt mix used in the production of Frogurt contains non-fat milk solids, honey, fructose, no preservatives, no fat or salt and only natural colouring from beetroot and elderberries. The natural, healthy and low-calorie features of Frogurt will appeal to all consumers whose health awareness levels have been or are increasing. The delicious flavours and toppings coupled with the product's originality are features which will appeal to consumers regardless of their health interest.

Product

There will be five yoghurt flavours to choose from. This range of flavours will change from day to day. Complementing this variety will be 7–10 different types of topping which will be a fixed range. The on-the-spot nature of the manufacturing process means that once the outlet has closed and the machines have been cleaned out, a new flavour may be used the following day. The flavours available from our suppliers can be found in the appendix (not included here). The proposed toppings are as follows:

- fruit salad;
- crushed nut;
- chocolate chip;
- mini marshmallow;
- raisins or sultanas;
- granola;
- Smarties.

The product will be served in small, medium and large sizes.

Price

Prices will vary according to the size of yoghurt serving. There will be one price charged for any of the toppings, which will be optional. Given a cost of approximately 20 pence for a 3.5 ounce serving and an expected gross profit margin of 75 per cent, the average price of the product is 80 pence. The expected prices per serving are as follows:

- small   60p
- medium 80p
- large   100p
- toppings 20p

Further analyses of costings, projections and competitors' prices are shown in the appendix.

Promotion

These techniques and ideas are being evaluated for the promotional aspect of the business:

● A large emphasis will be placed on hygiene at each outlet and this will be portrayed by specifically designed fixtures and fittings.

● All the positive aspects of the product will be conveyed to the consumer in point of sale displays making specific claims about the product, eg non-fat. Emotive wording will be used to create the healthy image as well as to show the product's originality.

● All toppings will be attractively displayed within the service counter, either on a bed of ice for perishable types or in vertical compartments for non-perishables.

● Initially, a flyer distributed to passers-by will serve to inform consumers about the outlet, the product and its benefits. It will also serve to entice customers to try the product for free on production of the flyer – this will entail a tiny serving.

● Editorial coverage in local and tourist press will be sought to announce the opening of each outlet, and to describe the product, its price and the free tastings available.

Place

Location. The targeted market segments described earlier in the book show that an area must be picked to ensure the presence of the particular age groups and socioeconomic classes required to form the customer base. The three main areas chosen as possible locations are:

● busy shopping centres;

● underground and mainline train stations;

● international airports.

These three possible locations each have two vital characteristics:

● High levels of consumer traffic. This means that awareness levels concerning the outlet and its product will rise quickly, as well as serving to ensure high turnover levels.

● Captive markets. None of the above targeted locations will be exposed to the elements. This will ensure the protection of turnover levels from the harmful effects of seasonality, as well as creating the scenario for the 'impulse buy' to take place as consumers window-shop or await trains and flights.

Premises. The premises will have an area of approximately 300 square feet with as large a frontage as possible – approximately 15 feet. The frontage will act as the counter over which customers will be served; this will be transparent so that customers can see what toppings are available. There will be no seating facilities provided as the frontage will face directly on to the main concourse of the shopping centre, station or airport. The premises must have a water supply to enable washing facilities to be installed and an electricity supply to run the machinery and lighting. Fixtures and fittings will be designed to convey an exciting, new and healthy image.

The 300 square feet will be divided into:

● a service area containing washing, storage, staff and refrigeration facilities;

● the area exposed to the general public containing the machines involved in the on-the-spot manufacturing process, fixtures and fittings, the toppings and counter unit and the staff themselves.

In the next three assignments we will look more closely at the remaining key elements of the marketing mix, to build on your product/service differentiation and focus, to avoid the trap of launching too similar products into tired existing markets.

Assignment 7

Pricing

The most frequent mistake made when setting a selling price for the first time is to pitch it too low. This mistake can occur either through failing to understand all the costs associated with making and marketing your product, or through yielding to the temptation to undercut the competition at the outset. Both these errors usually lead to fatal results, so in preparing your business plan you should guard against them.

These are the important issues to consider when setting your selling price.

COSTS

Make sure you have established all the costs you are likely to incur in making or marketing your product. Don't just rely on a 'guess' or 'common sense' – get several firm quotations, preferably in writing, for every major bought-in item. Don't fall into the trap of believing that if you will initially be working from home, you will have no additional costs. Your phone bill will rise (or you will fail!), the heating will be on all day and you'll need somewhere to file all your paperwork.

One potential entrepreneur, when challenged as to why there were no motoring expenses budgeted for in his business plan, blandly replied that he already owned his car and paid its running expenses. It had not occurred to him that the average personal mileage per annum is 12,000, whereas for the self-employed businessperson that rises to nearly 30,000. Similarly, his insurance could nearly double as a business user, his service charges and petrol would increase directly with the increased mileage, and the expected useful life of his car would be reduced from six years to three. The net effect of this was to wipe out his projections for a modest profit in the first year and push his break-even out to the second year.

Also make sure you analyse the effect of changes in turnover on your costs. This can be done by breaking down your costs into direct and indirect (see Assignment 20 for an explanation of break-even analysis, as this area is sometimes referred to).

CONSUMER PERCEPTIONS

Another consideration when setting your prices is the perception of the value of your product or service to the customer. His or her opinion of value may have little or no relation to the cost, and he or she may be ignorant of the price charged by the competition, especially if the product or service is a new one. In fact, many consumers perceive price as a reliable guide to the quality they can expect to receive. The more you pay, the more you get. With this in mind, had Dyson launched his revolutionary vacuum cleaner, with its claims of superior performance, at a price below that of its peers, then some potential customers might have questioned those claims. In its literature Dyson cites as the inspiration for the new vacuum cleaner, the inferior performance of existing products in the same price band. A product at six times the Dyson price is the one whose performance Dyson seeks to emulate. The message conveyed is that, although the price is at the high end of general run-of-the-mill products, the performance is disproportionately greater. The runaway success of Dyson's vacuum cleaner would tend to endorse this argument.

COMPETITION

The misconception that new and small firms can undercut established competitors is usually based on ignorance of the true costs of a product or service, such as in the example given above; a misunderstanding of the meaning and characteristics of overheads; and a failure to appreciate that 'unit' costs fall in proportion to experience. This last point is easy to appreciate if you compare the time needed to perform a task for the first time with that when you are much more experienced (eg changing a fuse, replacing a Hoover bag, etc).

The overheads argument usually runs like this: 'They (the competition) are big, have a plush office in Mayfair, and lots of overpaid marketing executives, spending the company's money on expense account lunches, and I don't. Ergo I must be able to undercut them.' The errors with this type of argument are, first, that the Mayfair office, far from being an 'overhead' in the derogatory sense of the word, is actually a fast-appreciating asset, perhaps even generating more profit than the company's main products (department stores, restaurants and hotels typically fit into this category), and second, the marketing executives may be paid more than the entrepreneur, but if they don't deliver a constant stream of new products and new strategies they'll be replaced with people who can.

Clearly, you have to take account of what your competitors charge, but remember price is the easiest element of the marketing mix for an established company to vary. They could follow you down the price curve, forcing you into bankruptcy, far more easily than you could capture their customers with a lower price.

ELASTICITY OF DEMAND

Economic theory suggests that, all others things being equal, the lower the price, the greater the demand. Unfortunately (or perhaps not!), the demand for all goods and services is not uniformly elastic – that is, the rate of change of price versus demand is not similarly elastic. Some products are actually price inelastic. For example, Apple's iPhone and Bentley Motors would be unlikely to increase sales if they knocked 5 per cent off the price – indeed, by losing 'snob' value they might even sell fewer. So, if they dropped their price they would simply lower profits. However, people will quite happily cross town to save 2p in the £1 on a litre of petrol.

So setting your price calls for some appreciation of the relative elasticity of the goods and services you are selling.

COMPANY POLICY

The overall image that you try to portray in the marketplace will also influence the prices you charge. However, within that policy there will be the option of high pricing to skim the market and lower pricing to penetrate. Skim pricing is often adopted with new products with little or no competition and is aimed at affluent 'innovators'. These people will pay more to be the trend setters for a new product. Once the innovators have been creamed off the market, the price can be dropped to penetrate to 'lower' layers of demand.

The danger with this strategy is that high prices attract the interest of new competitors, who see a good profit waiting to be made.

Opening up with a low price can allow you to capture a high market share initially, and it may discourage competitors. This was the strategy adopted by Dragon Lock, Cranfield enterprise programme participants (the executive puzzle makers), when it launched its new product. Its product was easy to copy and impossible to patent, so it chose a low price as a strategy to discourage competitors and to swallow up the market quickly.

BUSINESS CONDITIONS

Obviously, the overall conditions in the marketplace will have a bearing on your pricing policy. In 'boom' conditions, where products are virtually being rationed, the overall level of prices for some products could be expected to rise disproportionately. From 2002–07, house prices, for example, rose sharply ahead of general price inflation. However, during the recession of 1990–92 house prices fell rapidly, in real terms, as they did again in the winter of 2007/08.

Seasonal factors can also contribute to changes in the general level of prices. A turkey, for example, costs a lot less on the afternoon of Christmas Eve than it does at the start of Christmas week.

CHANNELS OF DISTRIBUTION

Your selling price will have to accommodate the mark-ups prevailing in your industry. For example, in the furniture business a shop may expect to set a selling price of double that charged by its supplier. This margin is intended to cover its costs and hopefully make a profit. So if your market research indicates that customers will pay £100 for a product bought from a shop, you, as the manufacturer selling to a shop, would only be able to charge £50.

CAPACITY

Your capacity to 'produce' your product or service, bearing in mind market conditions, will also influence the price you set. Typically, a new venture has limited capacity at the start. A valid entry strategy could be to price so high as to just fill your capacity, rather than so low as to swamp you. A housewife who started a home ironing service learnt this lesson on pricing policy to her cost. She priced her service at £5 per hour's ironing, in line with competition, but as she only had 20 hours a week to sell she rapidly ran out of time. It took six months to get her price up to £10 an hour and her demand down to 20 hours a week. Then she was able to recruit some assistance and had a high enough margin to pay some outworkers and make a margin herself.

MARGINS AND MARKETS

According to *Management Today*, nearly 80 per cent of UK companies price by reference to costs: either using a cost plus formula (eg materials plus 50 per cent) or a cost multiplier (eg three times material costs). Whatever formula you use, as accountant Brian Warnes has pointed out, you should endeavour to ensure that you achieve a gross profit margin of at least 40 per cent (sales price less the direct materials and labour used to make the article, the resulting margin expressed as a percentage of the sales price). If you do not achieve such margins, you will have little overhead resource available to you to promote and build an effective, differentiated image for your company.

Your competitive analysis will give you some idea as to what the market will bear. We suggest you complete a comparison with your competitors (Table 7.1) to give you confidence that you can match or improve upon your competitors' prices. At the very least you will have arguments to justify your higher prices to your customers and, importantly, your future employees.

Price is, after all, the element of the marketing mix that is likely to have the greatest impact on your profitability. It is often more profitable for a new company to sell fewer items at a higher price while you are getting your organization and product offerings sorted out (remember Henry Ford); the key is to concentrate on obtaining good margins, often with a range of prices and quality (eg Marks & Spencer has a tiered catalogue of three main price ranges: easy, medium and upper). And if you have to increase prices? Try to combine the increase with some new feature (eg new design, colour scheme) or service improvement (eg the Post Office reintroducing Sunday collections at the same time as a 1p increase in price).

Table 7.1 Product comparison with competitors

(Score each product factor from –5 to +5 to justify your price versus the competition)

Rating score: \\\\		Much worse	Worse	Same or nearly so	Better	Much better
Product attributes		–5	–4 –3 –2	–1 0 +1	+2 +3 +4	+5
Design						
Performance						
Packaging						
Presentation						
Appearance						
After-sales service						
Availability/ distribution						
Delivery methods/ time						
Colour/flavour						
Odour/touch						
Image/street cred.						
Specification						
Payment terms						
Other						
Total						

REAL-TIME PRICING

The stock market works by gathering information on supply and demand. If more people want to buy a share than sell it, the price goes up until supply and demand are matched. If the information is perfect (that is, every buyer and seller knows what is going on), the price is optimized. For most businesses this is not a practical proposition. Their customers expect the same price every time for the same product or service – they have no accurate idea what the demand is at any given moment.

However, for the internet company, computer networks have made it possible to see how much consumer demand exists for a given product at any time. Anyone with a point-of-sale till could do the same, but the reports might come in weeks later. This means online companies could change their prices hundreds of times each day, tailoring them to certain circumstances or certain markets, and so improve profits dramatically. EasyJet.com, a budget airline operating out of Luton, does just this. It prices to fill its planes, and you could pay anything from £30 to £200 for the same trip, depending on the demand for that flight. Ryanair (Stansted) and Eurotunnel (Waterloo) have similar price ranges based on the simplest rule of discounted low fares for early reservations and full fares for desperate late callers!

Bigmack Health Food

The average mark-up by Bigmack Health Food Co's (BHFC) competition is 300 per cent. This mark-up is necessitated by the high cost of their locations and the cost of personnel. After careful analysis of the costs involved, BHFC has determined that it could use a mark-up of only 200 per cent and still make a sizeable profit. BHFC will be able to do this because:

- Its location costs will be one-third less than that of the major competition. This is due to its ability to focus on a specific market segment made up of aware customers who are prepared to buy from smaller, secondary locations (market research has confirmed this view).

- The employee costs of BHFC will be only 20 per cent of the costs incurred by the competition. This is due to the fact that BHFC's customers will be almost entirely long-time health food devotees who will not need assistance or advice to select their purchases. The competition, on the other hand, has a constant stream of people who are novice health food consumers or who are not interested in health food but want to purchase, on a one-time basis, a particular product. These types of people require a lot of advice and instruction and thus several employees must be working at all times.

The company will sell on credit to several health food restaurants. It will require that they pay cash on delivery (COD) for the initial order but will allow a 'net 30 day' account thereafter if their credit is adequate. All other sales will be on a cash basis.

Policy

BHFC will adopt an introductory pricing policy using a 300 per cent mark-up, offering selective new customer discounts for the first month that will bring the mark-up down to 200 per cent.

In this way we can test the market at the higher price level and only come down if we have to, and so achieve the optimum revenue.

WORKSHEET FOR ASSIGNMENT 7: PRICING

1. List all the costs you are likely to incur in making or marketing your product.
2. Refer forward to Assignment 20 and then calculate the fixed and variable costs associated with your product.
3. Using the costs as calculated above and your profit objective, calculate the optimal price you should charge.
4. What price do your competitors charge?
5. Compared with your product/service how much better/worse are those of your competitors?
6. Are any of your possible market segments less price-sensitive than others?
7. Does your answer to question 6 lead you to believe that there is an opportunity to sell at different prices in each market segment – so enhancing profits?

SUGGESTED FURTHER READING

Berends, W (2004) *Price and profit: the essential guide to product and service pricing and profit forecasting*, Berends & Associates, Ontario

Gregson, A (2007) *Pricing strategies for small business*, Self-Counsel Press, Canada

Mackenzie, R (2008) *Why popcorn costs so much at the movies: and other pricing puzzles*, Springer-Verlag, New York

Advertising and promotion

In this section of your business plan, you should discuss your planned advertising and promotion programme. A major decision is to choose a method of advertising that will reach most of your customers for the least cost. Advertising is a specialized field and, whenever possible, you should use an advertising agency, but if you're like most small businesses, advertising agencies and market research firms are often not affordable. Contact several local agencies to discuss your needs and resources before deciding that you are unable to afford them. You will learn a lot about the business of advertising in the process, and you may even alter your own plans.

PROMOTION/ADVERTISING CHECKLIST

Advertising is to some extent an intangible activity, although the bills for it are certainly not. It is, as Lord Bell, formerly of Saatchi & Saatchi, has described it, 'essentially an expensive way for one person to talk to another!' We assume you know the target customers you wish to reach. The answers to these five questions should underpin the advertising and promotional aspects of your business plan:

- What do you want to happen?
- How much is that worth?

- What message will make it happen?
- What media should be used?
- How will results be checked?

What are your advertising objectives?

There is no point in informing, educating or pre-selling unless it leads to the opportunity in a significant number of instances for a sale to result. So what do potential customers have to do to enable you to make these sales? Do you want them to visit your showroom, to phone you, to write to your office, to return a card or to send an order in the post? Do you expect them to have an immediate need to which you want them to respond now, or is it that you want them to remember you at some future date when they have a need for whatever it is you are selling?

The more you are able to identify a specific response in terms of web hits, orders, visits, phonecalls or requests for literature, the better your promotional effort will be tailored to achieve your objective, and the more clearly you will be able to assess the effectiveness of your promotion and its cost versus its yield.

The more some particular promotional expenditure cannot be identified with a specific objective but is, for example, to 'improve your image' or 'to keep your name in front of the public', then the more likely it is to be an ineffective way of spending your money. Prospective financiers will be particularly wary of advertising expenditure detailed in your business plan, as this money, once spent, is gone for ever, unlike expenditure on cars, equipment or even stocks, which have at least some recoverable element.

How much is it worth to achieve your objective?

Once you know what you want a particular promotional activity to achieve, it becomes a little easier to provide for it in your business plan. In practice, four methods are most commonly used, and they each have their merits, with the exception of the first.

The *'what can we afford?'* approach has its roots in the total misconception of promotional activity, which implies that advertising is an extravagance. When times are good, surplus cash is spent on advertising and when times are bad this budget is the first to be cut back. In fact, all the evidence points to the success of businesses that increase promotional spending during a recession, usually at the expense of their meaner competitors.

The '*percentage of sales*' method very often comes from the experience of the entrepreneur or his or her colleagues, or from historical budgets. So if a business spent 10 per cent of sales last year, it will plan to spend 10 per cent in the next, particularly if things went well. This method at least has some logic and provides a good starting point for preparing the overall budget.

'*Let's match the competitors*' becomes a particularly important criterion when they step up their promotional activity. Usually this will result in your either losing sales or feeling threatened. In either case you will want to retaliate, and increasing or varying your promotion is an obvious choice.

The '*cost/benefit*' approach comes into its own when you have clear and specific promotional goals and an experience base to build on. If you have spare capacity in your factory or want to sell more out of your shop, you can work out what the 'benefit' of those extra sales is worth.

Suppose a £1,000 advertisement is expected to generate 100 enquiries for our product. If our experience tells us that on average 10 per cent of enquiries result in orders, and our profit margin is £200 per product, then we can expect an extra £2,000 profit. That 'benefit' is much greater than the £1,000 cost of the advertisement, so it seems a worthwhile investment.

In practice, you should use all of these last three methods to decide how much to spend on promoting your products.

What message will help to achieve the objectives?

To answer this question you must look at your business and its products/ services from the customer's standpoint and be able to answer the hypothetical question, 'Why should I buy your product?' It is better to consider the answer in two stages.

1. 'Why should I buy your *product* or *service*?' The answer is provided naturally by the analysis of factors that affect choice. The analysis of buying motives or satisfactions is an essential foundation of promotional strategy.
2. 'Why should I buy *your* product or service?' The only logical and satisfactory answer is: 'Because it is different.' The difference can arise in two ways:
   – We – the sellers – are different. Establish your particular niche.
   – It – the product or service – is different. Each product or service should have a unique selling point, based on fact.

Your promotional message must be built around these factors and must consist of facts about the company and about the product.

The stress here is on the word 'facts', and while there may be many types of facts surrounding you and your products, your customers are only interested in two: the facts that influence their buying decisions, and the ways in which your business and its products stand out from the competition.

These facts must be translated into benefits. There is an assumption sometimes that everyone buys for obvious, logical reasons only, when we all know of innumerable examples showing this is not so. Does a woman only buy a new dress when the old one is worn out? Do bosses have desks that are bigger than their subordinates' because they have more papers to put on them?

Having decided on the objective and identified the message, now choose the most effective method of delivering your message.

WHAT MEDIA SHOULD YOU USE?

Your market research should produce a clear understanding of who your potential customer group are which in turn will provide pointers as to how to reach them. But even when you know who you want to reach with your advertising message its not always plain sailing. The *Fishing Times*, for example, will be effective at reaching people who fish but less so at reaching their partners who might be persuaded to buy them fishing tackle for Christmas or birthdays. Also the *Fishing Times* will be jam-packed with competitors. It might just conceivably be worth considering a web ad on a page giving tide tables to avoid going head-to-head with competitors, or getting into a gift catalogue to grab that market's attention.

Another factor to consider in making your choice of media is the 'ascending scale of power of influence', as marketers call it. This is a method to rank media in the order in which they are most likely to favourably influence your customers. At the top of the scale is the personal recommendation of someone whose opinion is trusted and who is known to be unbiased. An example here is the endorsement of an industry expert who is not on the payroll, such as an existing user of the goods or services, who is in the same line of business as the prospective customer. While highly effective, this method is hard to achieve and can be expensive and time-consuming. Further down the scale is an approach by you in your role as a sales person. While you may be seen to be knowledgeable you clearly stand to gain if a sale is made, so you can hardly be unbiased. Sales calls, however they are made, are an expensive way to reach customers, especially if their orders are likely to be small and infrequent.

Further down still comes advertising in the general media: websites, press, radio, television and so forth. However whilst these methods may be lower down the scale, they can reach much more of the market, and if done well can be effective.

How will the results be checked?

A glance at the advertising analysis in Table 8.1 will show how to tackle the problem. It shows the advertising results for a small business course run in London. At first glance the Sunday paper produced the most enquiries. Although it cost the most, £3,400, the cost per enquiry was only slightly more than for the other media used. But the objective of this advertising was not simply to create interest; it was intended to sell places on the course. In fact, only 10 of the 75 enquiries were converted into orders – an advertising cost of £340 per head. On this basis the Sunday paper was between 2.5 and 3.5 times more expensive than any other medium.

Table 8.1   Measuring advertising effectiveness

Media used	Cost per advert £	Number of enquiries	Cost per enquiry £	Number of customers	Advertising cost per customer £
Sunday paper	3,400	75	45	10	340
Daily paper	2,340	55	43	17	138
Posters	1,250	30	42	10	125
Local weekly paper	400	10	40	4	100

Judy Lever, co-founder of Blooming Marvellous, the upmarket maternity-wear company, believes strongly not only in evaluating the results of advertising, but in monitoring a particular media capacity to reach her customers:

'We start off with one-sixteenth of a page ads in the specialist press,' says Judy, 'then once the medium has proved itself we progress gradually to half a page, which experience shows to be our optimum size. On average there are 700,000 pregnancies a year, but the circulation of specialist magazines is only around the 300,000 mark. We have yet to discover a way of reaching all our potential customers at the right time – in other words, early on in their pregnancies.'

Measuring advertising effectiveness on the internet

Seeing the value from internet advertising can be a difficult proposition. The first difficulty is seeing exactly what you are getting for your money. With press advertising you get a certain amount of space, on television and radio you get airtime. But on the internet there are at least three new ways to measure viewer value, aside from the largely discredited 'hits', used only because there was no other technique available. (Hits measured every activity on the web page, so every graphic on a page as well as the page itself counts as a hit.)

- *Unique visitors*: This is more or less what it says – new visitors to a website. What they do once there and how long they stay is not taken into account, so it's a bit like tracking the number of people passing a billboard. Could be useful, but perhaps they just stumbled across the site by accident. Also if users clear their cookies and clean up their hard drive there is no way to identify new and old visitors.

- *Time spent*: Clearly if a visitor stays on a website for a few minutes they are more likely to be interested or at least informed about your products and services than if they were there for a second or two.

- *Page views*: Much as in hard copy world, a page on the web can now be recognized and the number of viewers counted.

Nielson, a market-leading audience and market research measurement company, decided in July 2007 that 'time spent' was the best way to measure advertising effectiveness, other of course than actual sales if you can trace them back to their source. The order of the world-wide top websites is changed radically using this measure. For example in January 2008 Google ranked second for 'unique visitors' and 'page views', but only third for time spent.

ADVERTISING AND PROMOTION OPTIONS

In practice most new ventures have little to spend on advertising and there are an awful lot of options. For example if consumers already know what they want to buy and are just looking for a supplier then, according to statistics, around 60 per cent will turn to print, *Yellow Pages* (or similar); 12 per cent will use a search engine; 11 per cent will use telephone directory enquiries and 7 per cent online Yellow Pages. Only 3 per cent will turn to a friend. But if you are trying to persuade consumers to think about buying a product or service at a particular time, a leaflet or flyer may be a better option. Once again it's back to your objectives in advertising. The more explicit they are, the easier it will be to chose your medium.

The power of print

The printed word is probably still the way in which most organizations communicate with their publics. The rules for writing apply to advertising copy too. The content needs to be:

- Clear, using straightforward English, with short words, up to three syllables and short sentences, no more than 25–30 words. The text should be simply laid out and easy to read.

- Concise, using as few words as possible and be free of jargon or obscure technical terms.

- Correct, as spelling mistakes or incorrect information will destroy confidence in you and your product or service.

- Complete, providing all the information needed for the reader to do all that is required to meet *your* advertising objective.

Business cards and stationery

Everything you send out needs to be accompanied by something with all your contact details and a message or slogan explaining what you do. That includes invoices, bills, price lists and technical specifications. This may be all that anyone ever sees of you and your business. If it is effective they will remember you by it, and better still, they will remember to pass the information on to anyone else they know who could be a customer.

Direct mail (leaflets, flyers, brochures and letters)

These are the most practical ways for a new business to communicate with its potential customers. These forms of communication have the merits of being relatively inexpensive, simple and quick to put into operation, can be concentrated into any geographic area, and can be mailed or distributed by hand. Finally, it is easy to monitor results.

CASE STUDY

Goldsmith's (Northern) Ltd

Mark Goldsmith and Simon Hersch started their catering wholesaling business from halls of residence while still students at Manchester University. Taking advantage of a catering strike, they began supplying the student union with portioned cakes sourced from Robert's Fridge Factory, a small London-based manufacturer known to them. Buoyed on by their initial success, they produced a single-sheet leaflet entitled 'Earning more bread is a piece of cake', with a smart Goldsmith's Ltd logo, and itemizing on the reverse side the various small food items they could provide. This was distributed to small snack outlets in the vicinity of the university, and became their primary marketing tool and calling card. Goldsmith's (Northern) Ltd continued to provide Simon and his 40 employees with an interesting and rewarding lifestyle until its sale to Spring Fine Foods (www.springfine foods.com)!

These organizations can provide information that will help you with leaflets, brochures and all other forms of direct mail:

● Christian Aid has a useful guide to basic leaflet writing (http://pressure works.org/usefulstuff/how/leaflet.html) aimed at charities and pressure groups, but useful for a home-based business on a tight budget.

● The Direct Marketing Association (www.dma.org) is the trade association for all direct marketing activities. Their directory catalogue of lists (www.dma.org>DMA LIST MANAGER) allows you to search their two list databases, Consumer and Business. From each of these you can search for a list by country around the world, by business sector, or for consumers by age, gender, income, interest, homeowner etc.

- Hewlett-Packard offers professional-looking business materials with their free, easy-to-use and customizable templates for creating leaflets, flyers, brochures and advertisements (http://welcome.hp.com/country/ uk/en/welcome.html > Small and Medium Business > Printing Imaging Expertise Centre > In-house Marketing).

- Listbroker.com (www.listbroker.com; tel: 0870 120 1326) supplies lists of all types, including consumer and business-to-business, mostly in the United Kingdom but some overseas. All list details, including prices, are available on the site. The database is updated daily and offers consumer and business-to-business lists with over 1.6 billion names for rental. To use the search facilities you have to register, but there is no charge. You can put in your specific requirements and see the types of list that are available. They can be useful for constructing market research survey populations.

Newspapers, magazines and classified ads

You can get readership and circulation numbers and the reader profile directly from the journal or paper or from BRAD (British Rate and Data), www.brad.co.uk, which has a monthly classified directory of all UK and Republic of Ireland media. You should be able to access this through your local business library. The National Readership Survey (www.nrs.co.uk> Top Line Readership) produces average readership data on around 260 UK titles and a host of other data, much of which is free and available online to non-subscribers.

However, national newspapers, except for the classified ads sections, are likely to be outside the budget of most new businesses. If that is the case don't despair as local papers have a substantial readership (around 40 million adults a week) and they cost significantly less to advertise in and have a much more focused readership. Hold The Front Page (www. holdthefrontpage.co.uk>Newspaper websites) has links to the 200 or so local daily and weekly papers, from the *Aberdeen Evening Express* to the *York Herald*. For journals and magazines a good starting point is the directory of the 500 or so published listed at SWPP (www.swpp.co.uk>Find Newspapers and Magazines). Everything from *A Place in The Sun* to *Zurich Club Newspaper*, through *Your Cat* and the *Security Times*, is listed with web links.

Directories

General directories such as *Yellow Pages* and *Thomson Local*, both online and in printed form, and any of the hundreds of specialist directories that abound, are a durable place for small businesses to advertise if the budget is modest. A couple of hundred pounds will get an entry in most directories for a year's visibility. Three out of every four people and businesses looking for information reach for a directory first: they can be good value.

The Data Publishers Association (www.dpa.org.uk>Members Directory) has an index of directories on its site, as has the European Association of Directory and Database Publishers (www.eadp.org>Directories). You should also be able to find a copy of Current British Directories (www.cbd research.com) listing over 2,899 directories, yearbooks and guides published in the United Kingdom.

Posters, billboards and signs

If you know where your audience are likely to pass you could put a poster or billboard somewhere in their line of sight. This could be something as simple and inexpensive as an A4 sheet in the local newsagent window, bus shelter or supermarket message board, or a more costly and elaborate structure as are seen by the roadside.

There are rules governing positioning billboards as one young business starter learnt to his cost. Steve Sayer, a 13-year-old from Cheddar, hit upon the idea of selling manure from his father's stables, over the internet. Priced at £2.50 a bag his product was a hit with local gardeners. Rather than spend heavily on getting his website to the top of the search page he put a large board up in a field on their land adjoining a road. His business was flying and he had banked over £2,000 before the district council made him take the sign down.

Most businesses have a sign outside their door telling passers by what they do. If the premises has a high footfall with lots of people passing, this can get a lot of visibility for very little money. Obviously you don't have a free hand to put up any size or colour of sign you like; it needs to be in keeping with the local environment. Your local council's planning department will be able to advise you on the rules and regulations prevailing in your area.

You could also consider advertising on taxis and buses, where costs are well within a small firm's budget. For information and advice on all outdoor advertising matters visit the Outdoor Advertising Association of Great Britain's website (www.oaa.org.uk).

Using other media

Increasingly media such as television and radio, once the prerogative of big business, have filtered down the price band as they have further segmented their own markets with the introduction of digital technology.

Barking a Lot

Barking a Lot, a pet-boarding service, used Spot Runner (www.spotrunner. com), an internet-based ad agency franchised in the United Kingdom since 2006, which has revolutionized access to television advertising. For around £300 to create the ad from Spot Runner's ad database and £1,500 in ad time, Barking a Lot ran its ads 144 times over two weekend periods on local cable television. The quality is achieved by customizing from one of the several thousand ads Spot Runner has created for specific industry segments. Customer calls shot up by 20 per cent and the company has earmarked £20,000 for future television advertising.

Local radio, television and cinema

These media are priced out on a cost per listener/viewer basis, and you will need to be certain that the audience profile matches that of the market segment you are aiming at. As these media, unlike the written word, are not retained after the event, you will also need to support these media with something like local press advertising or an entry in a directory that you can signpost people too. 'See our entry in Yellow Pages/our advertisement in this week's *Cornishman*' are messages that radio, television and cinema audiences can retain and act on.

The Radio Advertising Bureau (www.rab.co.uk) and the Advertising Association (www.adassoc.org.uk) give further information on these media and contact details for professional firms operating in the sector. Rajar (Radio Joint Audience Research Ltd) publishes radio audience statistics quarterly (www.rajar.co.uk).

Internet and blogs

Your website (see Assignment 14, Building a 'website') is an obvious place to advertise, but the millions of other websites and search engines provide plenty of opportunities to get your message in front of your market. The normal rules of advertising apply in cyberspace as in any other medium. The main options are:

- Search engine advertising comes in two main forms. PPC (pay per click) is where you buy options on certain key words so that someone searching for a product will see your 'advertisement' to the side of the natural search results. Google, for example, offers a deal where you only pay when someone clicks on your ad, and you can set a daily budget stating how much you are prepared to spend, with US$5 a day as the starting price.

- E-mail marketing is just like conventional direct mail sent by post, except this way e-mail is the medium and you buy targeted e-mail databases.

- Display advertising, like advertising in newsprint, takes the form of words and images or varying sizes on websites that people looking for your product are likely to come across. The Audit Bureau of Circulations Electronic (www.abce.org.uk) audits website traffic.

- Viral marketing is the process of creating something so hot the recipients will pass it on to friends and colleagues, creating extra demand as it rolls out, using jokes, games, pictures, quizzes and surveys.

- Blogs are online spaces where the opinions and experiences of particular groups of people are shared. Online communities, MySpace for example, are an extension of this idea. Neilson NetRatings reported in 2007 that over 1.8 billion community sites are viewed every month in the United Kingdom alone. Wikis – sites such as Wikipedia – are special types of blogs that allow users to contribute and edit content. This provides a space where you can make sure your product or service gets some visibility. Newsgator (www.newsgator.com) and (www.measuremap.com) have blog indexing services to help you search out those appropriate to your business sector.

- Podcasts, where internet users can download sound and video free, are now an important part of the e-advertising armoury.

The Internet Advertising Bureau (www.iabuk.net) has a wealth of further information on internet advertising strategies as well as a directory of agencies that can help with some or all of these methods of promoting your business. Neilson NetRatings (www.neilson-netratings.com>Resources> Free Data and Rankings) provides some free data on internet advertising metrics.

Attending trade shows and exhibitions

Exhibitions are a way to get your product or business idea in front of potential customers face-to-face. That gives you first-hand knowledge of what people really want as well as providing a means of gathering market research data on competitors.

UK Trade & Investment (www.exhibitions.co.uk, sponsored by UK Trade & Investment) is the UK government organization responsible for all trade promotion and development work. It provides a comprehensive listing of all the consumer, public, industrial and trade exhibitions to be held in major venues around the United Kingdom. You can search the list by exhibition type, by exhibition date, by exhibition organizer or by exhibition venue. There is also a complete list of main subject categories and subject headings, the main UK exhibition venues, and exhibition organizers.

The site covers all exhibitions being held in the United Kingdom for two or more years ahead. The data is updated regularly twice a month.

Creating favourable publicity

This is about presenting yourself and your business in a favourable light to your various 'publics' – at little or no cost. It is also a more influential method of communication than general advertising – people believe editorials.

CASE STUDY

Chantal Coady

Chantal Coady, the Harrods-trained chocolatier who founded Rococo, was 22 when she wrote the business plan that secured her £25,000 start-up capital. The cornerstone of her strategy to reach an early break-even point lay in a carefully developed public relations campaign. By injecting fashion into chocolates and their packaging, she opened up the avenue to press coverage in such magazines as *Vogue, Harpers & Queen* and the colour supplements. She managed to get over £40,000 worth of column inches of space for the cost of a few postage stamps. This not only ensured a sound launch for her venture but eventually led to a contract from Jasper Conran to provide boxes of chocolates to coordinate with his spring collection.

Writing a press release

To be successful, a press release needs to get attention immediately and be quick and easy to digest. Studying and copying the style of the particular paper, magazine or website you want your press release to appear in can make publication more likely.

- *Layout.* The press release should be typed on a single sheet of A4. Use double spacing and wide margins to make the text both more readable and easy to edit. Head it boldly 'Press Release' or 'News Release' and date it.

- *Headline.* This must persuade the editor to read on. If it doesn't attract interest, it will be quickly 'spiked'. Editors are looking for topicality, originality, personality and, sometimes, humour.

- *Introductory paragraph.* This should be interesting and succinct, and should summarize the whole story; it could be in the form of a quote and it might be the only piece published. Don't include sales-oriented blurb as this will 'offend' the journalist's sense of integrity.

- *Subsequent paragraphs.* These should expand and colour the details in the opening paragraph. Most stories can be told in a maximum of three or four paragraphs. Editors are always looking for fillers, so short releases have the best chance of getting published.

- *Contact.* List at the end of the release your name, mobile and other telephone numbers and e-mail address as the contact for further information.

- *Style.* Use simple language, short sentences and avoid technical jargon (except for very specialized technical magazines).

- *Photographs.* While you can send a standard photograph of yourself, your product or anything else relevant to the story being pitched, you should also give the journalist concerned the option of having a digital version e-mailed.

● *Follow-up.* Sometimes a follow-up phone call or e-mail to see whether editors intend to use the release can be useful, but you must use your judgement on how often to do so.

Find out the name of the editor or relevant writer/reporter and address the envelope to him or her personally. Remember that the target audience for your press release is the professional editor; it is he or she who decides what to print. So, the press release is not a 'sales message' but a factual account designed to attract the editor's attention. These organizations can help you research for appropriate media for your press release: Hollis Press & Public Relations Annual (www.hollis-pr.com; tel: 020 8977 7711). BRAD Group (www.brad.co.uk; tel: 020 7505 8273). The Chartered Institute of Public Relations (www.ipr.org.uk>PR Directory>PR Matchmaker; tel: 020 7766 3333) has a free search facility to find a PR consultant either in your area or with expertise in your business sector. PR Made Easy (www.prmadeeasy. com> Guides) provides 40 free guides to a range of PR topics as well as templates to help you write a press release.

WORKSHEET FOR ASSIGNMENT 8: ADVERTISING AND PROMOTION

1. Prepare a leaflet describing your product/service to your main customers. (Don't worry if you don't plan to use a leaflet – the exercise will serve to ensure you have put your offer in terms that recognize customers' needs, rather than simply being a technical specification.)
2. Write a press release announcing the launch of your venture. List the media to whom you will send the release.
3. Prepare an advertising and promotional plan for the upcoming year, explaining:
    (a) what you want to happen as a result of your advertising;
    (b) how much it's worth to you to make that happen;
    (c) what message(s) you will use to achieve these results;
    (d) what media you will use and why;
    (e) how the results of your advertising will be monitored;
    (f) how much you will spend.
4. If you have already done some advertising or promotional work, describe what you have done and the results you have achieved. Has your work on this assignment given you any pointers for future action?

SUGGESTED FURTHER READING

Goldsmith's fine foods, case history, parts 1, 2 & 3. Start-up and Growth, teaching note (Reference: 596-025-1), available from the European Case Clearing House, Cranfield, Beds MK43 0AL; tel: 01234 750903; fax: 01234 751125; website: www.ecch.cranfield.ac.uk; e-mail: ecch@cranfield.ac.uk

Hammond, J (2008) *Branding your business: promoting your business*, Kogan Page, London

Patton, D (2008) *How to market your business: a practical guide to advertising, PR, selling, direct and online marketing*, Kogan Page, London

Plummer, J, Rapport, S, Hall, T and Barocci, R (2007) *The online advertising playbook: proven strategies and tested tactics from the Advertising Research Foundation*, Wiley, New York

Place and distribution

'Place' is the fourth 'P' in the marketing mix. In this aspect of your business plan you should describe exactly how you will get your products to your customers. If you are a retailer, restaurateur or garage proprietor, for example, then your customers will come to you. Here, your physical location will most probably be the key to success. For businesses in the manufacturing field it is more likely that you will go out to 'find' customers. In this case it will be your channels of distribution that are the vital link.

Even if you are already in business and plan to stay in the same location, it would do no harm to take this opportunity to review that decision. If you are looking for additional funds to expand your business, your location will undoubtedly be an area prospective financiers will want to explore.

LOCATION

From your market research data you should be able to come up with a list of criteria that are important to your choice of location. Here are some of the factors you need to weigh up when deciding where to locate:

- Is there a market for the particular type of business you plan? If you're selling a product or service aimed at a particular age or socioeconomic group, analyse the demographic characteristics of the area. Are there sufficient numbers of people in the relevant age and income groups?

Are the numbers declining or increasing?

- If you need skilled or specialist labour, is it readily available?

- Are the necessary back-up services available?

- How readily available are raw materials, components and other supplies?

- How does the cost of premises, rates and utilities compare with other areas?

- How accessible is the site by road, rail, air?

- Are there any changes in the pipeline that might adversely affect trade, eg a new motorway bypassing the town, changes in transport services, closure of a large factory?

- Are there competing businesses in the immediate neighbourhood? Will these have a beneficial or detrimental effect?

- Is the location conducive to the creation of a favourable market image? For instance, a high-fashion designer may lack credibility trading from an area famous for its heavy industry but notorious for its dirt and pollution.

- Is the area generally regarded as low or high growth? Is the area pro-business?

- Can you and your key employees get to the area easily and quickly?

You may even have spotted a 'role model' – a successful competitor, perhaps in another town, who appears to have got his or her location spot on.

Using these criteria you can quickly screen out most unsuitable areas. Other locations may have to be visited several times, at different hours of the day and week, before screening them out.

CASE STUDY

Chantal Coady

Chantal Coady, founder of Rococo, stated in her business plan:

> Location is crucial to the success or failure of my business, therefore I have chosen the World's End section of the King's Road, Chelsea, at the junction of Beaufort Street. This is conveniently located for the Chelsea/

Knightsbridge clientele. There is a good passing trade, and a generally creative ambience on this road, and no other specialist chocolate shop in the
vicinity.

World's End was not chosen on a whim; it was the subject of a most
careful study. While Chantal was confident that her 'Rococo' concept
was unique, she was enough of a realist to recognize that at one level
it could be seen as just another upmarket chocolate shop. As such, her
shop needed its own distinctive catchment area. She drew up a map of
chocolate shops situated in central London, which verified her closest
competitors to be in Knightsbridge – in Central London terms, another
world.

A further subject of concern was the nature of the passing trade in
the vicinity of the proposed World's End shop. The local residents could
be polled by direct leafleting, but she decided to find out more about
the passing trade by means of a questionnaire. About half the people
questioned responded favourably to the 'Rococo' concept.

When writing up this element of your business plan keep these points in
mind:

- Almost every benefit has a cost associated with it. This is particularly
  true of location. Make sure that you carefully evaluate the cost of each
  prospective location against the expected benefits. A saving of a couple
  of hundred pounds a month in rent may result in thousands of pounds
  of lost sales. On the other hand, don't choose a high-rent location unless
  you are convinced that it will result in higher profits. Higher costs do
  not necessarily mean greater benefits.

- Choose the location with the business in mind. Don't start with the
  location as a 'given'. You may think it makes sense to put a bookshop
  in an unused portion of a friend's music shop since the marginal cost
  of the space is zero. The problem with this approach is that you force
  the business into a location that may or may not be adequate. If the
  business is 'given' (ie already decided upon), then the location should
  not also be given. You should choose the best location (ie the one that
  yields the most profit) for the business. 'Free' locations can end up
  being very expensive if the business is not an appropriate one.

  On the other hand, if you have a 'given' location, you should try to
  find the right business for the location. The business should not also be

predetermined. What business provides the highest and best use of the location?

- When you write your business plan as a financing tool, you often may not have the specific business location selected prior to completion of the business plan. This is fine, since there is no point in wasting time deciding on a location until you know you will have the money to start the business. Besides, even if you do select a location before obtaining the money, it is very possible that the location will already be gone by the time you get through the loan application process and have the business firm enough to sign a lease or purchase agreement. Another consideration is that you may wear out your welcome with an estate agent if you make a habit of withdrawing from deals at the last minute, due to lack of funds.

It will suffice if you are able to explain exactly what type of location you will be acquiring. Knowing this, you will be able to make a good attempt at cost and sales estimates, even though the specific location has yet to be determined.

OUTSOURCING

The most important choice at the outset of planning how much space you will need when starting a business is to decide what you will do in-house and what you will buy. The process of getting others to do work for you rather than simply supplying you with materials for you to work on is called 'outsourcing'. There is little in terms of business functions that can't be outsourced. It would be prudent to consider outsourcing, at least initially, any activity that requires a substantial amount of capital.

You can read up on the sorts of activities a small home-based business can outsource, how to chose outsourcing partners and how to draw up a supply agreement with outsource suppliers at this Business Link site (www.businesslink.gov.uk>Grow your business>Growth through strategic outsourcing > Outsourcing).

PREMISES

In your business plan you will need to address these issues with respect to premises.

Can the premises you want be used for your intended business?

The main categories of 'use' are retail, office, light industrial, general industrial and special categories. If your business falls into a different category from that of a previous occupant you may have to apply to the local authority for a 'change of use'.

An unhappy illustration of this came from a West Country builder who bought a food shop with living accommodation above. His intention was to sell paint and decorative products below and house his family above. Within three months of launching his venture he was advised that as his shop stock was highly flammable, the house would need fire-retardant floors, ceilings and doors – at a cost of £20,000, even doing the work himself. The business was effectively killed off before it started.

There are many regulations concerning the use of business premises. You should contact the Health & Safety Executive to ensure that whatever you plan to do is allowed. Two useful leaflets to refer to are PLM54 and INDG220, available from: Health & Safety Executive (www.hse.gov.ulc; tel: 01787 881165).

If you will be working with materials that are flammable, toxic, give off fumes or are corrosive you should check on the website of the Health and Safety Executive (www.hse.gov.uk>Businesses>Small businesses>Topics>Hazardous substances), where you will find detailed guidance and advice.

Will you be making any structural alterations?

If so, planning permission may be needed and building regulations must be complied with. Any structural alterations, increase in traffic, noise, smells or anything such as operating unreasonable hours or any disturbance that could affect nearby homes or other businesses may need permission.

You can find out whether approval is likely informally from your local council before applying, and the Communities and Local Government website (www.communities.gov.uk>Planning, building and the environment) has detailed information on all these matters. You can also get free answers to specific questions using UK Planning's Planning Doctor (www. ukplanning.com>The Planning Doctor), a service supported by some 20 UK councils.

Securing permissions to alter property or its uses takes time and will incur costs that should be allowed for in your cash-flow projections.

Are the premises the appropriate size?

It is always difficult to calculate just how much space you will require, since your initial preoccupation is probably just to survive. Generally, you won't want to use valuable cash to acquire unnecessarily large premises. However, if you make it past the starting post you will inevitably grow, and if you haven't room to expand, you'll have to begin looking for premises all over again. This can be expensive, not to say disruptive.

To calculate your space requirements, prepare a layout that indicates the ideal position for the equipment you will need, allowing adequate circulation space. Shops require counters, display stands, refrigeration units, etc. In a factory, machinery may need careful positioning and you may also have to consider in great detail the safe positioning of electricity cables, waste pipes, air extractors, etc.

The simplest way to work out space requirements is to make cut-out scale models of the various items and lay these on scaled drawings of different-sized premises – 400 square feet, 1,000 square feet, etc.

By a process of trial and error you should arrive at an arrangement that is flexible, easy to operate, pleasant to look at, accessible for maintenance, and comfortable for both staff and customers. Alternatively you can use space planning software such as SmartDraw (www.smartdraw.com>downloads), InstantPLANNER (www.instantplanner.com), Autodesk (www.autodesk. com) or plan3D (www.plan3D.com), all of which have free or very low cost tools for testing out your space layout.

Only now can you calculate the likely cost of premises to include in your business plan.

Will the premises conform with existing fire, health and safety regulations?

The Health and Safety at Work Act (1974), the Factories Act (1961), the Offices, Shops and Railway Premises Act (1963) and the Fire Precautions Act (1971) set out the conditions under which most workers, including the self-employed and members of the public at large, can be present. (The Health & Safety Commission (www.hse.gov.aboutus/hsc/; tel: 01787 881165) can advise.)

Will you be working from home?

If you plan to work from home, have you checked that you are not prohibited from doing so by the house deeds, or whether your type of activity is likely to irritate the neighbours. This route into business is much in favour with sources of debt finance, as it is seen to lower the risks during the vulnerable start-up period. Venture capitalists, on the other hand, would probably see it as a sign of 'thinking too small' and steer clear of the proposition. Nevertheless, working from home can make sound sense.

CASE STUDY

For example, Peter Robertson, aged 20, who founded Road Runner Despatch, started out running his business as a very domestic affair operated from his home in Brightlingsea, Essex. His mother answered the telephone and frequently his father used the family car to make collections. Within two years he was employing 10 full-time motorcycle riders. Only at this stage did Robertson put together a plan, which involved raising £100,000 capital, to open an office on a central site, complete with a state-of-the-art radio-telephone system.

Will you lease or buy?

Purchasing premises outright frequently makes sense for an established, viable business as a means of increasing its asset base. But for a start-up, interest and repayments on the borrowings will usually be more than the rental payments. But leasing itself can be a trap; eg a lease rental of £5,000 a year may seem preferable to a freehold purchase of say £50,000. But remember, as the law currently stands, if you sign and give a personal guarantee on a new 21-year lease (which you will be asked to do), you will remain personally responsible for payments over the whole life of the lease. Landlords are as reluctant to allow change in guarantors as they are to accept small business covenants. You could then be committing yourself, in these circumstances, to a minimum £105,000 outlay! Some financiers feel that your business idea should be capable of making more profit than the return you could expect from property. On this basis you should put the capital to be raised into 'useful' assets such as plant, equipment, stocks, etc.

However, some believe that if you intend to spend any money on converting or improving the premises, doing so to leased property is simply improving the landlord's investment and wasting your (their) money. You may even be charged extra rent for the improvements, unless you ensure that tenant improvements are excluded from the rent reviews.

In any event, your backers will want to see a lease long enough to get your business firmly established and secure enough to allow you to stay on if it is essential to the survival of your business. Starting up a restaurant in short-lease premises, for example, might be a poor investment proposition but, as Bob Payton proved, it might actually be a sensible way to test your business at minimum risk. The ideal situation, which can sometimes be obtained when landlords are in difficulties, is to negotiate a short lease (say one or two years) with an option to renew on expiry. All leases in Singapore and Malaysia are for two years, with options to renew at prevailing rates, which might seem much more helpful to encourage new business start-ups. It may be best for you to brief a surveyor to help you in your search and negotiation (their charge is normally 1 per cent, with payment only by result).

If appropriate, you could consider locating in a sympathetic and supportive environment

For example, universities and colleges often have a science park on campus, with premises and starter units for high-tech ventures. Enterprise agencies often have offices, workshops and small industrial units attached. In these situations you may have access to a telex, fax, computer, accounting service and business advice, on a pay-as-you-use basis. This would probably be viewed as a plus point by any prospective financial backer. UK Business Incubation (www.ukbi.co.uk) and United Kingdom Science Park Association (UKSPA) (www.ukspa.org.uk) have directories of incubators or innovation centres, as these new business friendly starter units are known.

What opening/works hours do you plan to keep, and why?

Many new retailers survive by working very long hours; be careful with many of the new shopping 'malls', where hours of opening are strictly controlled, thereby preventing you from 'being different' by having unusual operating hours.

Check on insurance

Any personal insurance policy you have will not cover business activity so you must inform your insurer what you plan to do. You can find out more about business insurance cover and where to find an insurance company on this Business Link website (www.businesslink.gov.uk>Health, safety, premises>Insurance>Insure your business and assets-general insurances).

CHANNELS OF DISTRIBUTION

If your customers don't come to you, then you have the following options in getting your product or service to them. Your business plan should explain which you have chosen and why.

- *Retail stores*. This general name covers the great range of outlets from the corner shop to Harrods. Some offer speciality goods such as hi-fi equipment, where the customer expects professional help from the staff. Others, such as Marks & Spencer and Tesco, are mostly self-service, with customers making up their own mind on choice of product.

- *Wholesalers*. The pattern of wholesale distribution has changed out of all recognition over the past two decades. It is still an extremely important channel where physical distribution, stock holding, finance and breaking bulk are still profitable functions.

- *Cash and carry*. This slightly confusing route has replaced the traditional wholesaler as a source of supply for smaller retailers. In return for your paying cash and picking up the goods yourself, the 'wholesaler' shares part of its profit margin with you. The attraction for the wholesaler is improved cash-flow, and for the retailer it is a bigger margin and a wide product range. Hypermarkets and discount stores also fit somewhere between the manufacturer and the marketplace.

- *Mail order*. This specialized technique provides a direct channel to the customer, and is an increasingly popular route for new small businesses.

Rohan

Paul Howcroft, who built his clothing 'casuals with toughness and durability' business, Rohan, from modest beginnings when he had just £60 in the bank, to a £7 million business in less than a decade, puts much of his success down to changing distribution channels. For the first two years most of his sales were to retail shops, which either wouldn't take enough produce or didn't pay up when they did. He set up his mail-order branch, using his box of enquiries and letters built up over the years as a mailing list. He moved a year's sales in two months, getting all the cash in up front.

Other direct from 'producer to customer' channels include:

- *Internet.* Revenue generation via the internet is big business and getting bigger. In some sectors – advertising, books, music and video – it has become the dominant route to market. There is no longer any serious argument about whether 'bricks' or 'clicks' is the way forward, or whether service businesses work better on the web than physical products. Almost every sector has a major part to play, and it is increasingly unlikely that any serious 'bricks' business will not have or be building an internet trading platform too. Dixon's, a major electrical retailer, has shifted emphasis from the high street to the web and Tesco has build a billion-pound-plus home delivery business on the back of its store structure. Amazon, the sector's pioneer, now has in effect the first online department store, with a neat sideline in selling on secondhand items once the customer has finished with the product. See Assignment 14, 'Building a website', for the nuts and bolts of operating online.

Liberty Control Networks

A Cornish company won a £150,000 order from South Africa for high-tech equipment just over 12 months after it was established. Liberty means freedom but not for thousands of criminals in an African prison soon to be secured by a locking system supplied by Liberty Control Networks. David and Sharon Parker established their firm just over a year ago at St Austell, in mid-Cornwall, and gained the big order in South Africa via their website. A prison management team thousands of miles away was 'surfing the net' to find someone who could supply a state-of-the-art jail locking system. Liberty Control Networks was one of four companies to respond to the challenge, with the Parkers providing the best solution.

Mr Parker said:

> As with any new company, long hours are expected, and at about 11.30 pm one Friday evening in January, I finished work by checking my e-mails before going to bed. I found this enquiry from South Africa. They were asking for 500 of this, 100 of that and so on. Needless to say, I didn't go to bed but put together our proposal.

Burning the midnight oil produced a bumper dividend, resulting in the first of what hopefully will be a series of orders, each in excess of £150,000.

- *Door-to-door selling*. Traditionally used by vacuum cleaner distributors and encyclopedia companies, this is now used by insurance companies, cavity-wall insulation firms, double-glazing firms and others. Many use hard-sell techniques, giving door-to-door selling a bad name. However, Avon Cosmetics has managed to sell successfully door-to-door without attracting the stigma of unethical selling practices.

- *Party plan selling*. This is a variation on door-to-door selling that is on the increase, with new party plan ideas arriving from the United States. Agents enrolled by the company invite their friends to a get-together where the products are demonstrated and orders are invited. The agent gets a commission. Party plan has worked very well for Avon and other firms that sell this way.

  On a more modest scale, one man turned his hobby of making pine bookcases and spice racks into a profitable business by getting his wife to invite neighbours for coffee mornings where his wares were prominently displayed.

- *Telephone selling*. This too can be a way of moving goods in one single step, from 'maker' to consumer. Few products can be sold easily in this way; however, repeat business is often secured via the phone.

Selecting distribution channels

These are the factors you should consider when choosing channels of distribution for your particular business:

- *Does it meet your customers' needs?* You have to find out how your customers expect their product or service to be delivered to them and why they need that particular route.

TWS

TWS, a window systems manufacturer, wanted to increase its sales. A customer survey was commissioned which revealed that 80 per cent of TWS customers did not have forklift trucks, resulting in manual offloading of deliveries by employees at its customers. The TWS solution was to order delivery vehicles, complete with their own fork-lift, facilitating unloading at customer premises in 15 minutes instead of 2 hours, giving faster turnaround time and requiring no customer assistance. This, in turn, did not waste the valuable time of customer employees and encouraged extra orders from existing TWS customers as well as opening up new customer possibilities.

- *Will the product itself survive?* Fresh vegetables, for example, need to be moved quickly from where they are grown to where they are consumed.
- *Can you sell enough this way?* 'Enough' is how much you *want* to sell.

Atrium

Atrium a £5 million annual turnover company whose executives attended Cranfield's Business Growth Programme, uses an actively managed website to have periodic sales. The company sells modern furniture, mostly via architects who have been retained to build or refurbish business premises. Atrium has products on display in its London showroom, and from time to time these have to be sold off to make way for new designs. But having hundreds of people milling around looking for bargains in a sale is not quite the atmosphere that is conducive to an architect and his or her client reviewing plans for a new project.

So, 'sale' products are displayed and sold on Atrium's website saleroom. 'Enough' products are sold with no disruption to the normal showroom activity.

- *Is it compatible with your image?* If you are selling a luxury product, then door-to-door selling may spoil the impression you are trying to create in the rest of your marketing effort.

- *How do your competitors distribute?* If they have been around for a while and are obviously successful, it is well worth looking at how your competitors distribute and using that knowledge to your advantage.

- *Will the channel be cost-effective?* A small manufacturer may not find it cost-effective to sell to retailers west of Bristol because the direct 'drop' size – that is, the load per order – is too small to be worthwhile.

- *Will the mark-up be enough?* If your product cannot bear at least a 100 per cent mark-up, then it is unlikely that you will be able to sell it through department stores. Your distribution channel has to be able to make a profit from selling your product too.

- *Push–pull.* Moving a product through a distribution channel calls for two sorts of selling activity. 'Push' is the name given to selling your product in, for example, a shop. 'Pull' is the effort that you carry out on the shop's behalf to help it to sell your product out of that shop. That pull may be caused by your national advertising, a merchandising activity or the uniqueness of your product. You need to know how much push and pull are needed for the channel you are considering. If you are not geared up to help retailers to sell your product, and they need that help, then this could be a poor channel.

CASE STUDY

Historical Connections

Historical Connections, a new company established to market educational wallcharts, faced conflicting distribution issues. Its products had to be securely and economically packed in such a way that the charts could be unrolled, crease free, by the end user; at the same time the product had to occupy an acceptable amount of shelf space in a crowded gift shop, for example.

A cardboard tube was the obvious answer to these problems; however, that rendered the true 'value' of the product invisible to shoppers. This problem was overcome by providing retailers with a framed chart, positioned by Historical Connections' salespeople, when the account was opened. This simple 'point of sale' display was an elegant and cost-effective 'pull'.

- *Physical distribution.* The way in which you have to move your product to your end customer is also an important factor to weigh up when choosing a channel. As well as such factors as the cost of carriage, you will also have to decide about packaging materials. As a rough rule of thumb, the more stages in the distribution channel, the more robust and expensive your packaging will have to be.

- *Cashflow.* Not all channels of distribution settle their bills promptly. Mail order customers, for example, will pay in advance, but retailers can take up to 90 days or more. You need to take account of this settlement period in your cashflow forecast.

WORKSHEET FOR ASSIGNMENT 9:
PLACE AND DISTRIBUTION

1.   What type and size of premises are required for your business?
2.   Describe the location.
3.   Why do you need this type of premises and location? What competitive advantage does it give you?
4.   If freehold what is/are the:
     –   value?
     –   mortgage outstanding?
     –   monthly repayments?
     –   mortgage with whom?
5.   If leasehold:
     –   What is the unexpired period of lease?
     –   Is there an option to renew?
     –   What is the present rent payment?
     –   What is the date of rent payment?
     –   What is the date of the next rent review?
6.   What rates are payable on your business premises?
7.   What are the insurance details:
     –   sum insured?
     –   premium?
8.   Are these premises adequate for your future needs? If not, what plans do you have?
9.   If you have not found your premises yet, what plans do you have to find them?
10. What channels of distribution are used in your field; which do you plan to use and why?

SUGGESTED FURTHER READING

Bird, D (2007) *Commonsense direct and digital marketing*, Kogan Page, London

Portman, J and Stenigold, F (2006) *Negotiate the best lease for your business*, NOLO, Berkley, Calif, USA

Rushton, A, Croucher, P and Baker, P (2006) *The handbook of logistics and distribution management*, Kogan Page, London

Phase 4

Operations

INTRODUCTION

Operations is the general name given to all the activities required to implement strategy. So, for example, once you have decided what to sell, to whom and at what price, you may still need to find someone to make your product, sell it and deliver it. You may also need to take out insurance, draw up contracts of employment, print stationery, establish a web presence, set up your office and communications systems and recruit staff, for example.

Of necessity, the emphasis you put on each element of this assignment will depend entirely on the nature of your business. Your business plan need not show the complete detail of how every operational activity will be implemented. Clearly, you and your colleagues will need to know, but for the business plan it is sufficient to show that you have taken account of the principal matters that concern your venture, and have a workable solution in hand.

This section discusses some of the most important operational issues to be addressed in your business plan. Assignments 10–15 are intended to help you to bring your customers, competitors and the marketplace more sharply into focus, and to identify areas you have yet to research.

The selling methods plan

Anyone considering backing your plans will look long and hard at how you plan to sell. Unbelievably, it is an area often dismissed in a couple of lines in a business plan. That error alone is enough to turn off most investors. Just because customers know you are in the market is not in itself sufficient to make them buy from you. Even if you have a superior product at a competitive price they can escape your net.

Getting people to sign on the dotted line involves selling, and this is a process that anyone championing a new proposition will have to use in many situations other than in persuading customers to buy. They have to 'sell' to their bank manager the idea that lending them money is worthwhile, to a potential partner that he or she should team up with them; and eventually to employees that working for their company is a good career move.

HOW SELLING WORKS

There is an erroneous view that salespeople, like artists and musicians, are born, not made. Selling can be learnt, improved and enhanced just like any other business activity. First you need to understand selling's three elements.

- Selling is a *process* moving through certain stages if the best results are to be achieved. First you need to listen to the customers to learn what they want to achieve from buying your product or service; then you should demonstrate how you can meet their needs. Often entrepreneurs launch into a pitch about their product from the outset without listening first. Often this results in a missed opportunity to stress particular relevant benefits, or worse still, alienates the potential customers as the impression is given that their needs are secondary. The next stage in the selling process is handling questions and objections; this is a good sign as it shows that the customer is sufficiently interested to engage. Finally comes 'closing the sale'. This is little more than asking for the order with a degree of subtlety. Once again many owner managers feel too embarrassed to push for a conclusion. This stage is a bit like fishing; pull before the hook is in and you lose the fish. You need a bite, a buying signal, before you close.

● Selling requires *planning* in that you need to keep records and information on customers and potential customers so that you know when they might be ready to buy or reorder. This is particularly important if you have to travel any distance to visit them. You need to plan your territory so that your time is used efficiently and you don't end up criss-crossing the country wasting hours in travel time. Second, you need to plan each sales pitch, trying to anticipate needs and objections beforehand, so that you can have answers to hand and close the sale.

● Selling is a *skill* that can be learnt and enhanced by training and practice, as shown in the case study. The Sales Training Directory (www.sales-training-courses.co.uk>Directory) lists sales course providers in the United Kingdom.

1E

When Sumir Karayi started up in business in the spare room of his flat in West Ealing, London, he wanted his business to be distinctive. He was a technical expert at Microsoft, and with two colleagues he set up 1E (www.1e.com) as a commune aiming to be the top technical experts in their field. The business name comes from the message that appears on your screen when your computer has crashed. Within a year of starting up the team had learnt two important lessons. Businesses need leaders, not commune, if they are to grow fast and prosper; and they need someone to sell.

On the recommendation of an advisor Karayi went on a selling course, and within months he had won the first of what became a string of blue-chip clients. The company is now one of the 10 fastest-growing companies in the Thames Valley, with annual turnover approaching £15 million, profits of 30 per cent, and partners and reseller partners worldwide.

USING AGENTS

If you are not going to be your business's main salesperson you need to brace yourself for costs of around £50,000 a year to keep a good salesperson on the road, taking salary, commission and expenses into account. The problems with employing your own salespeople is that initially they won't sell enough to cover their costs, and you may get the wrong person and so end up with just a big bill and no extra sales.

A less risky sales route is to outsource your selling to freelance salespeople. Here you have two options.

- Employ a sales outsourcing company such as Selling People (www. sellingpeople.biz) or People per Hour (www.peopleperhour.com), which can find and manage a salesperson for you on a short-term basis.

- Find an agent yourself, ideally with existing contacts in your field, who knows buyers personally and can get off to a flying start from day one. The Manufacturers Agents Association (www.themaa.co.uk >Finding an Agent) has a directory of commission agents selling in all fields of business. You have to pay £150 plus £26.25 VAT by credit card for an MAA Net Search allowing you to contact up to 20 agents in one search.

CASE STUDY

Howard Fabian

Howard Fabian's business was designing and selling greetings cards. His main market was London and the south-east of England, where there were 120 important shops to be sold to. He planned to sell to these accounts himself. This meant visiting all the outlets once at the outset.

He could make four to five calls a day, so it would take between four and five weeks to cover the ground. After that he would visit the most important 30 every month, the next 30 every two months, and he would phone or visit the remainder from time to time, and send samples of new designs in the hope of encouraging them to order. While on an enterprise programme at Cranfield he took a professional selling skills course.

Outside London and the south-east, Howard proposed to appoint agents, based in the principal provincial cities. To recruit these he planned to use the trade press and the Manufacturers Agents Association. Each appointment would be made on a three-month trial basis, and he had an agency contract explaining this business relationship drawn up. He proposed to set each agent a performance target based on the population in this catchment area. Sales within 25 per cent of target would be acceptable; outside that figure he would review the agent's contract.

Initially he was looking for 10 agents, whom he would visit and go out with once a quarter. As selling time in a shop was short, it was important that he and his agents should have a minimum set agenda of points to cover, and a sales presenter to show the range quickly and easily from the standing position.

GETTING PAID

The sale process is not complete until, as one particularly cautious sales director put it: 'the customer has paid, used your product and not died as a consequence'. You do have responsibilities for the safety of everyone involved in your business, including customers, the legal aspects of which are dealt with at the end of this chapter. One of the top three reasons that new businesses fail is because a customer fails to pay up in full or on time. You can take some steps to make sure this doesn't happen to you by setting prudent terms of trade and making sure the customers are creditworthy before you sell to them.

Checking creditworthiness

There is a wealth of information on credit status for both individuals and businesses of varying complexity, at prices from £5 for basic information through to £200 for a very comprehensive picture of credit status. So there is no need to trade unknowingly with individuals or businesses that pose a credit risk.

The major agencies that compile and sell personal credit histories and small-business information are Experian (www.UKexperian.com), Dun & Bradstreet (www.dnb.com), Creditgate.com (www.creditgate.com) and Credit Reporting (www.creditreporting.co.uk/b2b). Between them they offer a comprehensive range of credit reports instantly online, including advice on credit limit and CCJs (county court judgments).

Setting your terms of trade

You need to decide on your terms and conditions of sale, and ensure they are printed on your order acceptance stationery. Terms should include when and how you require to be paid, and under what conditions you will accept cancellations or offer refunds. The websites of the Office of Fair Trading (www.oft.gov.uk) and Trading Standards Central (www.tradingstandards. gov.uk) contain information on most aspects of trading relationships.

CASE STUDY

One unfortunate entrepreneur felt that his business, a management training consultancy, had got off to a good start when his first client, a major US computer company, booked him for three courses. Just three weeks prior to the first of these courses, and after he had carried out all the preparatory work and prepared relevant examples, handouts, etc, the client cancelled the order. The reason given was a change in 'policy' on training dictated by the overseas parent company.

If this entrepreneur had included in his standard terms and conditions a cancellation clause, then he would have received adequate compensation. In fact, he was operating on a 'wing and a prayer', had no terms of trade, and wasn't even aware there was an industrial 'norm'. Most of his competitors charged 100 per cent cancellation fee for cancellations within three weeks, 50 per cent within six weeks, 25 per cent within eight weeks, and for earlier cancellations no charge.

Cash or cheque

Cash has the attraction in that if you collect as you deliver your product or service you are sure of getting paid and you will have no administrative work in keeping tabs on what is owed you. However in many business transactions this is not a practical option, unless as in retailing for example, you are present when the customer buys. A cheque underwritten with a bank guarantee card is as secure as cash, assuming the guarantee is valid. But the cheque will take time to process. In practice you would be wise, until you have checked out the creditworthiness of the customer in question, to await clearance of the cheque before parting with the goods.

You need to be careful in interpreting banking terminology here. Your bank may state that the cheque is 'cleared' when in fact it is only in transit through the system. The only term in bank parlance that means your money is really there is 'given value'. If you have any concerns, ring your bank and ask specifically if you can withdraw funds safely on the cheque in question.

Credit cards

Getting paid by credit card makes it easier for customers to buy and makes it certain that you will get your money almost immediately. With a merchant account, as the process of accepting cards is known, as long as you follow the rules and get authorization the cash, less the card company's 1.5–3 per cent, gets to your bank account the day you charge.

You can get a merchant account without a trading history as a new venture, depending of course on your credit record. Streamline (www. streamline.com), part of the Royal bank of Scotland Group, Barclaycard Merchant Service (www.barclaysmerchantservices.co.uk) and HSBC (www. hsbc.co.uk/1/2/business/home>Credit Card Processing) offer services in the field, with set-up costs for a small business from around £150. They claim you can be up and running in a fortnight.

Dealing with delinquents

However prudent your terms of trade and rigorous your credit checks, you will end up with late payers and at worst nonpayers. There are ways to deal with them, but it must be said that experience shows that once something starts to go wrong it usually gets worse. There is an old investment saying, 'the first loss is the best loss', that applies here.

The most cost-effective and successful method of keeping late payers in line is to let them know you know. Nine out of 10 small businesses do not routinely send out reminder letters advising customers that they have missed the payment date. Send out a polite reminder to arrive the day after payment is due, addressed to the person responsible for payments, almost invariably someone in the accounts department if you are dealing with a big organization. Follow this up within five days with a phone call, keeping the pressure up steadily until you are paid.

If you are polite and professional, consistently reminding them of your terms of trade, there is no reason your relationship will be impaired. In any event the person you sell to may not be the person you chase for payment.

If you still have difficulty consider:

- Using a debt collection agency. You can find a directory of registered agents on the Credit Service Agency website (www.csa-uk.com/csa> Members list).

- Going to the small claims court offers a way for people whose claim is for relatively small sums (under £5,000) and would not be worth pursuing if you had to hire lawyers.

WORKSHEET FOR ASSIGNMENT 10: THE SELLING METHODS PLAN

Describe briefly the main operational aspects that are involved in ensuring that your strategy is successfully implemented. In particular, you should consider:

1. Who will conduct the selling for your business, and have they been professionally trained to sell?
2. What selling methods will they employ?
3. Will you use point-of-sale material – leaflets, brochures or videos, for example?
4. Who will manage, monitor and control your sales effort and how will they do so?
5. Describe the selling process, leading from an unaware prospect to a converted client, covering identification of decision makers, overcoming objections, gaining agreement, etc.
6. What procedures do you have for handling customer complaints?
7. What incentives are there for people to meet sales targets and how will you motivate them to do so?
8. Who will direct, monitor and control your sales effort and what experience/skills do they have?

9. How long is the process from becoming aware of your product or service to making the buying decision, receiving the product or service and finally paying for it? This will have an important bearing on your cash-flow and initial sales forecast
10. What sales volume and activity targets, such as calls per day, etc, have you set for each salesperson or selling method?
11. What processes will you use to ensure you are paid on time?

SUGGESTED FURTHER READING

King, G (2007) *The secrets of selling: how to win in any sales situation*, Financial Times/Prentice Hall, London

Swartz, M (2006) *The fundamentals of sales management for the newly appointed sales manager*, AMACOM, New York

Making, outsourcing and supplies

Organizations are usually, in fact almost invariably, in the business of adding value to bought-in resources. These may be as trivial as stationery for correspondence, packaging for software, or as complex as the many ingredients needed to make a computer or a motor vehicle, as in the case of Quantum Cars (see Assignment 6).

Your business plan needs to show how you have addressed these crucial issues, as in the first place you must demonstrate that you have thought through how to turn what is in effect at this stage a concept into a 'concrete' product or service that can be brought to market. You also need to show an awareness that value added is itself determined by the careful management of costs.

MAKING AND ASSEMBLING

If you need specific machinery, the general rule is that you should buy as little as possible as inexpensively as possible, as there is one certain fact about a new venture – after a few weeks or months of trading it will resemble less and less the business you planned to start. That in turn means that your initial investment in equipment could be largely wasted when you find you need to re-equip. Look back to the section on 'Outsourcing' in Assignment 9, and consider whether there are any less risky or costly methods of getting your product ready for market.

For machinery and equipment you should use a trade magazine to search out suppliers. Alternatively Friday-Ad (www.friday-ad.co.uk>For Sale>DIY & Tools), and Machinery Products UK (www.machineryproducts.co.uk) have secondhand machinery and tools of every description for sale.

If your business involves making or constructing products, then you should address the following issues in the business plan:

● Will you make the product yourself, or buy it in either ready to sell, or as components for assembly? You should also explain why you have chosen your manufacturing route.

CASE STUDY

One Cranfield graduate enterprise programme had these examples of different types of operation:

● Jenny Row designed her knitwear herself, but had it made up by out-workers. In this way she could expand or contract output quickly, paying only the extra cost of materials and production, for more orders. It also left her free to design new products to add to her existing range.

● Tim Brown sold computer systems tailor-made to carry out solicitors' conveyancing work. He commissioned software writers to prepare the programs, bought in computers from the manufacturer and selected a range of printers to suit individual customers' requirements. His end product was a total system, which he bought in 'kit' parts from his various subcontractors. Apart from IBM and a handful of giants, no one company could produce all these elements in-house.

● Graham Davy designed and manufactured his own range of furniture. He rented a Beehive workshop and bought in cutting, turning and polishing tools, and a finish spraying room. He bought in wood, and worked on it himself, producing batches of three or four of each design. The equipment needed for design and prototype work was also sufficient for small-batch production.

● Describe the manufacturing process to be used, and if appropriate explain how your principal competitors go about their manufacturing.

Jon Newall's company Escargot Anglais Ltd was set up to breed and market edible snails in the United Kingdom. The production system he adopted had already been used with some considerable success at one of the world's largest snail ranches in California. The stages of production are as follows:

1. *Commencing production.* Breeding snails will be fed on a compound with the essential requirements of a low copper content (below 13–14 mg/kg) and no anticoccidiostat, but with an appropriate calcium content for good shell disposition.
2. *Growing young snails.* These are grown in 25-litre buckets in batches of 150.
3. *Fattening and finishing.* At three months the snails will have attained market weight. They are then processed and frozen on site. For this, boiling and freezing equipment is needed, costing around £2,500 per line packaging. Finally, snails will be packaged in batches of six in a moulded aluminium foil dish, covered in shrink-wrap, with promotional material on the front and recipes on the back. Equipment for packaging will cost around £2,000.

● What plant and equipment will you need and what output limits will they have (see Table 11.1)?

● Provide a rough sketch of the layout of your manufacturing unit, showing the overall size of facility needed, the positioning of equipment, etc, and the path of materials and finished goods.

● What engineering support, if any, will you need?

● How will you monitor and control quality?

There are a number of well-regarded quality standards that may help you monitor and control your quality. The BS/ISO 9000 series are perhaps the best-known standards. They can ensure that your operating procedure will deliver a consistent and acceptable standard of products or services. If you are supplying to large firms they may insist on your meeting one of these quality standards, or on 'auditing' your premises to satisfy themselves. The British Standards Institution (389 Chiswick High Road, London W4 4AL; tel: 020 8996 9000; fax: 020 8996 7400; website: www.bsi-global.com) can provide details of these standards.

Table 11.1   Example showing goods needed, their purpose and cost

Plant/ equipment	Process (what does it do?)	Maximum volume	Cost	Do you already own it?

A number of commercial organizations will provide user-friendly guidelines and systems to help you reach the necessary standard. Searching the web using key words such as 'quality standards' (or 'measurement') will bring you some useful sites.

MATERIALS AND SOURCES OF SUPPLY

Your business plan should also explain what bought-in materials you require, who you will buy them from, and how much they will cost. Finding suppliers is not too difficult; finding good ones is less easy. Business-to-business directory, such as Kelly Search (www.kellysearch.co.uk), Kompass (www.kompass.co.uk) and Applegate (www.applegate.co.uk) between them have global databases of over 2.4 million industrial and commercial companies in 190 countries, listing over 230,000 product categories. You can search by category, country and brand name. You should check the supplier's:

- terms of trade;
- level of service;
- customer list, getting feedback from other customers;
- guarantees and warranties on offer;
- price, making sure that they are competitive;
- compatibility, ie that you will enjoy doing business with them.

To return to Escargot Anglais Ltd, Jon Newall explained in his business plan how he chose his main source of supply:

> The breeding snails were at first fed on vegetable waste obtained free in abundance from local greengrocers. While at first this seemed a very attractive proposition which I have seen work well in France and elsewhere, local supplies were unsatisfactory. The high water content led to difficulties in disposing of waste matter, but most importantly, residual pesticides, particularly in the more succulent leafy matter, led to a high snail fatality rate.
>
> After much experimenting I found a chicken feed, 'Pauls Traditional 18', that has all the essential ingredients. It can be bought from the local wholesaler for £4.60 per 25 kilogram bag. My original budgets were based on the assumption that free vegetable waste would be used; this is no longer valid and all feeding stuffs will have to be bought in. This will increase costs by about £7,000 per annum and so reduce gross profits. However, apart from capital expenditure on boiling, freezing and packaging equipment (total £4,500), the only non-labour cost apart from feeding stuffs is for packaging materials, butter and garlic. These will be bought in, locally at first; however, I am looking at the possibility of purchasing cheap EEC butter surplus.

- What major items of bought-in materials or services will you require?
- Who could supply those and what are the terms and conditions of sale?
- Why have you chosen your supplier(s)?

Keep stock cards so that you can identify fast- and slow-moving stock.

Other buying options

Aside from searching out suppliers through directories and word of mouth, consider one or more of the following strategies.

Bartering online

You can save using up your cash by bartering your products and services for those of other businesses. Organizations that can help you get started with bartering include Bartercard (website: www.bartercard.co.uk; tel: 01276 415739) and Barter Marketing (website: www.bartermarketing.com; tel: 0870 787 8100).

Buy online

There are over 200 price comparison websites covering computer hardware and software, phones, travel, credit cards, bank accounts, loans, utilities, electrical goods, office products including inkjet and printer supplies, and a few thousand more items a business might purchase. Paler.com, a quirky website run by Petru Paler (www.paler.com>UK Price Comparison Sites) has a directory listing these sites, with brief explanations and a helpful comment page where users have inserted more sites and additional information. There is a similar directory for international supplier comparison sites (www.paler.com>UK Price Comparison Sites>US/International).

Fitting out an office

You will need an 'office' to work from, but this should not be a costly affair at the outset. There are plenty of sources offering good-quality office furniture and equipment at a low cost. For new furniture supplied to most European countries and around the world, check out Amazon (www.amazon.co.uk> Home & Garden>Office), IKEA (www.ikea.com/gb/en/>Workspace) and Habitat (www.habitat.net>United Kingdom>Products>Home office). For second-hand office furniture search Wantdontwant.com (www.wantdont want.com), Green-Works (www.green-works.co.uk), which has outlets around the United Kingdom, and Office Furniture Desks and Chairs (www. officefurnituredesksandchairs.co.uk), where between them you could fit out a basic office for less than £50. See also Assignments 14 and 15 for information on equipping for communications and your website.

WORKSHEET FOR ASSIGNMENT 11: MAKING, OUTSOURCING AND SUPPLIES

Describe briefly the main 'manufacturing' aspects that are involved in ensuring that your strategy is successfully implemented. In particular, you should consider:

1. How much of your product or service do you plan to produce in-house?
2. If you are making a product, describe the production process; also explain how your principal competitors go about manufacturing.
3. What plant and equipment will you need, what can it do, how much will it cost and where will you get it from?
4. What bought-in materials and/or services will you need, where will you buy them from and how much will they cost?
5. How will you equip your office?

SUGGESTED FURTHER READING

Christodoulou, P, Fleet, D, Hanson, P and Phaal, R (2007) *Making the right things in the right places: a structured approach to developing and exploiting 'manufacturing footprint' strategy*, Institute for Manufacturing, University of Cambridge, UK

Hill, J (2007) *The FD's guide to outsourcing: from choosing the right partner to taking the plunge*, CRIPT at UCE, Birmingham

People and related administrative procedures

People are the most important element of any new venture. However good or innovative the idea or competitive the strategy, absolutely nothing can get done without people. Your business plan needs to show which people are important to your plan, how you will find, motivate and reward them, and what cover you have in the event of any key staff, including yourself, being unable to perform their duties.

RECRUITMENT AND SELECTION

No aspect of dealing with employees is particularly easy, and it's an interesting indictment that few people starting a second business after successfully selling their first actively search for one with more employees than they had before.

The starting point in the process is to decide what employees you need – someone with selling skills, or who can make deliveries for example – and set about finding them; and then get them to work effectively in your business doing what you want them to do because they want to do it.

Who do you need?

Working out the sort of person you need means more than just looking at existing problems. Taking on an employee may take weeks, even months, and employment laws means that once taken on shedding them without good reason will be difficult. So you need to look a year or so ahead, and decide on your growth objectives. Then it will be possible to determine the number of employees you are going to need, when you will need them and where the gaps in your organization are likely to appear.

Before rushing into looking for a full-time employee consider the possibility of using part-timers or job sharers. There are advantages going this route. In the first place you may tap into a better pool of job seekers. Those looking to work this way may well be recently retired, or returning to work after discharging family responsibilities; as such they may have valuable skills and knowledge. Second, you can put a toe into the world of becoming an employer and see if it is for you, before getting in too deep.

Settling on the job description

Often employers draw up the job description after they have found the candidate. This is a mistake; having it from the outset narrows down your search for suitable candidates, focuses you on specific search methods, and gives you a valid reason for declining unwelcome job requests from family and friends. In any event you have to give employees a contract of employment when you take them on, and the job description makes this task much easier. Start by listing what you would want to know if you were going to take on a new job, and you should cover the ground more than adequately. Include the following:

- The title, such as telesales person, bookkeeper or delivery van driver.

- The knowledge, skills and experience you expect them to have or acquire; such as 'You will have an HGV (Heavy Goods Vehicle) driving licence or take the test within four weeks of being appointed.'

- The main duties and measurable outputs expected. For example, 'You will be expected to generate £25,000 of new sales in the first three months' or 'You will keep the books to a standard that meets the requirements of HMRC's quarterly VAT return.'

- The work location and general conditions such as hours to be worked, lunch breaks and paid holiday arrangements.

- The pay structure and rewards.

- Who the employee will work for, if not for you.

WHERE CAN YOU FIND GREAT EMPLOYEES

There are many ways to find employees; when it comes to finding great employees the choices are more limited. Research at Cranfield revealed some alarming statistics. First, nearly two-thirds of all first appointments failed and the employee left within a year, having been found to be unsatisfactory. Second, there were marked differences in the success rate that appear to be dependent on the way in which employees are looked for.

Tapping into the family

Employing family members has a number of key advantages. First, they are a known quantity and you can usually vouch for their honesty and reliability. Second, you can ask them to work in conditions and for hours that would be neither acceptable nor legally allowed for any other employee. Against that, you need to weigh up the difficulties you may have if they can't do the work to the standard or in the manner you like.

Employing an agency or consultant

This is the least popular, most expensive and most successful recruitment method. The reasons for success are in part the value added by the agency or consultant in helping get the job description and pay package right; and in the fact that they have already pre-interviewed prospective employees before they put them forward. These organizations can help:

- Job Centre Plus (www.jobcentreplus.gov.uk>Need to fill a job?) is a free government-funded service to help UK firms fill full- or part-time vacancies at home or overseas. It can offer advice on recruitment and selection methods, local and trade pay rates, training, contracts of employment, and importantly for small firms, can offer interview facilities in some of its national network of offices.

- The Recruitment and Employment Confederation (www.rec.uk.com/employer>Choosing an Agency) is the professional association that supports and represents over 8,000 recruitment agencies and 6,000 recruitment professionals. As well as advice on choosing an agent there is a mass of information on employment law and a directory of members listed by business sector and geographic area.

Advertising in the press

You have a large number of options when it comes to press advertising. Local papers are good for generally available skills and where the pay is such that people expect to live close to where they work. National papers are much more expensive but attract a wider pool of people with a cross-section of skills, including those not necessarily available locally. Trade and specialist papers and magazines are useful if it is essential your applicant has a specific qualification, say in accountancy or computing.

The goal of a job advertisement is not just to generate responses from suitably qualified applicants, but also to screen out applicants who are clearly unqualified and leave a favourable impression of your business. You need to consider the following elements when writing the job advertisement.

- *Headline*. This is usually the job title, perhaps with some pertinent embellishment. For example, 'Dynamic sales person required'.

- *Job information*. This is a line or two about the general duties and responsibilities of the job.

- *Business information*. Always include something explaining what your business does and where it does it.

- *Qualifications*. Specify any qualifications and experience that are required. You can qualify some aspects of this by saying a particular skill would be useful but is not essential.

- *Response method*. Tell applicants how to reply and what information to provide. Make this as easy as possible so as not to put people off. One owner manager insisted that applicants phone him only after 6.30 pm. He did not encourage written applications as this meant work in reading them. Needless to say his recruitment was rarely successful.

You can find all the local and national newspapers listed at Newspapers. com (www.newspapers.com). From the individual newspaper weblink homepage you will find a signpost to 'Advertising' and from there you can find the readership demographics and advertising rate. For example for

Metro you would follow (www.metro.co.uk>Advertising.metro.co.uk>Who reads us?).

Using the internet

The internet's advantages are speed, cost and reach. You can get your job offer in front of thousands of candidates in seconds. The fees are usually modest, often less than regional paper job adverts, and in some cases such as with webrecruit.co.uk (www.webrecruit.co.uk), although the fee is a relatively high £595, they will reimburse you if they can't fill your job. Services through job boards range from the passive, where employers and employees just find each other, to the proactive where online candidate databases are searched and suitable candidates are made aware of your vacancy. Recruiter Solutions (www.recruitersolutions.co.uk>Job Boards) is a directory of job board websites, and whatjobsite.com (www.whatjobsite.com>Jobsite Directory) has a search facility that lets you look for job boards by country, region, and those that are most suited to the job on offer and the industry you are in.

Using your network

Nearly two out of every three very small businesses use business contacts and networks when they are recruiting. This route is favoured because it is cheap, informal and can be pursued without the bother of writing a job description, which can in effect be infinitely varied to suit the candidates that may surface.

Unfortunately the statistics indicate that two out of five appointments made through personal contacts fail within six months and the business is back in the recruiting game again. The reasons for this being an unsatisfactory route lie somewhere in the absence of rigour that the approach encourages, and the unlikelihood given the difficulty of finding good staff that any existing organization will happily pass them on.

HIRING PEOPLE

Once you have candidates for your vacancy the next task is to interview, select and appoint. If you have done your homework the chances are that you will have a dozen or more applicants, too many to interview, so this process is somewhat like a funnel, narrowing down until you have your ideal candidate appointed.

Selecting and appointing a candidate

You need to find at least two and ideally three people who could fill your vacancy to a standard that you would be happy with; this gives you contrast, which is always helpful in clarifying your ideas on the job, and a reserve in case the first candidate drops by the wayside or turns you down. The stages in making your selection are as follows:

- Make a shortlist of the three or four candidates that best suit the criteria set out in your job definition.

- Interview each candidate, ideally on the same day. Plan your questions in advance but be sure to let the candidates do most of the talking. Use your questions to plug any gaps in your knowledge about the candidate. Monster (www.monster.co.uk>Employers>Recruitment Centre>Monster Guides>Guide to interview technique) has a useful set of interview questions to ask, with some guidance on how to get the best out of the process.

- Use tests to assess aptitude and knowledge. Thousands of the most successful companies use them, and they claim to get better candidates and higher staff retention than they would otherwise achieve. Tests cost from £10 a candidate from companies such as Central Test (www. centraltest.co.uk); the British Psychological Society (www.bps.org.uk) and the Chartered Institute of Personnel and Development (www.cipd. co.uk) list various types of test, their purpose and how to use them and interpret results.

- Always take up references before offering the job. Use both the telephone and a written reference, and check that any necessary qualifications are valid. This may take a little time and effort, but if you are less than thorough you can set your growth plans back months if not years.

- Put the job offer in writing. While you may make the job offer on the telephone, face to face or in an email, always follow up with a written offer. The offer should contain all the important conditions of the job, salary, location, hours, holiday, work, responsibilities, targets and the all-important start date. This in effect will be the backbone of the contract of employment you will have to provide shortly after the person starts working for you.

MANAGING EMPLOYEES

Bringing a new employee into your business is a bit like carrying out a heart transplant. Even if the surgeon finds a compatible organ and the operation goes to plan, the new heart can be rejected because it doesn't quite fit in the surrounding parts. Even in the smallest of firms the 'rejection' rate of new employees is very high. One study of key staff appointments in small firms showed that over 50 per cent of first appointments failed in the first six months. The cost of failure in this area can be very high. It could set your plans back months or even years.

Aside from making a new employee welcome and to feel comfortable in what after all will be your home environment, you need to become a manager, a skill often alien to entrepreneurial types. What follows are the central elements that add up to successful management.

Delegate

At first when you start to delegate you may well feel you could do the job better and quicker yourself. You may even resent the time you have to invest to get a new employee up and running in the way you would like. But having appointed someone and given him or her a specific set of tasks, clear goals and a timetable, you need to step back and let the person get on with it.

Discreetly offer help and advice and set times aside, daily or weekly depending on the nature of the work, to review achievements and progress. But don't lean over the new employee's shoulder all day, scrutinizing every move. This is demotivating and counterproductive as you are depriving yourself of the main reason you took the person on in the first place – to free you up to do even more important work.

Motivate

Very often the problem is not so much that of motivating people, but of avoiding demotivating them! If you can keep off the backs of employees, it is quite possible that they will motivate themselves. After all, most of us want the same things: a sense of achievement or challenge, recognition of our efforts, an interesting and varied job, opportunities for responsibility, advancement and job growth. But in a small firm the potential for demotivation is high. Workloads invariable peak and there is never any slack in the systems of a small firm. Inevitably an employee will feel overloaded, neglected or just plain hard done by on occasions. You can motivate employees with some fairly basic techniques such as:

- Give praise as often as you can and minimize your reaction to bad results.

- Show an interest in what employees do.

- Train, coach and add to their skills. Employees rate this area as the greatest motivator. You can find a course on more or less anything anywhere in the United Kingdom on Course Plus's (www.courseplus. co.uk) directory of UK training courses, and find out about the prospects of getting government money to help pay for any learning from the Learning and Skills Council (www.lsc.gov.uk>Providers>Money to Learn).

Reward

People come to work to get paid, and if they achieve great results they expect great rewards. There is no single aspect of an employee's life more susceptible to gripes and complaints than pay. So how can you make sure that doesn't happen in your business?

First, make sure you are paying at least the going rate for the job in the area. Don't think you are getting a bargain if you get employees to work for less than that figure; if they do either they are not good at their job, or they are good and when they find they are being underpaid, they will feel cheated and leave. Look at advertisements for similar jobs in your area or visit PayScale (www.payscale.com>FOR EMPLOYERS) where you can get accurate real-time information on pay scales.

Include an element of incentive for achieving measurable goals. The Chartered Institute of Personnel and Development (www.cipd.co.uk >Subjects>Pay and reward) gives further guidance on a comprehensive range of reward options.

LEGAL ISSUES IN EMPLOYING PEOPLE

Employing people full- or part-time is something of a legal minefield, starting with the job advert and culminating with the point at which you decide to part company. Three comprehensive sources of information on the legal aspects of employment are:

- Acas (www.acas.org.uk>Our publications>Rights at work leaflets) is a link to free leaflets provided by the Advisory and Conciliation Service, which should know a thing or two about employment law.

- Business Link (www.businesslink.gov.uk>Employing people>Recruitment and getting started).

- TheSite.org(www.thesite.org>Work&Study>Working>Workers'Rights) is a site run by YouthNet UK, a charity that helps young people have access to high-quality, impartial information as an aid to making decisions. It covers everything to do with work including drug testing at work. While the site's centre of gravity is young people, the law as described applies to employers.

Also check out these sources for help with specific aspects of employment.

- As with any advertising you are governed by the *laws on discrimination and equal opportunities*. That means any reference to gender, age, nationality, sexual orientation or religion is not permitted. For tips on the descriptions you can use visit VizualHR.com (www.oneclickhr. com>HR Guide>Recruitment & Selection>Recruitment).

- *Contracts of employment.* You are required to give employees a contract of employment within two months of their starting work. Business Link (www.businesslink.gov.uk>Employing people>Paperwork> Create a written statement of employment) has an interactive tool to create a document of everything you are required by law to give new employees.

- *Employment records.* You need to maintain records on your employees, keeping note of absences, sickness, disputes, disciplinary matters, accidents, training, holidays and any appraisals or performance reviews. If you have an unsatisfactory employee and want to dismiss him or her this information will be vital. OyezWaterlow (www.oyezwaterlow. co.uk>HR Paper Forms) has a record-keeping system priced at £78.95. Software such as that provided by Vizual Management Solutions (www.vizualms.co.uk>Personnel Manager) will cost several times that of the paper version, and for most small businesses will add little value. If you can write a simple database programme using software such as Access then that is worth exploring.

- If you keep records on a computer you will need to be mindful of *the Data Protection Act* as it applies to employee records. You can get this information from the Information Commissioner's Office (www.ico. gov.uk>For organizations>Data protection guide).

● *Safety at work.* You have a 'duty of care' to ensure anyone working for you is working in a safe environment and is not exposed to possible health and safety hazards. You need to make an assessment of risk and working conditions, covering everything from fire exits to ensuring that ventilation, temperature, lighting and toilet facilities meet health and safety requirements. The Health and Safety Executive (www.hse. gov.uk>Businesses>Small businesses) has ready-made risk assessment forms and a basic guide to health and safety at work.

● *Unfair dismissal.* You can find a list of fair reasons for dismissing an employee on Monster's Employment Law (www.compactlaw.co.uk/ monster/empf9.html). Also Iambeingfired (www.iambeingfired.co.uk> Claim Evaluator) is worth examining as it gives the employee's side of the argument. The Claim Evaluator Tool takes an employee through a series of questions to see whether he or she has a case for unfair dismissal. The site also has comprehensive information on all aspects of employment law that impinge on the likelihood of being dismissed.

WORKSHEET FOR ASSIGNMENT 12: PEOPLE AND RELATED ADMINISTRATIVE PROCEDURES

Describe briefly the main 'people' aspects that are involved in ensuring that your strategy is successfully implemented. In particular, you should consider:

1. Who else apart from yourself does your venture need from the outset and in the first year of operations?
2. How will you go about recruiting them?
3. What pay and reward system will you use?
4. What steps will you take to manage them effectively?
5. Do you envisage any legal issues in recruiting and employing the staff you have in mind?

SUGGESTED FURTHER READING

Thorne, K and Pellant, A (2006) *The essential guide to managing talent: how top companies recruit, train and retain the best employees*, Kogan Page, London

Legal and regulatory factors affecting operations

The manner in which businesses and organizations operate, whether they are for profit, in the charity and not-for-profit sector, or even a public service, is governed by regulations. The UK government, for example, has explicitly recognized this burden of regulations and red tape when it renamed the Department of Trade and Industry as the Department for Business, Enterprise and Regulatory Reform.

All of these regulations have a major impact on cash-flow, the amount of start-up capital required and the profit margins that can be obtained. For example, electing to pay value added tax on a cash accounting basis can lower cash needs and speed up cash-flow, attractive attributes for any venture. However selling on credit, for which a licence is required, can increase funding needs and add to administrative costs. But if selling on credit is the norm in the business sector you plan to enter, or is a key ingredient of your competitive strategy, that burden has to be faced and prepared for.

These regulations can be loosely clustered under two headings: *customer facing*, those that deal with the rules concerning relationships with consumers; and *taxation*, those that deal with the various dues to the state that organizations have to either pay directly or to collect for onward transmission. Omitting the implications of these regulatory matters in your business plan will seriously weaken it and may even, when subsequently the financial implications are included, render a proposition unviable.

Other specific regulatory matters such as legal form, intellectual property, property consents and employment matters are covered in the relevant sections of this workbook.

CUSTOMER-FACING REGULATIONS

From the claims being made by some businesses and the shoddy treatment handed out to customers you might be forgiven for believing that *caveat emptor* (let the buyer beware) was the rule of the marketing road. Far from it. In fact, organizations are heavily regulated in almost every sphere of their operations. What follows are the main customer-facing regulations that you will need to take account of in running any venture.

Getting a licence or permit

Some businesses, such as those working with food or alcohol, employment agencies, mini-cabs and hairdressers, need a licence or permit before they can set up in business at all. Your local authority planning department can advise you what rules will apply to your business. You can also use a Business Link website (www.businesslink.gov.uk>Your type of business) from which you can obtain an interactive tool to find out which permits, licences and registrations will apply and where to get more information.

Complying with advertising and descriptive standards

Any advertising or promotion you undertake concerning your business and its products and services, including descriptions on packaging, leaflets and instructions and those given verbally, has to comply with the relevant regulations. You can't just make any claims you believe to be appropriate for your business. Such claims must be decent, honest, truthful and take into account your wider responsibilities to consumers and anyone else likely to be affected. If you say anything that is misleading or fails to meet any of these tests, you could leave yourself open to being sued.

The five bodies concerned with setting the standards and enforcing the rules are:

- The Advertising Authority (www.asa.org.uk>Advertising Codes) for printed matter, newspapers, magazines and so forth and the internet.

- Ofcom (wwwofcom.org.uk>About Ofcom>Compliance, Accessibility and Diversity) is responsible for ensuring advertisements on television and radio comply with rules on what can and cannot be advertised, including any special conditions such as the timing and content of material aimed at children.

- The Financial Services Authority (www.fsa.gov.uk>Being regulated> Financial Promotions) has the responsibility to see that financial promotions are clear, fair and not misleading.

- The Office of Fair Trading (www.oft.gov.uk>Advice and resources> Resource base>Approved codes of practice) is responsible for ensuring advertisements are not misleading or make unfair or exaggerated comparisons with other products and services, and to help consumers find businesses that have high standards of customer service.

- Trading Standards (www.tradingstandards.gov.uk>For business> guidance leaflets>Trade Descriptions) covers anything such as quantity, size, composition, method of manufacture, strength, performance, place of manufacture, date, brand name, conformity with any recognized standard or history.

Dealing with returns and refunds

Customers buying products are entitled to expect that the goods are 'fit for purpose' in that they can do what they claim to. Also, if the customer has informed you of a particular need the products must be suitable for that purpose. The goods also have to be of 'satisfactory quality', ie durable and without defects that would affect performance or prevent their enjoyment. For services you must carry the work out with reasonable skill and care, and provide it within a reasonable amount of time. The word 'reasonable' is not defined, and is applied in relation to each type of service. So for example, repairing a shoe might reasonably be expected to take a week, while three months would be unreasonable.

If goods or services don't meet these conditions customers can claim a refund. If they have altered an item or waited an excessive amount of time before complaining, or have indicated in any other way that they have 'accepted' the goods, they may not be entitled to a refund, but may still be able to claim some money back for a period of up to six years. Trading Standards (www.tradingstandards.gov.uk>For business>guidance leaflets>A Trader's Guide to the Civil Law Relating to the Sale and Supply of Goods and Services) provides a summarized guide to the relevant laws in clear plain English.

Distance selling and online trading

Selling by mail order, via the internet, television, radio, telephone, fax or catalogue, requires that you comply with some additional rules over and above those concerning the sale of goods and services described above. In summary, you have to provide written information, an order confirmation, and the chance to cancel the contract. During the cooling-off period customers have the unconditional right to cancel within seven working days, provided they have informed you in writing by letter, fax or email.

There are, however, a wide range of exemptions to the right to cancel, including accommodation, transport, food, newspapers, audio or video recordings and goods made to a customer's specification. The Office of Fair Trading (www.oft.gov.uk>Advice and resources>Advice for businesses> Selling at a distance) publishes a guide for business on distance selling.

Protecting customer data

If you hold personal information on a computer on any living person, a customer or employee for example, then there is a good chance you need to register under the Data Protection Act. The rules state that the information held must have been obtained fairly, be accurate, held only for as long as necessary and held only for a lawful purpose.

You can check whether you are likely to need to register using the interactive tool on the Business Link website (www.businesslink.gov.uk>IT & e-commerce>Data protection and your business>Comply with data protection legislation).

Getting a consumer credit licence

If you plan to let your customers buy on credit, or hire out or lease products to private individuals or to businesses, then you will in all probability have to apply for a licence to provide credit. If you think you may need a licence read the regulations on the website of the Office of Fair Trading (www.oft. gov.uk>Advice and resources>Advice for businesses>Offering credit>Do you need a credit licence).

COMPUTING TAXES

Any organization handling money is responsible for paying a number of taxes and other dues to the government of the day, both on its own behalf and for any employees it may have, as well as being an unpaid tax collector required to account for end-consumers' expenditure.

There are penalties for misdemeanours and late payments, and more serious penalties for anything that could be construed as tax evasion – a crime, as opposed to tax avoidance, the prudent arrangement of your affairs so as to minimize taxes due. You are required to keep your accounting records for six years, so at any point should tax authorities become suspicious they can dig into the past even after they have agreed your figures. In the case of suspected fraud there is no limit to how far back the digging can go.

Value added tax (VAT)

VAT, a tax common throughout Europe though charged at different rates, is a tax on consumer spending, collected by businesses. Basically it is a game of pass the parcel, with businesses that are registered for VAT (see below) charging each other VAT and deducting VAT charged. At the end of each accounting period the amount of VAT you have paid out is deducted from the amount you have charged and the balance is paid over to HM Revenue & Customs (HMRC).

In the United Kingdom the standard rate is 17.5 per cent, while some types of business charge lower rates and some are exempt altogether. The way VAT is handled on goods and services sold to and bought from other European countries is subject to another set of rules and procedures. HM Revenue and Customs (www.hmrc.gov.uk >Businesses and Corporations>VAT) publishes a series of guides such as *Should you be registered for VAT?* and a *General Guide*.

Starting thresholds

You should register for VAT if your sales are expected to reach the threshold, which at April 2007 was £64,000. This level rises by £1,000 or so each year. You can register for VAT below that figure, as you could benefit from being able to recover VAT on your business expenses, such as purchasing equipment or paying for petrol.

You will be given a VAT number when you register, which should be stated on all your invoices. If you suspect a business charging you VAT is not registered, or that one should be but is not, you can contact the HMRC's National Advice Service on 0845 010 900. You can verify European VAT numbers at the European Commission website (http://ec.europa. eu>Taxation and Customs Union>VIES).

Payment methods

Normally VAT is paid each quarter but small businesses can take advantage of a number of schemes to simplify procedures or aid their cash-flow. The annual accounting scheme lets you pay monthly or quarterly estimated figures, submitting a single annual return at the end of the year with any balancing payment. The cash accounting scheme allows you to delay paying over any VAT until you have actually collected it from your customers. The flat-rate scheme allows you to calculate your VAT as a flat percentage of your total sales, rather than having to record the VAT charged on individual purchases and sales.

Accounting for profit

You will pay tax on any profit made in your business. The rate at which you will pay depends on the legal structure chosen. If you are a sole trader or in a partnership you will pay tax at your personal marginal rate, either 22 per cent or 40 per cent; limited companies pay at a rate of 20 per cent on profits of up to £300,000 and thereafter on a sliding scale up to 30 per cent. These tax rates are subject to change each year or so.

The financial year and payment dates

The financial year for tax purpose is usually 6 April to 5 April, although some businesses use different dates such as the calendar year end if it is more appropriate for their type of business. You need to get your tax return back to HMRC by 30 September if you want it to calculate the tax due, or by 31 January if you are happy for you or your accountant to do the sums. The tax itself is paid in two stages at the end of July and January. Companies have to calculate their own tax due and pay it nine months after their year-end. You will be fined and charged interest on any late tax payments.

Filing accounts for a company

A company's financial affairs are in the public domain. As well as keeping HMRC informed, companies have to file their accounts with Companies House (www.companieshouse.gov.uk/about/gbhtml/gb3.shtml). Accounts should be filed within 10 months of the company's financial year-end. Small businesses (turnover below £5.6 million) can file abbreviated accounts which include only very limited balance sheet and profit and loss account information, and these do not need to be audited. You can be fined up to £1,000 for filing accounts late.

Estimating tax due

Tax is due on the profit of your business, which might not be the same amount as the figure arrived at in your profit and loss account. For example you will include depreciation, entertainment and perhaps other expenses in your profit and loss account. Although it is important for you to know how much and on what they were incurred, these are not allowable expenses for tax purposes. Your accountant will be able to give you a good steer in this area. Bytestart.co.uk, the small business portal, has a useful Business Expenses Guide (www.bytestart.co.uk>Money & Tax>Business Expenses Guide) which has a section, 'Working from home', dedicated to issues specific to businesses run from home.

PAYE (pay as you earn)

Employers are responsible for deducting income tax from employees' wages and making the relevant payment to HMRC. If you trade as a limited company, then as a director any salary you receive will be subject to PAYE. You will need to work out the tax due. HMRC (www.hmrc.gov.uk/employers/employers-pack.htm) gives details on PAYE in its Employers Pack.

Dealing with national insurance (NI)

Almost everyone who works has to pay a separate tax – national insurance (NI) – collected by HMRC, which in theory at least, goes towards the state pension and other benefits. NI is paid at different rates, and self-employed people pay Class 4 contributions calculated each year on the self-assessment tax form.

The amount of NI paid depends on a mass of different factors: married women, volunteer development workers, share fishermen, self-employed and small earnings are all factors that attract NI rates of between 1 per cent and 12 per cent. HMRC (www.hmrc.gov.uk>Library>Rates & Allowances>National Insurance Contributions) provides tables showing the current contribution rates, and elsewhere on the site (www.hmrc.gov.uk>employers>National Insurance) you can download an Employers Annual Pack dealing with all the complexities of NI paperwork.

Help and advice with tax

Business Link has a beginner's guide to tax and accounts in the form of a series of questions, at the end of which you get a report telling you about the tax you have to pay and the accounts you have to keep (www.businesslink. gov.uk>Taxes, returns & payroll>Introduction to business taxes>Beginner's guide to tax and accounts).

HMRC has online guides for employers and business and corporations linked directly from its home page (www.hmrc.gov.uk). Tax Café (www. taxcafe.co.uk>UK Taxes>Corporation and Business Taxes) has a series of guides priced at around £25 each on such subjects as *Using a company to save tax* and *Salary vs dividends* as well as a tax and VAT question and answer service where for £90 you can ask any question and get an answer within three to five working days.

WORKSHEET FOR ASSIGNMENT 13: LEGAL AND REGULATORY FACTORS AFFECTING OPERATIONS

1. Does your venture require a licence to operate?
2. Will you be holding data on customers, suppliers and employees, and if so what are the implications of the Data Protection Act on your plans?
3. Does your proposed advertising, both print and website, comply with the various advertising regulations?
4. How will you handle refunds?
5. Will you have to register for VAT, or could it be to your advantage to do so?
6. If you have to register for VAT, which is the best scheme for you?
7. How much tax do you expect to have to pay?
8. Will you have to collect and pay tax for any employees?
9. How much national insurance will you be responsible for paying?
10. Have you incorporated the cost implications of these operating regulations in your financial forecasts?

SUGGESTED FURTHER READING

Clayton, P (2007) *Law for the small business: an essential guide to all the legal and financial requirements*, 12th edn, Kogan Page, London
Tolley's (2007) *Tolley's tax computations*, Butterworth Law, London

Assignment 14

Building a website

You might be forgiven for thinking that a website is just for those selling on the internet; that, however, is just one of the many uses a website can be put to. In fact, as the list below confirms, a well-thought-out website is the heart of operations in almost any venture of any size:

- *Generating advertising revenue*. Once you have a website you have 'readers' who other people will pay to reach, just as they would if you had a hard copy magazine. You can sell space on your website yourself, but you should be too busy running your business to get diverted with this type of distraction. The easiest way to get advertising revenue is to get someone else to do the hard work. Google (www.google. com>Business Solutions>Earn revenue with AdSense), for example, matches advertisements to your site's content and you earn money every time someone clicks on one. You can check out the dozens of other affiliate advertising schemes such as FastClick Ad Network, Click Bank and Revenue Pilot at internet Ad Sales (www.internetadsales. com>Online Ad Networks), a site that reviews all online advertising products and trends.

- *Recruitment*. When you start to grow your business you can advertise for staff on your own website. In that way you can be sure applicants will know something of your business, and you could cut out most of the costs of recruitment.

- *Market research.* By running surveys you can find out more about your customers' needs, check out whether new products or services would appeal to them, and monitor complaints and so prevent them becoming problems.

- *Save communication costs.* Businesses get dozens of phonecalls and letters asking essentially the same questions. By having an FAQ (frequently asked questions) section on your website you can head off most of those and save time and money.

- *Add value.* By putting information relating to your product, for example a weather chart or foreign currency calculator if you are selling holidays, you will make your service better and different from competitors who do not have such features. You do not have to do the work yourself. Check out Bizezia (www.bizezia.com), RSS Feed Reader (http://rssfeedreader.com) and Yahoo (http://finance.yahoo.com/badges) to see the range of articles, calculators, tax calendars, online tutorials and financial information you can link, often for free, to your website.

- *Sell online 24/7 and 365 without being there.* Once you have set up your shop front, got your shopping cart, arranged a payment system and organized fulfilment all you have to do is 'stack the shelves'.

Many small businesses start with a presence on the web and quickly become disillusioned with it. This is partly due to reasons explained by the MD of Microsoft UK: 'So many websites are just online brochures – a real e-commerce solution allows customers to buy and sell products and services just as they would in a traditional supply chain.' Moving away from a static, rarely updated website is clearly advisable, yet changing to a regularly updated shopping website such as that maintained by Gap can cost seven figures in Year 1 – Amazon's 'virtual shopping world' came with an eight-figure price tab from the outset!

CASE STUDY

Jane Means

Jane Means started her gift-wrapping business, (www.janemeans.co.uk) as part of a desire to do something less stressful than racing across the globe working in the travel industry. The germ of the idea came about when she was in Tokyo, where she came across a shop that took meticulous care in wrapping the products they sold in a most innovative and attractive manner, whatever their shape. She then started out herself showing people how to wrap things beautifully. Her business has expanded to include courses on wrapping for individuals and companies keen to boost their sales, who ask her to train their counter staff. Jane has some compelling statistics on how much gift wrapping increases a retailer's sales. Her up-to-date website, she claims, is not only a new business's best advertisement, but an essential tool for selling programmes and attracting corporate clients.

WEBSITE BASICS

The web has come a long way since Amazon and a handful of other brave souls blazed the way. For a home-based business a visible place in cyberspace is all but essential if it wants to make any impact on the wider business world. Alongside the greater use of the internet, just as with computers, the price of getting on it is dropping sharply and the power and quality of what those fewer bucks will buy is immeasurably improved.

To get some idea of what to include and exclude from your website, check out your competitors' websites and those of any other small business that you rate highly. You can also get some pointers from the Web Marketing Association's Web Awards (www.webaward.org>Winners>Search Winners Database). There you can see the best websites in each business sector. Also look at the Good Web Guide (www.thegoodwebguide.co.uk) whose site contains thousands of detailed website reviews.

Selling on the internet

Everything from books and DVDs, through computers, medicines and financial services to vehicles and real estate, is being sold or having a major part of the selling process transacted online. Holidays, airline tickets, software, training and even university degrees are bundled in with the mass of conventional retailers such as Tesco which fight for a share of the ever growing online market. The online gaming market alone has over 217 million users.

The value of web transactions in the United States in 2007 was over $350 billion and in the United Kingdom was £50.5 billion, up from £19 billion in 2002; the value of sales to households as opposed to businesses over the same period doubled to £14 billion; £78 in every £100 spent in 2007 on the internet was used to buy physical goods. In the United States, 16 million people visited jewellery websites, 35 million hit flower and gift sites and 42 million looked for travel-related products and services.

Not all business sectors are penetrated to the same extent by the internet; according to Forrester (www.forrester.com), the internet research company, although sales of clothing and footwear online is a multi-billion business it only accounts for 8 per cent of total sales. Contrast that with computers, where 41 per cent of sales occur online.

According to eMarketer (www.emarketer.com) 88 per cent of shoppers prefer online to conventional shopping because they can shop at any time; 66 per cent like being able to shop for more than one product and in many outlets at the same time; 54 per cent claim to be able to find products they can only find online; 53 per cent like not having to deal with salespeople; 44 per cent reckon product information is better online; and perhaps the most revealing statistic of all, only 40 per cent preferred online to offline because they expected to find lower prices.

Doing your own selling

While selling online may be a sound way into market, you still have a choice. You could tag along with someone else, much as you would if you were selling a product into a shop, or you could set up shop yourself. The procedures of selling on the internet, aside from having your own website, require systems for showing and describing the goods and services on offer, as well as ordering, payment and fulfilment facilities. These topics are the subject of the other sections in this chapter.

The main advantage of setting up your own selling procedures is that you have greater control over where your products appear, which can be important to people who are passionate about their venture; and you get to keep the whole profit margin rather than sharing it with others in the channels of distribution. In varying ways you could end up passing on up to a quarter of your margin in this way. Against that, setting up your own online sales operation will require several thousand pounds of investment upfront and a continuing stream of investment to keep your systems up to date, much as a retailer would need new shop fittings.

Piggybacking on other websites

There is, however another way of getting your goods and services to internet markets: by piggybacking on established ready built e-tail platforms. The best known of these is eBay, which is covered in the Appendix on sources of business help information at the end of this book. There are also dozens of other sites that you can sell on, with or without going through the auction process. UK sales generated through sales on other providers' websites were estimated to be around £1.5 billion, up from £600 million in 2004.

Getting a storefront, a shopping cart and fulfilment system

If you were selling from a shop you would set out your window display and have a basket for customers to drop their shopping into prior to checking out and paying. Your online store has much the same features, with buttons and boxes around your order page allowing customers to select colours, sizes and quantities, place their order, pay and track the progress of their delivery. You need to decide what you want your online store to do, as with linkages to other services you can arrange payment, delivery and even stock reordering (all of which come at an increasing price, however, eating into your profit margin).

There are dozens of companies in the field such as Altcom (www.altcom. co.uk>Ecommerce), Easy Shop Maker (www.easyshopmaker.com) and ekm powershop(www.ekmpowershop.com) which have turnkey online shop fronts from £19.99 a month.

Getting paid online: PayPal et al

If you are going to trade on the internet then some form of online payment such as a credit card merchant account is essential. An alternative is one of a new breed of businesses tailored expressly for the internet. The leader of the pack is PayPal (www.paypal.com>Merchant Services). It claims to have 100 million accounts around the world, and firms using its services get an average 14 per cent uplift in sales.

Using PayPal you can in effect get a merchant account with all major credit and debit cards in one bundle without set-up fees or a lengthy application process, and start accepting payments within minutes. PayPal isn't free; you pay £0.20 per transaction and a sliding charge ranging from 3.4 per cent if your transactions amount to £1,500 in any month down to 1.4 per cent if sales are above £50,000 a month.

Other similar services are offered by WorldPay (www.worldpay. com>Small Business), Click and Buy (www.clickandbuy.com>Become a merchant) and Durango (www.durangomerchantservices.com).You can keep up with all the various services by reading the Merchant Account Forum (www.merchantaccountforum.com), a free newsletter set up by

Richard Adams who was so frustrated in his efforts to set up a merchant account for his first online business he decided to set up a site to review merchant accounts.

DESIGNING YOUR WEBSITE

Good website design is essential, with short loading time (use graphics, not photographs), short and sweet, legible text and an attractive layout. Research indicates that within three clicks, visitors must be captivated or they will leave. So clear signposting is necessary, including a menu on every page so that visitors can return to the homepage or move to other sections in just one click.

Promote your website by acquiring links on other commercial websites, using key words to ensure you can be found, and promoting outside the internet – feature your website address on all products and publications. Fill your homepage with regularly updated 'success stories', give discounts to first-time buyers, ask customers to 'bookmark' your site or add it to their list of 'favourites' on their browser. You could also try partnering with manufacturers and distributors in related business fields.

These are the do's and don'ts in website design. Do:

- think about design: create a consistent visual theme grouping elements together so that your reader can easily follow the information you are presenting;

- prepare your content: it should be focused on the needs of your target audience, and be credible, original, current and varied;

- plan your site navigation: your pages need to be organized intuitively so they are easy to navigate;

- consider usability and accessibility: use graphics sparingly as not everyone has super access speeds;

- optimize your HTML, especially on your home page, to minimize file size and download time by removing excess spaces, comments, tags and commentary;

- optimize for searching: build in key words and tags and markers so your site will be found easily.

Don't:

- have long pages: content beyond the first one and a half to two page lengths is typically ignored;

- have pointless animation: many of these are distracting, poorly de-signed in terms of colour and fonts, and add unnecessarily to file size, slowing down your reader's search;

- use the wrong colours, since colour choice is crucial; black text on a white background is the easiest to read whilst other colours such as red's and greens are harder to read (check out Visibone's website (www.visibone.com/colorblind) for a simulation of the web designer's colour palette of browser-safe colours);

- have stale information anywhere, especially on your homepage: nothing turns readers off so much as seeing information that relates to events long gone (recipes for Christmas pudding at Easter, for example);

- waste your readers' time: making readers register on your site may be useful to you, but unless you have some compelling value to offer, don't – or if you absolutely must, keep registration details to a couple of lines of information.

Check out Bad Website Ideas (www.badwebsiteideas.com) to see how to avoid the biggest howlers, and in consequence how to get your website design right.

Doing it yourself

You probably already have a basic website writing tool with your Office software. If you use Microsoft, then at Microsoft Office Live (http://office.microsoft.com>Microsoft Office Live) you will find links to free web design tools. Also you will find literally hundreds of packages from £50 to around £500 that with varying amounts of support will help you create your own website. Web Wiz Guide (www.webwizguide.com>Knowledgebase>De signing a Web Site) has a tutorial covering the basics of webpage design and layout. BT Broadband Office (www.btbroadbandoffice.com/businesstoday/0,9737,cats-5528530,00.html) is a direct link to dozens of articles on how to improve your website design. Top Ten Reviews (www.toptenreviews.com>Software>Website Creation) provides an annual report on the best website creation software rated by ease of use, help and support, value for money and a score of other factors. The best buy when this book was being written was a third of the price of the third-ranking programme.

Getting outside help

There are literally thousands of consultants who claim to be able to create a website for you. Prices start from £499, where an off-the-peg website package will be tweaked slightly to meet your needs, to around £5,000 to get something closer to tailor-made for you. The Directory of Design Consultants (www.designdirectory.co.uk>Design Category>internet) and Web Design Directory (www.web-design-directory-uk.co.uk) list hundreds of consultants, some one-person bands, others somewhat larger. You can look at their websites to see whether you like what they do. Web Design Directory has some useful pointers on choosing a designer. If you are working within a set budget you could consider auctioning off your web design project. With sites such as Get a Freelancer (www.getafreelancer. com), you state how much you are prepared to pay, with a description of the project, and freelancers around the world bid under your price, with the lowest bidder winning.

GETTING SEEN

Nine out of 10 visitors reach internet sites via a search engine or equivalent, so you need to fill the first page with 'key terms' that search engines can latch on to. This process is know as SEO (search engine optimization), where your website is 'optimized' so that it improves its position in search engine rankings. It also helps if you know a little about how search engines work.

How search engines work

Online searching services are often grouped under the single heading of 'search engines'. There are, however, two distinct services, 'directories' and ' search engines', which both contain the key to unlocking the wealth of information contained in billions of webpages throughout the internet. Directories and search engines differ mainly in the way each compiles its database of information.

Directories

These depend on people for compiling their information. You and millions of other people from around the world submit their website URLs (uniform resource locator – your website address – for example, www.mybusiness. com) with a brief description of your content. Volunteer editors view the website, see if it's appropriate for their directory and then place it in a category. Each category is further subdivided into more specific categories. For example clicking on the category ' business' will lead you to a further score of subheadings. Dmoz (www.dmoz.org) claims to be the largest and most comprehensive human-edited directory on the web, followed in size and range by WoW (www.wowdirectory.com). Web Directory List (www. webdirectorylist.com) is a guide to directory and related services.

Search engines

Unlike directories, no human interaction takes place with the websites submitted. Instead search engines have three major elements which attempt, with varying degrees of success, to arrive at the end result the 'surfer' is trying to achieve. The first of these elements is the spider (also called the crawler). The spider visits a webpage, reads it and then follows links to other pages within the site. The spider is looking for HTML (hypertext mark-up language) 'tags' or markers which can be woven into a webpage, making it more likely that a particular page will be detected by the spider. Everything the spider finds goes into the second part of the search engine, the index. The index can best be thought of as a colossal digital book holding a copy of every webpage found by the spider. This 'book' is updated every time a webpage changes. Until a webpage is entered into the index it is not available to those searching with a search engine. Hence the longer the intervals between a site being 'spidered', as this process is known, the less likely it is that information searched for will be relevant or current. Search engine software is the third element of a search engine. This is the program that sifts through the millions of pages recorded in the index to find matches to a search. It will also rank those matches according to certain criteria, to suggest which pages are most relevant.

Finding a search engine

While Google is one of the best-known search engines it is certainly not the only one, nor is it necessarily the best for every type of business. Yahoo!, Ask, MSN, AOL and AltaVista are among the hundreds of others. The Search Engine Guide (www.searchengineguide.com>internet Search Engines) lists search engines by business sector, some of which may be better for your products and services than the market leaders. Search Engine Watch (www.searchenginewatch.com) provides tips and information that can help website owners to improve their likelihood of being found in search engines.

You can track user satisfaction with search engines, a good indication of whether or not it is worth investing effort in getting onto their site, at the American Customer Satisfaction Index (www.theacsi.org>ACSI SCORES & COMMENTARY>Scores By Industry>internet Portals/ Search Engines) established by the University of Michigan. The latest survey ranks Yahoo! top and rising, followed by Google in second place and falling.

You can also track the market share of searches by search engine at comScore, a global internet information provider (www.comscore.com> Press Center>Key Measurements). In September 2007 for example Google had 55.2 per cent of the market, Yahoo! 23.5 per cent and Microsoft 12.3 per cent.

Getting listed

If you want to be sure of getting listed appropriately in a search engine, first make a list of the words that you think a searcher is most likely to use when looking for your products or services. For example a repair garage in Penzance could include keywords such as car, repair, cheap, quick, reliable, insurance, crash and Penzance in the home page to pull in searchers looking for a competitive price and a quick repair. As a rule of thumb, for every 300 words you need a keyword or phrase to appear between 10 and 15 times. Search engines thrive on content, so the more relevant content, the better. You can use products such as that provided by Good Keyword (www.goodkeyword.com), which has a free Windows software program to help you find words and phrases relevant to your business and provides statistics on how frequently those are used. Keywords Gold is its paid-for product (priced at $49) which has several additional filters and tools to help you refine your keyword lists.

Search engine algorithms also like important, authoritative and prestigious terms. So while you may not be able to boast 'by Royal Appointment' if you can get your press releases quoted in the *Financial Times*, your comments included in postings on popular blogs or your membership of professional institutes and associations into your homepage, your chances of being 'spidered' will rise accordingly.

Next on the list of strategies is to get your website linked to other sites with related but not competing information. So if you are selling garden pots, websites selling plants, gardening tools, fencing or compost are likely to have people hitting them who are of value to you. Being linked to dozens of other sites improves your chances of being spotted by a search engine. You can offer the sites in question a link to your site as a quid pro quo, and you could both benefit from the relationship.

Don't forget to submit the URL of your website domain name to search engines and reregister on a regular basis. Check on the search engine websites for the section headed 'submit your site'. For example for Yahoo! this is http://search.yahoo.com/info/submit.html and to register is free. Most search engines offer a premium registration service which involves a fee of some sort, but does guarantee a better degree of exposure. Yahoo! Directory Submit (www.yahoo.com/dir/submit/intro) cost $299 a year and claims to put you ahead of the herd, and its sponsored search service paid for by the 'click' aims to get you even more visibility.

Submitting to each search engine repeatedly is time-consuming so, as you might expect, the process can be automated using URL submission software such as that provided by WebPosition (www.webposition.com) or web ceo (www.webceo.com) for US$150–400. These programs will not only ensure your entry in search engines is kept up to date, but will provide tips on improvement and tools to report on your search engine ranking.

Using a submission service

While you can build words into your website that will help search engines find you, there are also professionals whose job it is to move you up the rankings. Submission services such as those provided by Submit Express (www.submitexpress.xo.uk), Rank4u (www.rank4u.co.uk) and Wordt8racker (www.wordtracker.com) have optimization processes that aim to move you into the all important top 10 ranking on key search engines. Payment methods vary: for example Rank4u has a 'no placement, no fee' deal where it only gets paid once it has achieved the positioning you want. 123 Ranking (www.123ranking.co.uk) has optimization packages aimed at small and new businesses from £199 per annum. Search Engine Guide (www.searchengineguide.com>Search Engine Marketing) has a guide to all aspects of search engine marketing.

Paid inclusion and placement

If you don't want to wait for search engines to find your website you can pay to have your webpages included in a search engines directory. That won't guarantee you a position, so for example if your page comes up at 9,870 in Google's list then the chance of a customer slogging their way to your page is zero. The only way to be sure you appear early – in the first page or two of a search – is to advertise in a paid placement listing. For major search engines such as Google AdWords (www.google.com>Business

Solutions>Earn revenue with AdWords), Yahoo Search Marketing (http://searchmarketing.yahoo.com) and Microsoft adCenter (https:adcenter. Microsoft.com) you will be invited to bid on the terms you want to appear for, by way of a set sum per click.

CHOOSING AN INTERNET SERVICE PROVIDER (ISP)

An ISP keeps you connected to the internet. Without a fast, reliable, cost-effective and well-supported service your website may not realize its full potential. Upload and download speeds of 1 Mbps (slow) to 24 Mbps (fast) are available, with 8 Mbps currently being the norm. Some ISPs restrict the amount of information you can download in any month, but look out for suppliers with no such restrictions. Set-up costs, monthly charges, length of contract and support are also factors to look out for.

Broadband Finder (www.broadband-finder.co.uk) and Broadband Checker (www.broadbandchecker.co.uk) provide information and rate ISPs according to your criteria.

WORKSHEET FOR ASSIGNMENT 14: BUILDING A WEBSITE

1. Do your competitors or other similar organizations have websites, and if so what functions are carried out there?
2. Will you sell some or all of your products and services on your website, and if so which and why?
3. What other operational activities could you carry out via a website?
4. If you do plan to sell on the internet, will you sell your self or through an intermediary and why?
5. How will you get paid and fulfil web-based business?
6. What steps will you take to drive traffic to your website?
7. Are there any revenue-generating opportunities other than selling that you can pursue?
8. Who will design your website?
9. How will you upload new information to your website, keeping it current and topical?
10. Have you incorporated the cost implications of building and running your website in your financial forecasts?

SUGGESTED FURTHER READING

Meerman, S (2007) *The new rules of marketing and PR: how to use news releases, blogs, podcasting, viral marketing and online media to reach buyers directly,* Wiley, New York

Sahlin, D and Snell, C (2007) *Building websites all-in-one desk reference for dummies,* Wiley, New York

Communication systems

With the exception of retail businesses, customers, potential employees and suppliers for that matter, have their first experience of almost every other type of business on the phone, by post, e-mail or on the internet. Often that 'moment of truth' as this initial contact experience is known is the clincher that decides whether or not to go on and do business with that organisation. Injecting an element of professionalism at this stage can make your business stand out and stand tall.

The other major consideration from a business planning perspective is the cost of communication systems. On average the equivalent of 10 per cent of sales revenue is expended in these areas; that is about the same sum as a typical business makes in profit. Savings in the efficient structuring of communication systems drop straight to the bottom line of the profit and loss account. This can make a new venture more viable and more certain of success. This chapter outlines the communication equipment that you are likely to need, as a bare minimum, and how to establish their costs for inclusion in your business plan.

TELEPHONE SYSTEMS

If you will be working full-time at your business and want to exude professionalism, having broadband internet, a business phone number and a spare line for a fax/answer machine would be a good starting specification.

Obviously if your business is in telemarketing you may need much more substantial provision. Ofcom (www.ofcom.org.uk/consumeradvice/landline/residential) and USwitch (www.uswitch.com>Home phone>Home phone guides) give overviews of the landline options available at any particular time, and guidelines on how to chose between them. BT (http://sme.bt/startingabusiness) has a guide to its products for business start-ups including its BT Business One Plan.

Mobile phones

Mobile phones have two valuable uses. First, they let you operate your business from anywhere: the car, train and even on an increasing number of airplanes. Second, they give you an additional 'landline' facility, for example if your mainline is handling a fax or being used by someone working with you.

The cost of mobile services is ever-changing, with a mass of bundling of landlines, internet and television making comparisons difficult. That is particularly the case if you expect to be making or receiving many international calls. Money Supermarket (www.moneysupermarket.com>MOBILE PHONES), Fone-Deals (www.fone-deals.co.uk) and Before You Buy (www.beforeyoubuy.co.uk>PHONE) are price comparison websites that give tariff and cost details based on the information you provide on your likely usage – calls, texts, video, internet usage and so forth.

VoIP (voice over internet protocol)

Increasingly it is becoming possible to use the internet as a connection route for making telephone calls. This gives you instantly as many 'lines' as you need at zero or very little cost. Companies such as Skype (www.skype.com) provide a free piece of software which once installed allows all users to speak free anywhere around the world. Aside from speech, text, landline and mobile phone calls and message answering services can be added for a modest cost. To find out what developments are in this field go to www.voireview.org, ww.voip-news.com and www.voip.org.uk.

Toll-free numbers

Customers are three times more likely to call a freephone number than to make a standard paid-for call. Free numbers come in all shapes and sizes, ranging from totally free from anywhere, to the price of a local call from anywhere. Calls from mobile phones will be variable dependent on the network either you or your customer is using.

Companies such as Planet Numbers (www.planet-numbers.co.uk) and SKYCOM (www.skycomuk.com) provide a mass of services, claiming that you need only pay around 5p for every call received. You can use your own landline number, a mobile phone or pick your own phone number from a menu of options. You can change the destination number of the incoming call so you can receive calls anywhere you happen to be.

You can get a private phone number in almost any country in the world, thus giving you a 'local' presence in that country, and have those calls redirected to your business landline or mobile phone. The caller in the country in question can get the call for free or at local call rates, with you picking up the balance. American International Telephonics (www. aittelephone.com) and Callagenix (www.callagenix.com) can provide you with international phone numbers and supporting services.

ABSENT MESSAGING

If you work alone and are away from your office or immersed in tasks from which you don't want to be interrupted, this does not mean that customers, suppliers and others you work with don't want to contact you by phone. The classic way to handle this is to have some form of automated answering system that can either take and give a message such as 'I am away until 11 am; call my mobile number; or leave a message and I'll get back to you later today.' Whatever system you use the cardinal rules are:

- Let callers know your message is relevant. For example, 'You are through to Instant Interiors. It is Thursday 5 September and I am away from my desk or in meetings until 3.30 pm. I will return your call after then.'

- Call them back as arranged.

The simplest and cheapest thing to do is to buy an old-fashioned answering machine. For around £20 you can get a machine that will do everything a small business could reasonably require, including being able to access and change messages from anywhere. Your telephone company will be able to offer a similar service without involving any hardware at your end. The most basic of these services, such as BT's Answer 1571 Free, takes up to 10 messages, but does nothing else. For more facilities expect to pay around £5 a month.

An answering machine uses your phone line, so when someone calls no one else can get through and you can't call out. Voice mail can handle at least 10 simultaneous calls, even when you are checking the messages. You can call in, pick up messages or get texts or e-mails with an MP3 file attachment so you can hear the calls from any computer or internet café.

Voice mail services start at around £100 per annum, but can be used by the month if you just want to cover a busy period, such as during a promotional campaign. Companies such as Premier Voicemail Ltd (www. premiervoicemail.co.uk; tel: 020 8236 0236) and X-on Voicemail (www.x-on.co.uk; tel: 0870 345 5577) offer the full range of voicemail services.

Using an answering service

The systems described so far take and give messages but don't involve a 'warm body' response. You can get a real person to answer your phone without having him or her in your home. This could be a valuable service if the calls you will be receiving are complicated, for example asking for one of several information packs, asking for a visit or placing an order. It could also be useful if you are expecting a large volume of high-value calls in a short period of time or if you need 24/7 cover to support your product or service.

Office Response (www.office-response.co.uk; tel: 0800 197 0286) and Office Answers (www.office-answers.co.uk; tel: 0207 11 11 085) both offer a variety of services that amount to having a 'virtual receptionist'. Prices start from £17 a month, with a £25 set-up cost. Office Answers offers a one-week free trial, after which if you are happy to proceed, you commit to its minimum term of three months.

Fax

The fax machine still has a part to play in business life when you want to transmit pictures, diagrams and complex text such as price lists, or if the recipient doesn't have a computer. You will get the best value if you buy the fax as part of an answer machine or printer combination package, but in any event the cost will be minimal. Expect to pay upwards of £30, with the most sophisticated costing around £100. Amazon (www.amazon.co.uk) has over 500 fax machines listed.

E-mail

E-mail is now more or less universal and can be used as the host for almost any communication system, from being a basic telephone (VoIP), to sending and receiving faxes and other documents and providing an answering service. E-mail has a number of key advantages for business users:

- If you have broadband internet connection e-mails are more or less free.

- E-mailing can save time sending as many copies of the same message as you like all at the same time.

- You can do e-mail when it suits you best whereas phone calls can interrupt the day.

- You have a written record, unlike with any telephone-based message, which should reduce the possibilities of confusion or error.

- You can e-mail from anywhere.

Your ISP will almost certainly bundle in a dozen or more e-mail addresses free with its service. Hotmail (www.hotmail.com), Google Mail (www.google.co.uk>more>Google Mail) and Yahoo (www.yahoo.com>Free mail) all offer free e-mail services with masses of free storage – 2GB up to 8GBs. See also the section in Assignment 14 on 'Choosing an internet service provider'.

POSTAL MATTERS

While technology has helped business communications it has not supplanted the good old-fashioned 'snail mail' arriving through the letterbox. If you are going to be working alone or are likely to be away from your office for long periods, the Post Office (www.postoffice.co.uk) has a number of services to make life easier for you. Keepsafe holds mail for up to two months at a cost of around £8 a month, or for £57.85 a year you can have a PO box. In using the box service, you can have in effect a new address for your post, which you have to pick up monthly (or as frequently as you like). This can create a professional image and let you decide when to handle the post, rather than have it dumped on your doorstep at what may be an inconvenient time.

Private companies such as Inter Post Box (www.interpostbox.com; tel: 020 7278 4846) and PostBox Shop (www.postboxshop.com; tel: 0845 602 3594) offer a prestigious address and either a call-in service or mail forwarding for from £21 a month for a yearly contract.

Other postal matters

If you do expect to have to handle a large volume of post these are some other matters to consider:

- Machine franking is a way to ensure you never run out of stamps and always have the right value of stamp for the size of letter and its destination. When postal tariffs change these systems automatically update. Machine providers claim to save up to 20 per cent on postage costs, and at the very least offer a 2p saving on standard postage rates. Franking machines cost from around £500 to buy or £20 a month to rent. The Royal Mail offers a SmartStamp service that you can run from your computer and printer for as little as £5 a month, downloading stamps as you need them.

- Automated letter opening or folding may be useful if you are mailing or receiving a large volume of post. These machines cost upwards of £250.

- Shredding confidential papers may become important once you start your business. Any document with information on your bank account, supplier discounts, customer addresses or any document you would prefer competitors not to see should be shredded. Office shredders cost upwards of £40.

The Royal Mail (www.royalmail.com>Business customers>Small and Medium Business) has a guide to its services and a directory of approved franking and mailroom equipment providers. UK Office Direct (www. ukofficedirect.co.uk) has a comprehensive range of mailroom machines and guides to choosing which is right for your needs.

COMPUTERS, HARDWARE, SOFTWARE AND SECURITY SYSTEMS

Computers and their software are the single most important tools for almost any type of business. These have in effect levelled the playing field between big established businesses and new entrants. In fact as prices have dropped steeply and specifications risen, anyone buying now will have a significant advantage over those buying a year or two back.

The general computer specification

To handle general business needs, run a basic website and design and print a newsletter you need an entry-level computer with this specification:

- For PCs look for one that has or can use the Windows Vista Business operating system. For Apple computers look for Mac OS X v 10.5, known as Leopard. The operating system is the intelligent link between the computer's hardware and software; the language used, in effect, to 'speak' to the computer. These two are the latest.

- Look for at least 80 GB hard drive, enough to hold 150,000 pages of text at any one time. Capacity of 200 GB or more will be necessary if you are working with multimedia applications.

- Random access memory (RAM) is the memory available to work the programs as opposed to storing data. You need at least 1 GB of RAM, and double that if you will be editing high-end graphics.

- Opt for a 17 inch flat-screen monitor which will allow for preparing and editing price lists, newssheets and leaflets.

- CD/DVD drives that allow copying and writing are standard on computers today. You should look for a drive that writes at 52X to keep copy times down.

- Graphics and sound cards determine the quality of sound and visual output, and have their own separate memory. Look for an integrated graphics card with 256 MB of video memory and a separate graphics card with 128 MB memory.

- At least three USB ports.

- Core Duo architecture that in essence squeezes two independent computer drives onto a single CPU (central processing unit) which means it handles doing two tasks at the same time a whole lot better than with single architecture.

To keep on top of what the latest specs and offers are read *PC World* (www. pcworld.com>Hardware Reviews), CNET (www.cnet.com>Reviews) and IT Reviews (www.itreviews.co.uk). For Apple visit Apple.com (www. apple.com/mac)

Laptops versus desktops

Buying a laptop rather than a desktop means electing for portability over price and performance. There is virtually nothing that you are likely to want a computer for as a business owner that cannot be done on a laptop, but as a rough rule of thumb the latter will cost 20 per cent more and be 20 per cent less powerful. If you will be travelling a lot then it may just be worth the additional cost, but with laptops selling in supermarkets for £299 you could consider having both.

There are just a couple of further considerations. Being portable a laptop is more likely to get broken or stolen. So you will need to make sure your insurance will cover these eventualities.

You can keep abreast of developments in the laptop world at Laptop Magazine (www.laptopmag.com>Reviews) and What Laptop (www.what laptop.co.uk).

PDAs

Personal digital assistant was a rather pretentious name for what used to be little more than an electronic diary and address book. Today you can get PDAs that have sufficient memory to hold all the files you are working on (including PowerPoint presentations and spreadsheets); connect to the internet; send and receive e-mails; synchronize with your computer; work as a mobile phone; enable you to watch movies and listen to your music; operate as a digital camera; and act as a GPS navigation mapping system.

Prices start from £70 for the basic Palm Z22 and range up to around £400 for a BlackBerry or Hewlett-Packard. You can get all the benefits of both PDA and laptop when you travel by subscribing to a service such as GoToMyPC (www.gotomypc.com). By paying £107.79 a year and leaving your computer on and connected to the internet you can access data on your computer from any other computer with an internet connection.

You can keep abreast of developments in the PDA field at Brighthand (www.brighthand.com) and Mobile Tech Review (www.mobiletechreview. com).

SECURITY AND BACK-UP SYSTEMS

The cardinal rule in working with computers is to do frequent back-ups and hold copies of your work somewhere other than on the drive of the machine you are working on at the time. There are a myriad of options, so there is no excuse other than absentmindedness or laziness, neither of which are behaviours that entrepreneurs should cultivate. Viruses, theft, computer crashes and physical damage are the most likely problems that cause data loss. Working at home only magnifies the opportunities for any of these problems to arise.

At the very least back-ups of the files you have been working with should be done at the end of every day, and of your whole system once a week. These are the main options:

- Use the CD/DVD drive on the computer to back up to a disk. These cost around 50p for a rewritable disk that can be used up to 1,000 times.

- Back up to a laptop, if you have one. This has the merit that you can work with the files if something has gone wrong with your main computer. If the computer is vital to your business this is the favourite option, but will cost at least £300 for a new laptop.

- Use an online back-up system; the provider's software is installed on your computer, and detects any changes or additions to your files and automatically makes copies in real time. This service costs from £35 a month for up to 50 GB of data and you can usually get a 15-day free trial. Backup Direct (www.backupdirect.net; tel: 0800 0 789 437) and SecuriData (www.securidata.co.uk; tel: 08712 71 29 29) provide this service. Check whether your ISP offers this service, which may come free.

- Use a separate hard drive such as those provided by Iomega (www. iomega.com) or Western Digital (www.wdc.com). Prices start at £50, and you can expect to pay £80 for 500 GB.

- Use a USB pen drive. These have up to 4 GB storage on a small cigarette-lighter-sized implement that slots into a USB port. Sandisk has a 'Smart' flash drive, as these disks are usually referred to, that will automatically back up your e-mail, diary, My Documents folder, Internet Favourites and Skype phone system. Priced from around £4 and £18 for the Sandisk Cruiser (www.sandisk.com), a system that automatically backs up data. Amazon (www.amazon.co.uk) offers one of the widest ranges of these products at very competitive prices.

Power support systems

If you use a laptop then losing power will not be too big a problem; not for an hour or two at least, until the battery runs flat. However, your desktop computer will shut instantly and you could lose everything you were working on. You can get a basic back-up power system for between £40 and £140, which will give you up to an hour's use of a computer, kicking in automatically when your power goes off; more than enough time to make a back-up, save vital e-mails and find the fuse box. Maplin (www.maplin. co.uk) and Adept Power Solutions (www.adeptpower.co.uk) have a range of products to handle power interruptions.

It is also useful to have a surge protector, which acts as a 'brake' making sure that whatever happens to the power source, the actual power to your equipment stays within safe limits. If you use an uninterruptible power system for your computer system it will almost certainly have surge protection built in, but for other equipment such as printers, fax machines and scanners, you should consider buying a protector. A protector that will cope with up to six pieces of equipment will cost around £15. Dabs (www. dabs.com), Maplin and Adept Power Solutions offer surge protectors.

Other hardware needs

Your computer will not be much use on its own without other pieces of equipment to connect to, or ways to connect to the internet. These are the most common elements to make up a complete office computer system.

Networks

If you are going to be working in different parts of your business premises or using several computers you should consider installing a local area network (LAN) using a router; a small transmitter connected to your telephone. This is a wireless way to connect your computers to the internet and to each other, and can be a useful way to share a printer, scanner or any other device between several users.

Your ISP will in all probability give you the transmitter and installation instructions, or you can buy one from the suppliers listed above under 'Power support systems', for around £35.

An alternative is to use a Powerline Network, a system that uses your electricity power circuit to transmit data. You connect one plug to a router and other plugs can be used to link computers to the internet wherever they are on that electric circuit. This could be useful if there are areas where you want internet reception, but cannot get it via the router alone. Homeplugs (www.homeplugs.co.uk) and Maplin (www.maplin.co.uk>Computers>Ne tworking Over The mains) provide these systems.

Printers and copiers

Printers and copiers do much the same task but for printers the input comes directly from a computer. You have two main options:

- *Inkjet* (sometimes known as bubble jet) where ink is squirted in thousands of minute dots onto paper to form text or pictures. The advantages of inkjet are that the printers are inexpensive and they can print in colour. The drawbacks are that replacement ink cartridges are expensive, print speeds are slow and the print quality may not be that great.

- *Laser* printers use a drum and toner, produce crisper copies, faster and at a much lower cost per copy. The machines cost more than inkjets, and if you want colour the machine will be more expensive still.

If what you print or copy is for in-house consumption only, an inkjet printer will meet all your needs. If you send documents to customers and quality is vital, or if you make thousands of copies, consider going for a laser printer. ITWEEK (www.itweek.co.uk>Reviews>Printers) and Trusted Reviews (www.trustedreviews.com>Printers) produce regular evaluations of printers so that you can make a comparison of specifications and prices.

Scanners

Normally you will input data into your computer using a keyboard. There may be occasions when you want to transfer something from paper onto your computer, a picture or image, for example. The cost of scanners ranges from £30 for basic machines up to around £500 for scanners that will handle extremely high-resolution films and even remove dust and scratches from damaged photos. In the top price range scanners come with the software needed to edit text and pictures, otherwise you will need to buy a program such as Textbridge or OmniPage, both available from suppliers such as Amazon (www.amazon.co.uk) for between £49 and £72.

THE VITAL SOFTWARE

These are the minimum programs that you are likely to require. (Accounting and business planning software are covered at the end of Assignment 25.)

Office program suites

This is the generic title for bundles of programs that usually include a word processor, spreadsheet, database, e-mail manager, diary/address book and much else besides. The most popular, at least in terms of sales, is Microsoft Office (http://office.microsoft.com>Products). Prices range between £100 for a Home and Student suite up to £400 for Microsoft Office 2007 Ultimate. There is a good chance if you buy a new computer that a version of Office will already be installed.

There are a few free suites of programs that will do much if not all of what a small business might require. Google (docs.google.com), think free (www.thinkfree.com) and Ajax 13 (www.ajax13.com) all offer free office suites, compatible with Microsoft. The catch is you have to be online to use them, but that in turn means you can use them anywhere on any computer.

If you want to be able to work offline, try OpenOffice (www.openoffice. org), whose free office programs are compatible with Microsoft and work in some 30 languages; or Sun Microsystems (www.sun.com>Products>Soft ware>Desktop>Office Productivity), whose Star Office 8 Writer, priced at $69.95, claims to match Microsoft's product for small businesses but at one-fifth the cost.

Publishing leaflets and price lists

Word processing programs will do almost everything a small business could ask for when it comes to preparing leaflets, newsletters and price lists. If you want something more sophisticated but don't want to pay, try Serif Europe (www.freeserifsoftware.com) which has a suite of desktop publishing and drawing programs absolutely free. If that doesn't quite fit the bill, try its more sophisticated products at www.serif.com, priced at £99.

Antivirus

There are nearly as many programs to protect your computer against viruses as there are viruses. A good free system that seems to work well is that from Grisoft (http://free.grisoft.com). Its AVG Anti-Virus Free edition provides basic protection, but without any technical support. To get that you will have to pay $52.95. Norton (www.symantec.com) and McAfee (www.mcafee.com) are the market leaders in this sector, but keep an eye on *Personal Computer World*'s regular reviews (www.pcw.co.uk>Reviews> Software>Antivirus & Firewalls).

WORKSHEET FOR ASSIGNMENT 15: COMMUNICATION SYSTEMS

1. What telephone and absent answering systems do you plan to use and why?
2. Determine the specification of your computer system.
3. How will you handle your incoming and outgoing mail?
4. What back-up systems will you use to ensure vital data is not lost?
5. Describe the software you will need to ensure your business can run effectively.
6. What hardware other than a computer will you require?
7. How will you ensure your computer system is kept virus free?

SUGGESTED FURTHER READING

Sobey, E (2007) *A field guide to office technology*, Chicago Review Press, USA

Phase 5

Forecasting results

INTRODUCTION

Once you have formulated a basic or new strategy for your business, you will have to make some forecast of the likely results of your endeavours. These projections are essential to show how much cash you will need and how much profit you could make, and to chart a safe financial strategy. This is the part of your business plan of greatest interest to potential backers and anyone else whose support is essential to your venture.

Your forecasts may well prove wrong, and initially at least, you may have little confidence in them being achieved. But the learning that comes from carrying out these projections will serve to increase the chances of ending up with a plan that you do believe in, and that has a good chance of achieving results that will ensure your venture survives.

The task in forecasting is to get your dart on the board, rather than to hit the bullseye first time. Once on the board you can correct your aim with subsequent throws. Remember these forecasts are being made before you commit resources, so in effect, you can have as many throws as you like at this stage, without the pain of the resultant consequences.

Assignment 16

The sales forecast

The precision of numbers often bears no relation to the facts.

Denis Healey, former chancellor of the Exchequer

The sales forecast is perhaps the most important set of numbers to come out of the business planning process. How much stock to hold, how many staff to employ, how much material to buy, are all decisions that hinge on the sales forecast. These sales figures are also used to predict the cash-flow forecast and hence the funding requirements of the business.

These projections are also the key to valuing the business, so they will determine whether or not bankers will lend and investors invest. Furthermore, they will give some guidance as to how much of an enterprise investors expect in exchange for funding.

Naturally enough, potential backers do not accept a sales forecast unchallenged as, in their experience, new ventures nearly always miss the target by a wide margin.

The Millennium Dome

How could a forecast of 12 million visitors have been made for the number of visitors to the Millennium Dome in Greenwich? Pierre-Yves Gerbeau, the French MBA brought in to stabilize the situation, explained:

> Few business plans show you can break even in Year 1. Yet the forecast was based on costs. How many visitors do we need to balance the books, was the question asked? The answer was 12 million! I am convinced now, half-way through the year, that we can reach 6 million. But with a 2 per cent of turnover marketing budget only (compared with an 8–12 per cent average in the attractions industry), don't shoot the Frenchman if we don't make it!

While forecasts may turn out to be wrong, it is important to demonstrate in your business plan that you have thought through the factors that will have impact on performance. You should also show how you can deliver satisfactory results even when many of these factors may be working against you. Backers will be measuring the downside risk to evaluate the worst scenario and its likely effects, as well as looking towards an ultimate exit route.

Here are some guidelines to help you make an initial sales forecast.

● *Check how others have fared*: your overall projections will have to be believable. Most lenders and investors will have an extensive experience of similar business proposals. Unlike yourself, they will have the benefit of hindsight, and are able to look back several years at other ventures they have backed to see how they fared in practice compared with the ventures' initial forecasts. You could gather some useful knowledge on similar businesses yourself by researching filed company accounts and trade magazines, or by talking with the founders of such ventures who will not be your direct competitors. Look back to Assignments 5 and 6 for guidance on how to research competitor performance.

Scoops

Edmund Bradley estimated that in its first year of trading, Scoops would generate £50,000 worth of sweet sales. The projection was based upon observation of the numbers of purchases made by a competitor's outlet in Bath (Confetti), over a one-week period. The number of customers per hour varied between 34 (during rainy weather) and 140 (when sunny), with an average expenditure per purchase of £1. Discussions with confectionery-shop owners revealed that the summer months of June, July and August, plus Christmas (December), accounted for half of the year's sales. In other months, purchases made on Saturdays accounted for half the weekly sales.

Based on a different town population (Taunton is half the size of Bath), Edmund estimated that Scoops would only attract half the customers of Confetti and would require an average of 25 customers per hour to reach his sales target. As well as working there himself, he planned to employ one full-time assistant, part-time help on Saturdays and student part-timers in the summer and Christmas vacations.

● *Work out market share*: how big is the market for your product or service? Is it growing or contracting? At what rate and percentage per annum? What is its economic and competitive position? These are all factors that can provide a market-share basis for your forecasts.

An entry market share of more than a few per cent would be most unusual. In spite of all the hype, after more than a decade of hard work the internet booksellers still account for less than 10 per cent of all books sold, and Amazon is just one of a score of major players. But beware of turning this argument on its head.

Many sales forecasts are made on the premise that 'If we capture just 1 per cent of the potential market, we'll be a great success.' This statement is made so that no time is wasted in doing basic market research – after all, the business only has to sell to this tiny percentage of possible buyers! In fact, this type of thinking leads to more business failures than any other single factor. If the market is so huge as to make 1 per cent of it very profitable, then inevitably there are large and established competitors. For a small firm to try to compete head on in this situation is little short of suicidal. It can be done, but only if sound research has clearly identified a market niche. No investor will be impressed by unsubstantiated statements such as 'In a market of £1 billion per annum, we can easily capture 1 per cent – £1 million a year.'

- *Think about your customers*: how many customers and potential customers do you know who are likely to buy from you, and how much might they buy? You can use many types of data on which to base reasonable sales projections: you can interview a sample of prospective customers, issue a press release or advertisement to gauge response and exhibit at trade shows to obtain customer reactions.

Werner Herker

Having arranged UK suppliers and fixed teams to install Victorian conservatories in Germany, qualified engineer and Cranfield MBA Werner Herker formed a company and placed a tiny advertisement in the leading German television listings magazine. With over 15 replies, and knowing that an average fitted installation costs at least £25,000, Werner was able to accurately forecast his first year's sales and accordingly launched a successful company.

- *Be aware of order cycles and timescales*: if your product or service needs to be on an approved list before it can be bought, then your forecast should confirm you have that approval.

- *Look at seasonality*: you should consider seasonal factors that might cause sales to be high or low in certain periods of the year. For example, 80 per cent of toys are sold in just three months of the year, leaving nine very flat months. If you were selling toys, this would have a significant effect on cash-flow projections.

- *Use rules of thumb where possible*: for some businesses, there are rules of thumb that can be used to estimate sales. This is particularly true in retailing, where location studies, traffic counts and population density are all known factors.

Using rules of thumb: Tim Brown

When Tim Brown founded his second restaurant, Alamo, in Los Angeles, with substantial backing from private investors, he used one such rule. In his experience, once a restaurant has served 25,000 clients it can expect sufficient repeat business to break even. In his first eight months of operation he had achieved 20,000.

● *Work out your desired income*: forecasts will accommodate the realistic aims of the proprietor. You could even say that the whole purpose of strategy is to ensure that certain forecasts are achieved. This is more likely to be the case in a mature company with proven products and markets than with a start-up. Nevertheless, an element of 'how much do we need to earn?' must play a part in forecasting, if only to signal when a strategy is not worth pursuing.

Working out desired income: Jane Jenkins

Jane Jenkins set up her business 18 months after finishing a college degree. At first she was not sure what business to start, but a friend with whom she lived wanted to set up a craft studio to teach students how to slip-cast (an ancient method of making pottery using liquid clay poured into a mould). Jane visited a number of potteries and discovered people with this skill. 'Their mug shapes were revolting, though. So I drew my own. I found, doing so, that all my frustration evaporated just like that. Suddenly I knew what I wanted to do.'

The next few months were spent driving around the country, staying in hotels normally frequented by travelling salespeople. She equipped herself with sponges and colours so that she could apply her designs to her mugs in the factories.

'At first people thought I was mad and were sceptical but helpful.' However, she soon won her first order, worth £600, from the General Trading Company and within two months she joined a lot of 'hysterical stallholders with lavender bags' at a trade fair.

Jane Jenkins was of the opinion that if she could not earn at least £40,000 per annum in the second year of her new business, she would not want to start up. Her predicted profit margin was 40 per cent, so this 'objective' called for a sales forecast of £100,000. She used her market research and the resultant strategies to satisfy herself (and her backers) that this was a realistic goal.

● *Relate the sales forecast to activity*: however they are arrived at, sales figures will convince no one unless they are related back to the specific activities that will generate business. For example, if, in your business, salespeople have to make visits to generate orders, then knowing how many calls need to be made to get one order and what the average order size could be are essential pieces of information to include in your sales forecast.

CASE STUDY

Making the sales forecast: Exploration Works

For the past two years, Anthea Cody has run a very successful outdoor clothing shop called Exploration Works. The business took on an agency from Asian Adventure Holidays, one of the largest and most respected tour operators in the market. With virtually no marketing effort, some 200 adventure holidays were sold in six months, netting £40,000 in commissions. Sales of insurance policies and other services added to this total and could potentially add much more.

When making her sales forecast, Anthea estimated that her enquiry-to-sale conversion rate on adventure travel holidays sold within the outdoor clothing shop to date had been 33 per cent. However, she revised her estimate downward in order to be conservative, assuming that only 20 per cent of enquiries would actually result in an adventure holiday being booked.

She expects a steady build-up of clients coming to the clothing shop to talk about holidays (see Table 16.1). She also thinks the number of new enquiries generated by promotional activity will build up during the year, gradually overtaking enquiries from the clothes shop. This is a trend she expects to continue. Based on the projection in Table 16.1, she is forecasting to sell 660 adventure travel holidays next year at an average price of £2,125.

Once insurance and other service sales are added, she can expect to generate an income of £160,948 over 12 months.

Table 16.1 Sales forecast projection

	Q1	Q2	Q3	Q4	Year total
Enquiries generated through promotion	200	425	425	750	1,800
Adventure shop enquiries	300	300	450	450	1,500
Total enquiries	500	725	875	1,200	3,300
Holidays sold	100	145	175	240	660
Average holiday's cost (£)	2,000	2,000	2,250	2,250	–
Commission received (£)	20,000	29,000	43,312	59,136	151,448
Commission on insurance & other services received (£)	1,000	2,000	3,000	3,500	9,500
Total commission & fees earned (£)	21,000	31,000	46,312	62,636	160,948

● *How far ahead should you forecast?* Opinions are divided between three and five years ahead. However, financiers we have talked to, while often asking for a five-year view, only pay serious attention to the first three years.

The arguments for looking this far ahead are twofold. First, most new ventures are at their greatest risk in the first few years, so investors and lenders want to see that the proprietors have a well-thought-out strategy to cover this period. Second, venture capitalists in particular want to look forward to the time when they can realize their investment and move on. Typically their exit route has to materialize between years 3 and 5 – they hope, during the earliest of the three.

The first two years of the sales forecast should be made on a monthly basis, and the remaining three years on a quarterly basis.

The examples below provide a flavour of the range of possible outcomes for the first few years of a new venture's life.

Graham Brown founded Oasis in Oxford a year after completing his economics degree, and two years later his second shop opened in Brighton. Finding that running two shops was very different from running one, he took on a partner, Andrew Thomas, who had learnt his retailing at Debenhams and Habitat. Two years later they raised £100,000 to open their Guildford store, and four years further on their Covent Garden flagship was opened. This cost £65,000 for shopfitting alone. Within a decade of starting up, turnover was up to £3.5 million a year.

Blooming Marvellous, a mail order company providing stylish and imaginative maternity clothes, is the brainchild of two successful businesswomen, Judy Lever and Vivienne Pringle. Started on a shoestring with £750 and only two dresses on offer, within two and a half years Blooming Marvellous had built up to an annual turnover of £120,000.

Brian Davies (a former sales manager) and his wife Anne bought the Rothesay, a middle-market 23-bedroomed private hotel at Llandudno, North Wales. They spent the summer of that year learning the ins and outs of the hotel trade under the guidance of the previous owners. Total turnover for their first year was £37,925. The following year Brian introduced a new sales strategy and cold-called coach tour companies to drum up new business. This succeeded in raising turnover for that year to £54,134. The third year saw Brian making improvements to the decor and restaurant facilities, but several coach cancellations left total revenue for the year at £60,816. By year four they consolidated past strategies and turnover rose to £64,844, but with some cost savings, profits grew faster than turnover. The strategy for their fifth year in business was to extend the season from its previous 17 weeks into the 20–22 range.

Unfortunately, unusually bad weather reduced the casual trade by 12 per cent but coach party sales were a record. The resultant sales level peaked at £73,950.

CASE STUDY

Maureen Davy and her husband Graham, a former Naval officer, the founders of Equinox designer furniture company, took £6,000 in revenue in their first year, £20,150 in their second, £63,280 in their third and £111,050 in their fourth year.

CASE STUDY

Former stockbroker David Stapleton was 40 when he bought Pinneys, a sleepy salmon-smoking business in the Scottish borders, for £20,000. Three years later Pinneys made its first real breakthrough, when it secured Marks & Spencer as a customer. It was a gamble for M&S, which at that time had never stocked products costing more than £3 per pound on its shelves before. But it paid off for both of them. Within 10 years of starting up, Stapleton had taken Pinneys' sales to £50 million pa and an estimated net worth of £15 million.

CASE STUDY

Former advising executive John Nettleton borrowed £1,800 from his four-year-old daughter's building society and set up his business in a tumbledown shed in Richmond. His company, MicroScent, uses micro-encapsulation technology to trap bubbles of fragrant oil on paper. Scratching or rubbing releases the scent over time. The principal application is scented drawer lining paper. His first year's turnover amounted to £30,000 with a nominal £1,000 loss. A friendly bank manager, enthused by the venture's prospects, advanced £70,000 for proper manufacturing equipment on the basis of a business plan and £10,000 collateral on his house. In his second year turnover was £204,000 with profits at £45,000; the third year turnover was £369,000; in his fourth year turnover rose to £680,000 with profits forecast at £130,000.

WORKSHEET FOR ASSIGNMENT 16: THE SALES FORECAST

1. Provide details of any firm orders on hand.
2. Provide details of all customers you expect to sell to over the forecast period, and how much you expect to sell to each.
3. Give market research data that support or verify these forecasts. This is particularly important for ventures in the retail field, for example, when names of customers are not necessarily known in advance.
4. Prepare a sales forecast by value and volume for each major product group (eg for a hotel: bedrooms, restaurant, off-licence) throughout the whole period of the business plan – eg up to five years (monthly for years 1 and 2 and quarterly thereafter).
5. Support your forecast with examples from other similar ventures started recently, and drawing from company accounts and other sources.
6. Give an estimate of the likely market share that these forecasts imply.

SUGGESTED FURTHER READING

Bolt, G (2007) *Market and sales forecasting*, Crest, New Delhi
Carlberg, C (2005) *Excel sales forecasting for dummies*, Wiley, New York.

Pro forma cash-flow statement

CASH-FLOW VERSUS PROFIT

It is a generally accepted principle that the purpose of business is to make a profit. There is, however a purpose that is even more important – survival. In the short term, a business can survive even if it is not making a profit as long as it has sufficient cash reserves, but it cannot survive without cash even though it may be making a profit. The purpose of the cash-flow projection is to calculate how much cash a business is likely to need to accomplish its objectives, and when it will need it in the business. These projections will form the basis of negotiations with any potential provider of capital.

Let us look at the following example to illustrate the difference between cash and profit and the need to start financial planning with both a cash-flow and profit projection.

Kensington Quick Fit

The Kensington Quick Fit Exhaust Centre has just started up, employing a young apprentice. It has to stock a basic range of spares for most European and Japanese cars. In January it fitted 100 exhausts at an average cost of £75 each to the customer, making total sales for the month of £7,500. These exhausts have cost Kensington on average £35 each to buy, and its total wages bill was £300. The company's position is as follows:

	£
Materials	3,500
Labour	300
Total direct cost	3,800

The gross profit in the month is £3,700 (sales of £7,500 less direct costs of £3,800), and after making provision for other business costs of £500 for heat, light, rates, insurance etc, Kensington Quick Fit has made a profit of £3,200.

However, the proprietor is a little concerned that although he is making a good profit, his bank balance is not so healthy; in fact it is worse than when he started. An examination of his operations reveals that when he buys in his exhaust systems his suppliers impose a minimum order quantity of 150 units, and since he needs two suppliers – one for the European car systems and one for the Japanese cars – he has to buy in 300 units at a time. He does, however, make sure that he has sufficient cash for his other outgoings before ordering these 300 units.

At the end of the month he has spent the following cash sums to meet his January sales:

	£
Materials	10,500
Labour	300
Total direct cost	10,800

During the month he has received cheques for £7,500 and made a profit of £3,500 but his cash at the bank has gone down by £3,300, and he still owes £500 for the other business expenses. He does have 200 exhaust systems in stock at a cost of £7,000, which accounts for his poor cash position, but these can only be converted into cash when they are fitted to customers' cars.

Kensington's proprietor was aware of the situation as he closely monitored the timing of the outflow of cash from the business and the inflow of cash from his customers, and he knew that the temporary decrease in his bank balance would not stop his business surviving. However, there was no escaping the fact that although his business made a profit in the month of January, the most immediate result was that his bank balance went down!

CASHFLOW ASSUMPTIONS

The future is impossible to predict with great accuracy, but it is possible to anticipate likely outcomes and be prepared to deal with events by building in a margin of safety. The starting point for making a projection is to make some assumptions about what you want to achieve and test them for reasonableness.

Take the situation of High Note, a new venture being established to sell sheet music, small instruments and CDs to schools and colleges, which will expect to be given trade credit, and members of the public, who will pay cash. The owners plan to invest £10,000 and to borrow £10,000 from a bank on a long-term basis. The business will be run initially out of a converted garage adjoining their home and will require £11,500 to install windows, heat, light, power, storage shelving and a desk and chairs. A further £1,000 will be needed for a computer, software and a printer. That should leave around £7,500 to meet immediate trading expenses such as buying in stock and spending £1,500 on initial advertising. They hope customers' payments will start to come in quickly to cover other expenses such as some wages for bookkeeping, administration and fulfilling orders. Sales in the first six months are expected to be £60,000 based on negotiations already in hand, plus some cash sales that always seem to turn up. The rule of thumb in the industry seems to be that stock is marked up by 100 per cent; so £30,000 of bought-in goods sell on for £60,000.

Forecasting cash needs

On the basis of the above assumptions it is possible to make the cash-flow forecast set out in Table 17.1. It has been simplified and some elements such as VAT and tax have been omitted for ease of understanding.

Table 17.1   High Note six-month cash-flow forecast

Month	April	May	June	July	Aug	Sept	Total
Receipts							
Sales	4,000	5,000	5,000	7,000	12,000	15,000	
Owners' cash	10,000						
Bank loan	10,000						
Total cash in	24,000	5,000	5,000	7,000	12,000	15,000	48,000
Payments							
Purchases	5,500	2,950	4,220	7,416	9,332	9,650	39,108
Rates, elec, heat							
tel, internet etc	1,000	1,000	1,000	1,000	1,000	1,000	
Wages	1,000	1,000	1,000	1,000	1,000	1,000	
Advertising	1,550	1,550	1,550	1,550	1,550	1,550	
Fixtures/fittings	11,500						
Computer etc	1,000						
Total cash out	21,550	6,500	7,770	10,966	12,882	13,240	
Monthly cash Surplus/deficit (–)	2,450	(1,500)	(2,770)	(3,966)	(882)	1,760	
Cumulative cash balance	2,450	950	(1,820)	(5,786)	(6,668)	(4.908)	

The maths in the table is straightforward; the cash receipts from various sources are totalled, as are the payments. Taking one from the other leaves a cash surplus or deficit for the month in question. The bottom row shows the cumulative position. So for example whilst the business had £2,440 cash left at the end of April, taking the cash deficit of £1,500 in May into account, by the end of May only £950 (£2,450 – £1,500) cash remains.

Based on these projections this business would require at least £6,668 of cash to meet the goals in its business plan. A margin of safety would be prudent, so the financing requirement for this venture would be somewhere between £8,000–10,000.

AVOIDING OVERTRADING

In the example above the business has insufficient cash, based on the assumptions made. An outsider, a banker perhaps, would look at the figures in August and see that the faster sales grew, the greater the cashflow deficit would become. We know, using our crystal ball, that the position will improve from September and that if the owners can only hang on in there for a few more months they should eliminate their cash deficit and perhaps even have a surplus. Had they made the cash-flow projection at the outset and either raised more money (perhaps by way of an overdraft), spent less on refurbishing the garage, or set a more modest sales goal, which would have meant a need for less stock and advertising, they would have had a sound business. The figures indicate a business that is trading beyond its financial resources, a condition known as overtrading, which is anathema to bankers the world over.

ESTIMATING START-UP CASH REQUIREMENTS

The example above takes the cash-flow projection out to six months. You should project your cash needs forward for between 12 and 18 months. Make a number of projections using differing assumptions (for example, seeing what will happen if you get fewer orders, people take longer to buy or adapting your office costs more). Finally when you arrive at a projection you have confidence in, and you believe you can justify the cash needed, build that figure into the financing needs section of your business plan.

If that projection calls for more money than you are prepared to invest or raise from outside, don't just steam ahead and hope for the best. The result could well mean that the bank pulls the plug on you when you are within sight of the winning post. There is a useful spreadsheet that will prompt you through the most common costs on the startups website (www. startups.co.uk>Business planning>Startup Costs).

You can do a number of 'what if' projections to fine-tune your cash-flow projections using a spreadsheet. Business Link (www.businesslink.gov. uk/Finance_files/Cash_Flow_Projection_Worksheet.xls) has a cash-flow spreadsheet that you can copy and paste into an Excel file on your computer; the Small Business Advice Service (www.smallbusinessadvice.org.uk>Free Downloads>Download Cash-flow Forecast) has a free spreadsheet you can download online. Alternatively you can use the template in Table 17.2.

PRE-TRADING CASH-FLOW FORECAST

Typically a new venture will take a few months to start generating income. Your cash-flow projections need to start from the moment you anticipate incurring costs or generating income. In other words day zero is the time

Table 17.2   Pro forma cash-flow statement by month

Business name: ....

	Month 1	Month 2	Month 3	Month 4	Month 5
Inflow					
_____	___	___	___	___	___
_____	___	___	___	___	___
_____	___	___	___	___	___
_____	___	___	___	___	___
_____	___	___	___	___	___
Total inflow	___	___	___	___	___
Outflow	___	___	___	___	___
_____	___	___	___	___	___
_____	___	___	___	___	___
_____	___	___	___	___	___
_____	___	___	___	___	___
_____	___	___	___	___	___
_____	___	___	___	___	___
_____	___	___	___	___	___
_____	___	___	___	___	___
_____	___	___	___	___	___
_____	___	___	___	___	___
_____	___	___	___	___	___
_____	___	___	___	___	___
_____	___	___	___	___	___
_____	___	___	___	___	___
Total outflow	___	___	___	___	___
Net inflow (outflow)	___	___	___	___	___
Cumulative in(out)flow	___	___	___	___	___

Year . . . (20XX)

Month 6	Month 7	Month 8	Month 9	Month 10	Month 11	Month 12	Total for year
——	——	——	——	——	——	——	[_____]
——	——	——	——	——	——	——	[_____]
——	——	——	——	——	——	——	[_____]
——	——	——	——	——	——	——	[_____]
——	——	——	——	——	——	——	[_____]
——	——	——	——	——	——	——	[_____]
——	——	——	——	——	——	——	[_____]
——	——	——	——	——	——	——	[_____]
——	——	——	——	——	——	——	[_____]
——	——	——	——	——	——	——	[_____]
——	——	——	——	——	——	——	[_____]
——	——	——	——	——	——	——	[_____]
——	——	——	——	——	——	——	[_____]
——	——	——	——	——	——	——	[_____]
——	——	——	——	——	——	——	[_____]
——	——	——	——	——	——	——	[_____]
——	——	——	——	——	——	——	[_____]
——	——	——	——	——	——	——	[_____]
——	——	——	——	——	——	——	[_____]
——	——	——	——	——	——	——	[_____]
——	——	——	——	——	——	——	[_____]
——	——	——	——	——	——	——	[_____]
——	——	——	——	——	——	——	[_____]
——	——	——	——	——	——	——	[_____]
——	——	——	——	——	——	——	[_____]
——	——	——	——	——	——	——	[_____]
——	——	——	——	——	——	——	[_____]
——	——	——	——	——	——	——	[_____]

expenses are incurred or a sale is made, even if such expenses or sales are made on a credit basis and are not due to be paid for a further month or more.

WORKSHEET FOR ASSIGNMENT 17: PRO FORMA CASH-FLOW STATEMENT

Using the format on the pro forma cash-flow statement sheet (Table 17.2) or using a spreadsheet (see above for sources of free cashflow spreadsheets):

1. Construct a cash-flow statement for the pre-trading period leading up to 'opening' day.
2. Construct a cash-flow statement for years 1, 2, 3, 4 and 5 assuming that you achieve the level of sales in your sales forecast.

Remember you should produce years 1 and 2 monthly and years 3, 4 and 5 quarterly. Do not forget to state the key assumptions that you have made in arriving at your figures.

SUGGESTED FURTHER READING

Barrow, C (2008) *Practical financial management: a guide to budgets, balance sheets and business finance*, 7th edn, Kogan Page, London

Barrow, C (2008) *Business accounting for dummies*, 2nd edn, Wiley, New York

Assignment 18

Pro forma profit and loss statement

You may by now be concerned about the financial situation at High Note as revealed in the preceding chapter. After all the business has sold £60,000 worth of goods that it only paid £30,000 for, so it has a substantial profit margin to play with. While £39,108 has been paid to suppliers only £30,000 of goods at cost have been sold, meaning that £9,108 worth of instruments, sheet music and CDs are still in stock. A similar situation exists with sales. High Note has billed for £60,000 but only been paid for £48,000; the balance is owed by debtors. The bald figure at the end of the cash-flow projection showing High Note to be in the red to the tune of £4,908 seems to be missing some important facts.

The profit and loss account, the subject of this assignment, and the balance sheet that follows in the next assignment, will complete our picture of this business's financial situation. In practical terms, the cash-flow projections and the profit and loss account projections are parallel tasks which are essentially prepared from the same data. They may be regarded almost as the 'heads' and 'tails' of the same coin – the profit and loss account showing the owner/manager the profit/loss based on the assumption that both sales income and the cost of making that sale are 'matched' together in the same month; and the cash-flow statement looking at the same transactions from the viewpoint that in reality the cost of the sale is incurred first (and paid for) and the income is received last, anywhere between one week and three months later.

Obviously, the implications for a non-cash business of this delay between making the sale and receiving the payment and using a service/buying goods and paying for them are crucial, especially in the first year of the business and when your business is growing quickly.

SOME GROUND RULES

The profit and loss account sets out to 'match' income and expenditure to the appropriate time period. It is only in this way that the profit for the period can be realistically calculated. Before we look at the structure of the profit-and-loss account, it might be helpful to look at the accounting concepts to help us to apply the matching principle. Further concepts govern the balance sheet, and these are given in Assignment 19.

The realization concept

A particularly prudent entrepreneur once said that an order was not an order until the customer's cheque had cleared, he or she had consumed the product, had not died as a result, and, finally, had shown every indication of wanting to buy again.

Most of us know quite different people who can 'anticipate' the most unlikely volume of sales. In accounting, income is usually recognized as having been earned when the goods (or services) are dispatched and the invoice sent out. This has nothing to do with when an order is received, or how firm an order is, or how likely a customer is to pay up promptly.

It is also possible that some of the products dispatched may be returned at some later date – perhaps for quality reasons. This means that income, and consequently profit, can be brought into the business in one period and have to be removed later on. Obviously, if these returns can be estimated accurately, then an adjustment can be made to income at the time.

So the 'sales income' figure that is seen at the top of a profit-and-loss account is the value of the goods dispatched and invoiced to customers in the period in question.

THE ACCRUAL CONCEPT

Suppose, for example, that you are calculating one month's profits when the quarterly telephone bill comes in. The picture might look like this:

Table 18.1   Example showing mismatched account

Profit-and-loss account for January 2008–09

	£
Sales income for January	4,000
Less telephone bill (last quarter)	800
Profit	3,200

This is clearly wrong. In the first place, three months' telephone charges have been 'matched' against one month's sales. Equally wrong is charging anything other than January's telephone bill against January's income. Unfortunately, bills such as this are rarely to hand when you want the accounts, so in practice the telephone bill is 'accrued' for. A figure (which may even be absolutely correct if you have a meter) is put in as a provision to meet this liability when it becomes due.

THE DIFFERENCE BETWEEN PROFIT AND CASH

Cash is immediate and takes account of nothing else. Profit, however, is a measurement of economic activity that considers other factors which can be assigned a value or cost. The accounting principle that governs profit is known as the 'matching principle', which means that income and expenditure are matched to the time period in which they occur. So for High Note the profit and loss account for the first six months is as shown in Table 18.2.

STRUCTURING THE PROFIT AND LOSS ACCOUNT

This account is normally set out in more detail for a business in order to make it more useful when it comes to understanding how the business is performing. For example although the profit shown in our worked example is £8,700, in fact it would be rather lower. As money has been borrowed to finance cash-flow there would be interest due, as there would be on the longer-term loan of £10,000.

Table 18.2   Profit and loss account for High Note for the six months Apr–Sept

	£	£
Sales		60,000
Less cost of goods to be sold		30,000
Gross profit		30,000
Less expenses:		
Heat, electric, tel, internet etc	6,000	
Wages	6,000	
Advertising	9,300	
Total expenses		21,300
Profit before tax, interest		
and depreciation charges		8,700

(See Assignment 19 for an explanation of depreciation.)

In practice we have four levels of profit:

- *Gross profit* is the profit left after all costs related to making what you sell are deducted from income.

- *Operating profit* is what is left after you take away the operating expenses from the gross profit.

- *Profit before tax* is what is left after deducting any financing costs.

- *Profit after tax* is what is left for the owners to spend or reinvest in the business.

For High Note this could look much as set out in Table 18.3.

MAKING PROFIT PROJECTIONS

While you may have been realistic in preparing your forecasts of sales and related costs, it is highly probable that during year 1 especially, your actual performance will not be as expected. This could be for one or more reasons, such as resistance to innovation (if a new product), overestimate of market

Table 18.3 High Note's extended profit and loss account

	£
Sales	60,000
Less the cost of goods to be sold	30,000
Gross profit	30,000
Less operating expenses	21,300
Operating profit	8,700
Less interest on bank loan and overdraft	600
Profit before tax	8,100
Less tax at 21%	1,827
Profit after tax	6,723

size, change in consumer demand, or slow take-up of product. All these could mean that sales forecasts are significantly wrong. It is advisable to pre-empt any potential investor's question, such as 'What happens if your sales are reduced by 20 per cent?', by asking yourself the question first and quantifying the financial effects in your business plan. You need not go into any great detail – it is sufficient to outline one or two scenarios.

You can make the above task a lot easier by using the online spreadsheet at SCORE's website (www.score.org>Business Tools>Template Gallery>Profit and Loss). Download in Excel format and you have a profit and loss account with 30 lines of expenses, the headings of which you can change or delete to meet your particular needs

WORKSHEET FOR ASSIGNMENT 18: PRO FORMA PROFIT AND LOSS STATEMENT

Using the format on the pro forma profit and loss account sheet (Table 18.4) or a spreadsheet (see above for source of a free spreadsheet):

1. Construct a profit and loss account for years 1, 2, 3, 4 and 5, assuming you achieve the level of sales in your sales forecast. Include a statement of key assumptions made.

Table 18.4 Pro forma profit-and-loss statement summarising yearly performance

Business name ....

	(20XX) Year 1	(20XX) Year 2
<u>Income</u>		
Sales		
Misc income	————	————
	————	————
Total income	————	————
Cost of goods sold	————	————
Gross profit	————	————
<u>Expenses</u>		
————————————	————	————
————————————	————	————
————————————	————	————
————————————	————	————
————————————	————	————
————————————	————	————
————————————	————	————
————————————	————	————
————————————	————	————
————————————	————	————
————————————	————	————
————————————	————	————
————————————	————	————
————————————	————	————
————————————	————	————
Total expenses	————	————
Profit before tax	————	————
Tax	————	————
Profit after tax	————	————

Summary of years 1 to 5:
Years ended:

(20XX) Year 3	(20XX) Year 4	(20XX) Year 5

2. Construct a four-line summary (sales, gross profit, operating profit and profit before tax) of your profit-and-loss accounts for the full five years (annually).
3. Carry out a sensitivity analysis, noting by how much each of the following must change seriously to affect the apparent viability of your business plan:
    (a) Sales lower by x per cent
    (b) Fixed costs higher by x per cent
    (c) Cost of goods sold higher by x per cent.

SUGGESTED FURTHER READING

Barrow, C (2008) *Practical financial management: a guide to budget, balance sheets and business finance*, 7th edn, Kogan Page, London

Barrow, C (2008) *Business accounting for dummies*, 2nd edn, Wiley, New York

Pro forma balance sheet

So far in our example the money spent on 'capital' items such as the £12,500 spent on a computer and on converting the garage to suit business purposes has been ignored, as has the £9,108 worth of sheet music etc remaining in stock waiting to be sold and the £12,000 of money owed by customers who have yet to pay up. An assumption has to be made about where the cash deficit will be made up, and the most logical short-term source is a bank overdraft. The balance sheet is the accounting report that shows at any moment of time the financial position taking all these longer-term factors into account.

For High Note, the example we have been using in the other finance chapters, at the end of September the balance sheet is set out in Table 19.1.

There are a number of other items not shown in this balance sheet that should appear, such as liability for tax and VAT that have not yet been paid and should appear as current liability. You will find a spreadsheet template to help you construct your own balance sheets at SCORE (www.score.org>Business Tools>Template Gallery>Balance Sheet (Projected).

THE LANGUAGE OF THE BALANCE SHEET

The terms used in financial statements often seem familiar but they are often used in a very particular and potentially confusing way. For example look at the balance sheet above and you will see the terms 'assets' and

Table 19.1   High Note balance sheet at 30 September

	£	£
Assets		
Fixed Assets		
Garage conversion etc	11,500	
Computer	1,000	
Total Fixed Assets		12,500
Working Capital		
Current Assets (CA)		
Stock	9,108	
Debtors	12,000	
Cash	0	
	21,108	
Less Current Liabilities (CL)		
Overdraft	4,908	
Creditors	0	
	4,908	
Working Capital (CA–CL)		16,200
Total Assets		28,700
Liabilities		
Owners' capital introduced	10,000	
Long-term loan	10,000	
Profit retained (from P&L account)	8,700	
Total Liabilities		28,700

'liabilities'. You may think that the money put in by the owner and the profit retained from the years trading are anything but liabilities, but in accounting 'liability' is the term used to show where money has come from. Correspondingly 'asset' means, in the language of accounting, what has been done with that money.

You will also have noticed that the assets and liabilities have been jumbled together in the middle to net off the current assets and current liabilities and so end up with a figure for the working capital. 'Current' in accounting means within the trading cycle, usually taken to be one year. Stock will be used up and debtors will pay up within the year, and an overdraft, being repayable on demand, also appears as a short-term liability.

Assets

Assets are 'valuable resources owned by a business'. You can see that there are two key points in the definition:

- To be valuable the resource must be cash, or of some use in generating current or future profits. For example, a debtor (someone who owes a business money for goods or services provided) usually pays up. When he or she does, the debtor becomes cash and so meets this test. If there is no hope of getting payment, then you can hardly view the sum as an asset.

- Ownership, in its legal sense, can be seen as being different from possession or control. The accounting use of the word is similar but not identical. In a business, possession and control are not enough to make a resource an asset. For example, a leased machine may be possessed and controlled by a business but be owned by the leasing company. So it is not an asset, but a regular expense appearing on the profit and loss account.

Liabilities

These are the claims by people outside the business. In this example only creditors, overdraft and tax are shown, but they could include such items as accruals and deferred income. The 'financed by' section of our example balance sheet is also considered in part as liabilities.

Current

This is the term used with both assets and liabilities to show that they will be converted into cash, or have a short life (under one year).

Now let's go through the main elements of the balance sheet.

Net assets employed

This is the 'what have we done with the money?' section. A business can only do three things with funds:

● It can buy *fixed assets*, such as premises, machinery and motor cars. These are assets that the business intends to keep over the longer term. They will be used to help to make profits, but will not physically vanish in the short term (unless sold and replaced, like motor cars, for example).

● Money can be tied up in *working capital*, that is, 'things' immediately involved in the business's products (or services), that will vanish in the short term. Stocks get sold and are replaced; debtors pay up, and creditors are paid; and cash circulates. Working capital is calculated by subtracting the current liabilities from the current assets. This is the net sum of money that a business has to fund the working capital. In the balance sheet this is called the net current assets, but on most other occasions the term 'working capital' is used.

● Finally, a business can put money aside over the longer term, perhaps in local government bonds or as an investment in someone else's business venture. In the latter case this could be a prelude to a takeover. In the former it could be a cash reserve for future capital investment. The account category is called *investments*. It is not shown in this example as it is a fairly rare phenomenon in new or small businesses, which are usually cash hungry rather than rich.

Financed by

This section of the balance sheet shows where the money came from. It usually has at least two subheadings, although larger companies can have many more.

● *Share capital.* This is the general name given to the money put in by various people in return for a part share in the business. If the business is successful they may get paid a dividend each year, but their principal reward will come from the expected increase in the worth of the business and the consequent rise in value of their share (more on this subject in Assignment 21).

The profit or loss for each year is added to or subtracted from the shareholders' investment. Eventually, once the business is profitable, it will have some money left each year to plough back into reserves. This term conjures up pictures of sums of cash stored away for a rainy day. It is important to remember that this is not necessarily so. The only cash in a business is that shown under that heading in the current assets. The reserves, like all the other funds, are used to finance a business and are tied up in the fixed assets and working capital.

⬤ The final source of money to finance a business is long- or medium-term loans from outside parties. These loans could be in the form of debentures, a mortgage, hire purchase agreements or long-term loans from a bank. The common features of all such loans are that businesses have to pay interest on the money and eventually repay the capital, whether or not the business is successful. Conversely, if the business is a spectacular success the lenders, unlike the shareholders, will not share in the extra profits.

SOME GROUND RULES

These ground rules are generally observed by accountants when preparing a balance sheet.

Money measurement

In accounting, a record is kept only of the facts that can be expressed in money terms. For example, the state of your health, or the fact that your main competitor is opening up right opposite in a more attractive outlet, are important business facts. No accounting record of them is made, however, and they do not show up on the balance sheet, simply because no objective monetary value can be assigned to these facts.

Expressing business facts in money terms has the great advantage of providing a common denominator. Just imagine trying to add typewriters and motor cars, together with a 4,000 square foot workshop, and arrive at a total. You need a common term to be able to carry out the basic arithmetical functions, and to compare one set of accounts with another.

Business entity

The accounts are kept for the business itself, rather than for the owner(s), workers, or anyone else associated with the firm. If an owner puts a short-term cash injection into his or her business, it will appear as a loan under current liabilities in the business account. In his or her personal account it will appear as an asset – money he or she is owed by someone else. So depending on which point of view you take, the same sum of money can be an asset or a liability. And as in this example the owner and the business are substantially the same person, the possibilities of confusion are considerable.

This source of possible confusion must be cleared up and the business entity concept does just that. The concept states that assets and liabilities are always defined from the business's viewpoint.

Cost concept

Assets are usually entered into the accounts at cost. For a variety of reasons, the real 'worth' of an asset will probably change over time. The worth, or value, of an asset is a subjective estimate on which no two people are likely to agree. This is made even more complex and artificial because the assets themselves are usually not for sale. So, in the search for objectivity, the accountants have settled for cost as the figure to record. It means that a balance sheet does not show the current worth, or value, of a business.

Depreciation

Fixed assets are usually depreciated over their working life rather than taken as one hit on the profit and loss account. There are accounting rules on the appropriate period to depreciate different assets over, usually somewhere between 3 and 20 years. If we believe the computer has a useful life of four years and the rules allow it, we take £250 a year of cost, by way of depreciation, as an expense item in the profit and loss account for the year in question. Depreciation, though vital for your management accounts, is not an allowable expense for tax purposes. The tax authorities allow a 'writing down' allowance say of 25 per cent of the cost of an asset each year which can be set as an expense for tax purposes. There are periods when the government of the day wants to stimulate businesses to invest, say in computers, and it will boost the writing-down allowance accordingly. This figure will almost certainly not correspond to your estimate of depreciation, so you need a profit for tax purposes and a profit for management purposes. You can see the effect of deprecation on the accounts in Table 19.2. Fixed assets reduce by £125 of depreciation and there is a corresponding reduction in profit retained for the year, thus ensuring the balance sheet balances.

One of the books you will keep will be a Capital Register, keeping track of the cost and depreciation of all fixed assets. Another accounting rule, that of 'materiality', comes into force here. Technically a pocket calculator costing £5 is a fixed asset in that it has been bought to use rather than sell and it has a life of over one year. But it is treated as an expense as the sum involved is too small to be material. There are no clear rules on the point at which a cost becomes material. For a big organization it may be for items costing a few thousand pounds. For a small business £100 may

Table 19.2 The changes to High Note's balance sheet to account for depreciation

Balance sheet	£
Asset changes	
Fixed assets at cost	12,500
Less depreciation for six months	125
Net book assets	12,375
Liability changes	
Profit from P&L account reduced by £125 to	8,575

be the appropriate level. You can find guidance on depreciation and on the layout of the balance sheet and profit and loss account as required by the Companies Act from the Accounting Standards Board (www.frc.org>ASB>Technical>FRSSE). Accounting Glossary (www.accountingglossary.net) and Accounting for Everyone (www.accountingfor everyone.com>Accounting Glossary) have definitions of all the accounting terms you are ever likely to need for running your own business.

Other assets, such as freehold land and buildings, will be revalued from time to time, and stock will be entered at cost, or market value, whichever is the lower, in line with the principle of conservatism (explained later).

Going concern

Accounting reports always assume that a business will continue trading indefinitely into the future, unless there is good evidence to the contrary. This means that the assets of the business are looked at simply as profit generators and not as being available for sale.

Look again at the motor car example above. In year 2 the net asset figure in the accounts, prepared on a 'going concern' basis, is £3,000. If we knew that the business was to close down in a few weeks, then we would be more interested in the car's resale value than its 'book' value; the car might fetch only £2,000, which is a quite different figure.

Once a business stops trading, we cannot realistically look at the assets in the same way. They are no longer being used in the business to help to generate sales and profits. The most objective figure is what they might realize in the marketplace. Anyone who has been to a sale of machinery will know the difference between book and market value!

Table 19.3 Pro forma balance sheet by year

Business name: ....

	Year 1 (20XX)			
	Qtr 1	Qtr 2	Qtr 3	Qtr 4
<u>Fixed assets</u>				
Cost	————	————	————	————
Accum depreciation	————	————	————	————
Net book value	————	————	————	————
<u>Current assets</u>				
Stock & WIP	————	————	————	————
Debtors	————	————	————	————
Bank & cash	————	————	————	————
<u>Current liabilities</u>				
Trade creditors	————	————	————	————
Bank overdraft	————	————	————	————
Short-term loan	————	————	————	————
<u>Net current assets</u>				
Total assets less current liabilities	————	————	————	————
Net assets	═══	═══	═══	═══
<u>Financed by</u>				
Called-up shares	————	————	————	————
Accum profits (deficit)	————	————	————	————
Loan capital	————	————	————	————
	═══	═══	═══	═══

Dual aspect

To keep a complete record of any business transaction we need to know both where money came from, and what has been done with it. It is not enough simply to say, for example, that someone has put £1,000 into their business. We have to show how that money has been used to buy fixtures, stock in trade, etc.

> ### WORKSHEET FOR ASSIGNMENT 19: PRO FORMA BALANCE SHEET
>
> Using the format on the pro forma balance sheet (Table 19.3) or a spreadsheet (see above for source of a free spreadsheet):
>
> 1. Construct a balance sheet for your business as it might look on the day before you start trading. This should be done now.
> 2. List and explain the assumptions underpinning your financial forecasts.
> 3. Construct a balance sheet at the end of years 1, 2, 3, 4 and 5 assuming you achieve the level of sales in your sales forecast. These should be done after you have completed the pro forma profit and loss account (Assignment 18) and pro forma cash-flow forecast (Assignment 17).

SUGGESTED FURTHER READING

Barrow, C (2008) *Practical financial management: a guide to budget, balance sheets and business finance*, 7th edn, Kogan Page, London

Barrow, C (2008) *Business accounting for dummies*, 2nd edn, Wiley, New York

Break-even analysis

CALCULATING YOUR BREAK-EVEN POINT

While some businesses have difficulty raising start-up capital, paradoxically one of the main reasons small businesses fail in the early stages is that too much start-up capital is used to buy fixed assets. While some equipment is clearly essential at the start, other purchases could be postponed. This may mean that 'desirable' and labour-saving devices have to be borrowed or hired for a specific period. This is obviously not as nice as having them to hand all the time, but if, for example, computers, word processors, photocopiers and even delivery vans are brought into the business, they become part of the fixed costs.

The higher the fixed-cost plateau, the longer it usually takes to reach break-even and then profitability. And time is not usually on the side of the small new business: it has to become profitable relatively quickly or it will simply run out of money and die. The break-even analysis is an important tool to be used both in preparing a business plan and in the day-to-day running of a business.

Difficulties usually begin when people become confused by the different characteristics of costs. Some costs, for instance, do not change however much you sell. If you are running a shop, the rent and the rates are relatively constant figures, quite independent of the volume of sales. On the other hand, the cost of the products sold from the shop is completely dependent on volume. The more you sell, the more it 'costs' to buy stock.

The former of these costs are called 'fixed' and the latter 'variable', and you cannot add them together to arrive at total costs until you have made some assumptions about sales.

BREAKING EVEN

Let's take an elementary example: a business plans to sell only one product and has only one fixed cost, the rent.

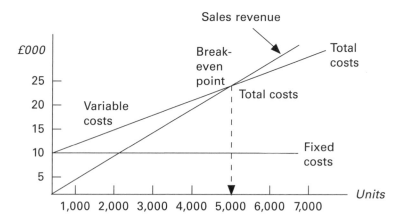

Figure 20.1 Graph showing break-even point

In Figure 20.1 the vertical axis shows the value of sales and costs in thousands of pounds, and the horizontal axis the number of 'units' sold. The second horizontal line represents the fixed costs, those that do not change as volume increases. In this case it is the rent of £10,000. The angled line running from the top of the fixed costs line is the variable costs. In this example the business plans to buy in at £3 per unit, so every unit it sells adds that much to its fixed costs.

Only one element is needed to calculate the break-even point – the sales line. That is the line moving up at an angle from the bottom left-hand corner of the chart. The business plans to sell out at £5 per unit, so this line is calculated by multiplying the units sold by that price.

The break-even point is the stage at which a business starts to make a profit. That is when the sales revenue begins to exceed both the fixed and variable costs. Figure 20.1 shows the example's break-even point is 5,000 units.

A formula, deduced from the figure, will save time for your own calculations.

$$\text{Break-even point} = \frac{\text{Fixed costs}}{\text{Selling price} - \text{Unit variable cost}}$$

$$\frac{10,000}{£5 - £3} = 5,000 \text{ units}$$

CAPITAL INTENSIVE VERSUS 'LEAN AND MEAN'

Look at two hypothetical new small businesses. They are both making and selling identical products at the same price, £10. They plan to sell 10,000 units each in the first year.

The owner of Company A plans to get fully equipped at the start. His fixed costs will be £40,000, double those of Company B. This is largely because, as well as his own car, he has bought such things as a delivery van, new equipment and a photocopier. Much of this will not be fully used for some time, but by buying it he will save some money now. This extra expenditure will result in a lower unit variable cost than Company B can achieve, a typical capital-intensive result. Its break-even chart will look like Figure 20.2.

Company B's owner, on the other hand, proposes to start up on a shoestring. Only £20,000 will go into fixed costs, but of course his unit variable cost will be higher, at £4.50. The variable cost is higher because, for example, he has to pay an outside carrier to deliver, while A uses his own van and pays only for petrol. So the break-even chart will look like Figure 20.3.

From the data on each company you can see that total costs for 10,000 units are the same, so total possible profits, if 10,000 units are sold, are also the same. The key difference is that Company B starts making profits after 3,636 units have been sold. Company A has to wait until 5,333 units have been sold, and it may not be able to wait that long.

This was only a hypothetical case, but the real world is littered with the corpses of businesses that spend too much too soon. The marketplace dictates the selling price, and your costs have to fall in line with that for you to have any hope of survival.

Company A: Capital intensive

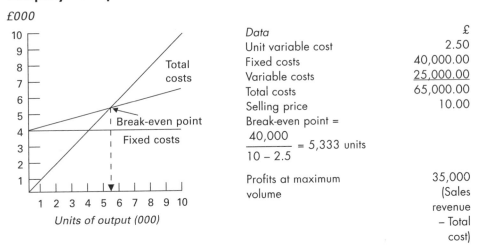

£000

Data	£
Unit variable cost	2.50
Fixed costs	40,000.00
Variable costs	25,000.00
Total costs	65,000.00
Selling price	10.00

Break-even point =

$$\frac{40,000}{10 - 2.5} = 5,333 \text{ units}$$

Profits at maximum volume 35,000 (Sales revenue – Total cost)

Figure 20.2 Example break-even chart for a capital-intensive company

Company B: Lean and mean

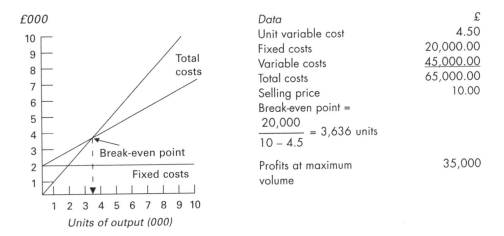

£000

Data	£
Unit variable cost	4.50
Fixed costs	20,000.00
Variable costs	45,000.00
Total costs	65,000.00
Selling price	10.00

Break-even point =

$$\frac{20,000}{10 - 4.5} = 3,636 \text{ units}$$

Profits at maximum volume 35,000

Figure 20.3 Example break-even chart for a 'lean and mean' company

PROFITABLE PRICING

To complete the break-even picture we need to add one further dimension – profit. It is a mistake to think that profit is an accident of arithmetic calculated only at the end of the year. It is a specific and quantifiable target that you need at the outset.

Let's go back to our previous example. You plan to invest £10,000 in fixed assets in a business, and you will need to hold another £5,000 worth of stock too – in all say £15,000. You could get £1,500 profit just leaving that money in a bank or building society, so you will expect a return of say £4,000 (equal to 27 per cent) for taking the risks of setting up on your own. Now let's see when you will break even.

The new equation must include your 'desired' profit, so it will look like this:

$$\text{Break-even profit point} = \frac{\text{Fixed costs} + \text{Profit objective}}{\text{Selling price} - \text{Unit variable cost}}$$
(BEPP)

$$= \frac{10,000 + 4,000}{£5 - £3} = 7,000$$

We know that to reach our target we must sell 7,000 units at £5 each and have no more than £10,000 tied up in fixed costs. The great strength of this equation is that each element can be changed in turn on an experimental basis to arrive at a satisfactory and achievable result. For instance, suppose you decide that it is unlikely that you can sell 7,000 units, but that 6,500 is achievable. What would your selling price have to be to make the same profit?

Using the BEPP equation you can calculate the answer:

$$\text{BEPP} = \frac{\text{Fixed costs} + \text{Profit objective}}{\text{Selling price} - \text{Unit variable cost}}$$

$$6,500 = \frac{10,000 + 4,000}{6,500} = £2.15$$

$$£x = \quad £2.15 + £3 \quad = £5.15$$

If your market will bear a selling price of £5.15 as opposed to £5, all is well; if it won't, the ball is back in your court. You have to find ways of decreasing the fixed and/or variable costs, or of selling more, rather than just accepting that a lower profit is inevitable.

FROM THE PARTICULAR TO THE GENERAL

The example used to illustrate the break-even profit point model was of necessity simple. Few if any businesses sell only one or two products, so a more general equation may be more useful if your business sells hundreds of products, as, for example a real shop does.

In such a business, to calculate your break-even point you must first establish your gross profit. If you are already trading, this is calculated by deducting the money paid out to suppliers from the money received from customers. If you are not yet trading, then researching your competitors will give you some indication of the sort of margins you should aim for.

For example, if you are aiming for a 40 per cent gross profit, your fixed costs are £10,000 and your overall profit objective is £4,000, then the sum will be as follows:

$$\text{BEPP} = \frac{10,000 + 4,000}{0.4^*} = \frac{14,000}{0.4}$$

$$= £35,000$$

So to reach your target you must achieve a £35,000 turnover. (You can check this out for yourself: look back to the previous example where the BEPP was 7,000 units, and the selling price was £5 each. Multiplying those figures out gives a turnover of £35,000. The gross profit in that example was 2/5, or 40 per cent, also.)

GETTING HELP WITH BREAK-EVEN

You have few options to get help with making break-even calculations. Your accountant can show you, and if your algebra is a bit rusty you can take a quick refresher at the BBC's Bite Size site (www.bbc.co.uk/schools/gcsebitesize/maths).

Alternatively there are a number of online spreadsheets and tutorials that will take you through the process. biz/ed (www.bized.co.uk>Virtual Worlds>Virtual Learning Arcade>Break-even Analysis) is a simulation that lets you see the effect of changing variables on a fairly complex break-even calculation. Score (www.score.org>Business Tools>Template Gallery>Break Even Analysis) and BizPep (www.bizpeponline.com/PricingBreakeven. html) sell software programs that calculate your break-even for prices plus or minus 50 per cent of your proposed selling price. You can tweak costs to see how to optimize your selling price and so hit your profit goal.

WORKSHEET FOR ASSIGNMENT 20: BREAK-EVEN ANALYSIS

Using the format on the break-even analysis sheet (Table 20.1):

Table 20.1

1. Calculate your gross profit

    Projected sales   £

    – Direct costs:
    Purchases (material costs)   £
    Labour costs   £
    = Gross profits   £   (A)

2. Calculate your gross profit margin

    Gross profit (A) £
    ―――――――――――――――――――   x 100

    Sales   £

    = Gross profit margin   % (B)

    _____

    Notes:

3. Calculate your overheads

    Indirect costs:

    Business salaries
    (including your own drawings)   £
    + Rent   £

+ Rates   £
+ Light/heating   £
+ Telephone/postage   £
+ Insurance   £
+ Repairs   £
+ Advertising   £
+ Bank interest/HP   £
+ Other expenses
(eg depreciation of fixed assets)   £
                                                 £
                                                 £
                                                 £
                                                 £
= Overheads   £   (C)
                                               _____

4. Calculate your actual turnover required to break even

Overheads (C)   £
────────────────────────────── x 100
Gross profit margin (B)   %

= Break-even sales £   (D)

5. Calculate the monthly target to break even

Break-even sales (D) £
──────────────────────────
              6
= Monthly break-even sales £ _____

6. Calculate your estimated profit
Projected sales   £
– Break-even sales (D)   £
+ Gross profit margin (B)   %
= Profit (for 12 months)   £
                           _____

1. Construct a break-even analysis for year 1 of your business from the figures calculated in the last three chapters. You can use the Wavendon example below as a guide, or use a spreadsheet as given above.
2. Estimate the effect of the following events on your break-even point for each year:
   (a) a 10 per cent rise/fall in sales volume;
   (b) a 10 per cent rise/fall in unit selling price;
   (c) a 10 per cent rise/fall in variable costs per unit of sale, eg a meal;
   (d) a 10 per cent rise/fall in fixed costs;
   (e) a requirement for achieving your profit objective by year 1 – now what 'volume' of product must you sell to break even?
3. Look back to Assignment 7 on Pricing, and review your proposed selling price in the light of work/research carried out during this assignment.

EXAMPLE: WAVENDON PLUMBING

Table 20.2   Wavendon Plumbing: 6-month financial projection

1. Calculate your gross profit
   Project sales   £75,000

   –Direct costs:
   Purchases (material costs)   £32,500
   Labour costs   £20,000
   = Gross profit   £22,500   (A)

2. Calculate your gross profit margin

   $$\frac{\text{Gross profit (A) £22,500}}{\text{Sales} \qquad \text{£75,000}} \times 100$$

   = Gross profit margin   30% (B)

   Note: For simplicity all figures shown are exclusive of VAT.

3. Calculate your overheads
   Indirect costs:
   Business salaries
   (including your own drawings)   £ 6,000

+ Rent	£ 2,000
+ Rates	£ 500
+ Light/heating	£ 500
+ Telephone/postage	£ 500
+ Insurance	£ 500
+ Repairs	£ 2,000
+ Advertising	£ 1,500
+ Bank interest/HP	£ 1,500
+ Other expenses	£ 1,500
(eg depreciation of fixed assets)	£
	£
	£
	£
	£
= Overheads	£16,500 (C)

4. Calculate your actual turnover required to break even

$$\frac{\text{Overheads (C)} \quad £16,500}{\text{Gross profit margin (B)} \quad 30\%} \times 100$$

$$\frac{= \text{Break-even sales} \quad £55,000 \text{ (D)}}{6}$$

= Monthly break-even sales   £9,167

6. Profits accumulate in favour of the business once the break-even point
    has been reached. As overhead costs have been provided for in the
    break-even calculation, profits accumulate at a rate of 30 per cent (ie
    the gross margin percentage) on projected sales over and above the
    break-even figure.

    In the case of the example, this is:

Projected sales	£75,000
– Break-even sales (D)	£55,000
× Gross profit margin (B)	30%
= Profit (for 6 months)	£6,000

    These figures can be affected by:

- actual level of sales achieved;
- increase/decrease in gross margin;
- increase/decrease in overheads.

SUGGESTED FURTHER READING

Barrow, C (2008) *Practical financial management: a guide to budget, balance sheets and business finance*, 7th edn, Kogan Page, London

Barrow, C (2008) *Business accounting for dummies*, 2nd edn, Wiley, New York

Financing requirements

Your business plan may look very professional, showing that you have a very high probability of making exceptional returns, but it will fall at the first hurdle if your funding requirements have not been properly thought out and communicated to potential lenders and investors. It is not sufficient for you to look at your pro forma cash-flow statement and, taking the maximum overdraft position, say:

> The management require £150,000 to commence business, which may come either from bank loans or a share capital injection. The cash-flow projections show that if the funding was by way of a loan it would be repaid within three years. If the funding came from an issue of share capital an excellent return would be available by way of dividends.

Such a statement leaves many questions unanswered, such as:

- Why do you need the money?
- What type of money do you need?
- When will you need it?
- Who is the best source of money for your venture?

The more successful you are, the more money you will need to finance and store stock if you are selling products or to pay wages if you are in a service business. To remain competitive and visible your products and services will need to be kept up to date as will your website, all of which will call for some additional investment.

WHY DO YOU NEED THE MONEY?

You probably have a very good idea of why you need the funds that you are asking for, but unless readers of your business plan have plenty of time to spare (which they have not) and can be bothered to work it out for themselves (which they can't), you must clearly state what you will use the funds received for. An example is:

A net investment of £150,000 is required, which will be used as follows:

	£
To purchase:	
Motor vehicle	5,000
Plant and equipment	100,000
To provide:	
Working capital for first 6 months	75,000
Total requirement	180,000
Less investment made by (you)	30,000
Net funding requirement	150,000

This statement clearly tells the reader how the funds will be used and gives clear pointers as to appropriate funding routes and timing of the funding requirements.

WHAT TYPE OF MONEY DO YOU NEED?

There are many sources of funds available to independent businesses. However, not all of them are equally appropriate to all firms at all times. These different sources of finance carry very different obligations, responsibilities and opportunities for profitable business. The differences have to be understood to allow an informed choice.

Most new ventures confine their financial strategy to bank loans, either long term or short term, viewing the other financing methods as either too complex or too risky. In many respects the reverse is true. Almost every finance source other than banks will to a greater or lesser extent share some of the risks of doing business with the recipient of the funds.

The great attraction of bank borrowings lies in the speed with which facilities can usually be arranged. Most small businesses operate without a business plan, so most events that require additional funds, such as sudden expansion or contraction, come as a surprise, either welcome or unwelcome. It is to this weakness in financial strategy that banks are ultimately appealing, so it is hardly surprising that many difficulties arise.

Lenders and investors compared

At one end of the financing spectrum lie shareholders: either individual business angels, or corporates such as venture capital providers. These share all the risks and vagaries of the business alongside the founder, and expect a proportionate share in the rewards if things go well. They are not especially concerned with a stream of dividends, which is just as well, as few small companies ever pay them. Instead they hope for a radical increase in the value of their investment. They expect to realize this value from other investors who want to take their place for the next stage in the firm's growth cycle, rather than from any repayment by the founder.

Investors in new or small businesses do not look for the security of buildings or other assets to underpin their investment. Rather they look to the founder vision and the core management team's ability to deliver results.

At the other end of the financing spectrum are the banks, which try hard to take no risk, but expect some reward irrespective of performance. They want interest payments on money lent, usually from day one. While they too hope the management is competent, they are more interested in securing a charge against any assets the business or its managers may own. At the end of the day (and that day can be sooner than the borrower expects), a bank wants all its money back – no more and certainly no less. It would be more prudent to think of banks as people who will help you turn a proportion of an illiquid asset such as property into a more liquid asset such as cash at some discount.

Understanding the differences in expectation between lenders, who provide debt, and investors, who provide equity, or share capital, is central to determining who to approach for funding. In a nutshell, lenders are risk averse, want security cover for any loan, expect to receive interest and for it to be paid on time, and want their money back in a predetermined period of time. Investors, on the other hand, have an appetite for risk, do not expect any payment until the business has grown substantially or has been sold, and rely on the founder's vision and business plan for their confidence in the proposal.

In between the extremes of shareholders and the banks lie a myriad of other financing vehicles that have a mixture of lending and investing criteria. A business needs to keep its finances under constant review, choosing the most appropriate mix of funds for the risks it plans to take and the economic climate ahead. The more risky and volatile the road ahead, the more likely it is that taking a higher proportion of risk capital will be appropriate. In times of stability and low interest, higher borrowings may be more acceptable.

SOURCES OF FINANCE

There are five main sources of finance for new and established ventures:

- your own money;

- loans from banks and other institutions or from family and friends;

- taking investors whom you know something about on board to share the risks and rewards alongside yourself;

- floating your business to the public at large on a stock market;

- 'free' money by way of grants or winning a competition.

USING YOUR OWN RESOURCES

The first port of call when looking to finance your business should be your own resources. This is usually easier to arrange, cheaper, quicker and less time-consuming than any other source of money. There is of course another important advantage in that if you don't tap into bank borrowing and the like you may get a better reception later on once your business is up and running.

Going for redundancy

Between 120,000 and 150,000 people are made redundant every month in the United Kingdom. High levels of redundancy are a continuing feature of the industrial landscape as the pace of change continues to accelerate. If you are in employment and could be eligible for redundancy, this could be a way of financing your business. In any event if your business takes off you are likely to have your hands full. These are the key factors to consider:

- Are you eligible for redundancy? This is a complex area but the Citizens Advice Bureau (www.adviceguide.org.uk/index/life/employment/redundancy.htm) has a summarized guide to the topic with useful links to other information.

- The first £30,000 of redundancy payment is normally-tax free and any sum above that level is taxed at your highest tax rate. Redundancy Help (www.redundancyhelp.co.uk/MonTax.htm) provides a guide to the taxation of redundancy payments.

- Your pension entitlement may be adversely affected if you draw your pension earlier than your designated retirement age. The Association of British Insurers and the Financial Services Authority have a pension calculator (www.pensioncalculator.org) which you can use to see what will happen to a pension by paying in for fewer years and retiring early.

Dipping into savings

If you have any savings put aside for a rainy day, you could also consider dipping into them now. You will need to discuss this with your financial adviser as there may be penalties associated with cashing in insurance policies early, for example. The Association of Investment and Financial Advisers (www.aifa.net) can help you to find an adviser in the United Kingdom or abroad.

Remortgaging

If you bought your present home five years or more ago the chances are that you are sitting on a large amount of equity – the difference between the current market value of your house and the amount you still owe the mortgagor. You can dip into this equity by remortgaging for a higher sum and taking out some cash. You should be able to take out between 80 and 90 per cent of the equity, although this may mean paying between 0.5 per cent and 1 per cent more for the whole mortgage as well as an arrangement fee of anything from £200 to £700. If you need a relatively small amount of finance or only need the money for a short period to finance working capital, this is probably not the best option.

You will find a guide to the whole subject at Mortgage Sorter (www. mortgagesorter.co.uk>Remortgages), where you will also find a Re-mortgage Quote service. The banks also offer advice on this subject (eg www. barclays.co.uk>mortgages>Remortgaging).

Using credit cards

Why would anyone pay 18 per cent interest when they could get a bank overdraft at a third of that cost? The simple answer is that banks put their borrowers through a fairly stringent credit check (see below), while credit card providers have built a large volume of defaulting customers into their margins. In other words you are paying over the odds to get fairly easy money.

Use a credit card by all means for travel and the like. Keep one to hand as part of your contingency planning to handle financial emergencies. But this type of money should not become part of the core funding of any business. Money Supermarket.com (www.moneysupermarket.com>MONEY>credit cards) has a comparison tool that lets you compare over 300 cards, and About Your Money (www.aboutyourmoney.co.uk>credit cards>Business Cards) has an a–z listing of business credit card providers and a comparison of the interest rates and other charges.

Earning sweat equity

If you work on your business for free the value put in is known as sweat equity. So if you build a prototype of your product, design a brochure or launch your website, the cost that would have been incurred had you paid for them can count as if you had put in the money yourself.

The attraction to this type of investment is that it is cost-free to the business. Also it might act as a spur to encourage bankers or outside investors to match your notional investment with their cash, much as they would have done if you had actually put the money in yourself.

Obviously you can't live on air, so you will need to 'moonlight' while still in employment. As long as you perform well in your daytime job this should pose no difficulties, as employers usually only place restrictions on your having another paid job. It means you will have to work 80-hour weeks, but that will be useful preparation for when your business gets going.

Using a local exchange trading scheme

Local exchange trading schemes (LETS) allow anyone who joins a scheme to offer skills or services, such as plumbing, gardening or the use of a photocopier, to other members. A price is agreed in whatever notional currency has been adopted, but no money changes hands. The system is more ambitious than straight barter. The provider receives a credit on his or her account kept by a local organizer, and a debit is marked up against the user. The person in credit can then set this against other services.

The benefits of using LETS are that you can start trading and grow with virtually no start-up capital. All you need are time and saleable skills – once you have 'sold' your wares, payment is immediate by way of a LETS credit. Also, using LETS means that the wealth is kept in the local community, which means customers in your area may be able to spend more with you. One of the keys to success in using LETS is to have an enterprising organizer who can produce, maintain and circulate a wide-ranging directory of LETS services and outlets. Find out from Letslink UK (www.letslinkuk.net) more about the system and how to find your nearest organizer.

BORROWING MONEY

Borrowing money is your main source of finance if you don't want to take in shareholders, or a partner (see Assignment 2 for information on types of partnership). Lenders for the most part will help you turn a proportion of an illiquid asset such as property, stock in trade or customers who have not yet paid up, into a more liquid asset such as cash, but of course at some discount. They rarely advance money without some form of collateral.

Using a bank

Banks are the principal, and frequently the only, source of finance for nine out of every 10 new and small businesses. Small firms around the world rely on banks for their funding. In the United Kingdom, for example, they have borrowed nearly £55 billion from the banks, a substantial rise over the past few years. When this figure is compared with the £48 billion that small firms have on deposit at any one time, the net amount borrowed is around £7 billion.

Bankers, and indeed any other sources of debt capital, are looking for asset security to back their loan and provide a near-certainty of getting their money back. They will also charge an interest rate that reflects current market conditions and their view of the risk level of the proposal.

Bankers like to speak of the 'five Cs' of credit analysis, factors they look at when they evaluate a loan request. When applying to a bank for a loan, be prepared to address the following points:

- *Character*. Bankers lend money to borrowers who appear honest and who have a good credit history. Before you apply for a loan, it makes sense to obtain a copy of your credit report and clean up any problems.

- *Capacity*. This is a prediction of the borrower's ability to repay the loan. For a new business, bankers look at the business plan. For an existing business, bankers consider financial statements and industry trends.

- *Collateral*. Bankers generally want a borrower to pledge an asset that can be sold to pay off the loan if the borrower lacks funds.

- *Capital*. Bankers scrutinize a borrower's net worth, the amount by which assets exceed debts.

- *Conditions*. Whether bankers give a loan can be influenced by the current economic climate as well as by the amount required.

Finding a business banker

The use among small firms of telephone and internet banking has increased significantly over the past few years. In 1998, 16 per cent of small firms used telephone banking, rising to 38 per cent by 2007. For internet banking the proportion has risen from 14 per cent to 34 per cent. Branch location seems less likely to be a significant factor to bank customers in the future, so you no longer have to confine your search for a bank to those with a branch nearby. All the major clearing banks offer telephone banking and internet services to their small business customers, or are in the process of doing so.

You can see a listing of business bank accounts at Find.co.uk the finance website (www.find.co.uk>Banking>Commercial>Business Banking), where the top six or so are star rated and reviewed, and there is also an A–Z listing. Move Your Account (www.moveyouraccount.co.uk>Business Banking) offer a free service claiming to find you the best current banking deal for a small business. You have to complete a dozen questions online and await the response. Startups (www.startups.co.uk>Finance management>Business bank accounts) offers a range of advice and tips on opening or changing a business bank account and what charges to look out for. The British Banking Association (www.bba.moneyfacts.co.uk) has a business bank account finder tool which also lets you compare your present bank against any others you may chose.

Giving bank guarantees

Where the assets of a business are small, anyone lending it money may seek the added protection of requiring the owner to personally guarantee the loan. In the case of limited companies, this is in effect stripping away some of the protection that companies are supposed to afford the risk-taking owner-manager. You should resist giving guarantees if at all possible. If you have to do so, try to secure the guarantee against the specific asset concerned only, and set clear conditions for the guarantee to come to an end, for example when your overdraft or borrowings go down to a certain level.

Remember, everything in business finance is negotiable, and your relationship with a bank is no exception. Banks are in competition too, so if yours is being unreasonably hard, it may be time to move on. Obviously, to be able to move on, you need to have some advance notice of when the additional funds are needed. Rushing into a bank asking for extra finance from next week is hardly likely to inspire much confidence in your abilities as a strategic thinker. That is where your business plan will come into its own.

Overdrafts

The principal form of short-term bank funding is an overdraft, secured by a charge over the assets of the business. A little over a quarter of all bank finance for small firms is in the form of an overdraft. If you are starting out in a contract cleaning business, say, with a major contract, you need sufficient funds initially to buy the mop and bucket. Three months into the contract they will have been paid for, and so there is no point in getting a five-year bank loan to cover this, as within a year you will have cash in the bank and a loan with an early redemption penalty!

However, if your bank account does not get out of the red at any stage during the year, you will need to re-examine your financing. All too often companies utilize an overdraft to acquire long-term assets, and that overdraft never seems to disappear, eventually constraining the business.

The attraction of overdrafts is that they are very easy to arrange and take little time to set up. That is also their inherent weakness. The key words in the arrangement document are 'repayable on demand', which leaves the bank free to make and change the rules as it sees fit. (This term is under constant review, and some banks may remove it from the arrangement.) With other forms of borrowing, as long as you stick to the terms and conditions, the loan is yours for the duration. It is not so with overdrafts.

Term loans

Term loans, as long-term bank borrowings are generally known, are funds provided by a bank for a number of years. The interest can either be variable, changing with general interest rates, or fixed for a number of years ahead. The proportion of fixed-rate loans has increased from one-third of all term loans to around half. In some cases it may be possible to move between having a fixed interest rate and a variable one at certain intervals. It may even be possible to have a moratorium on interest payments for a short period, to give the business some breathing space. Provided the conditions of the loan are met in such matters as repayment, interest and security cover, the money is available for the period of the loan. Unlike in the case of an overdraft, the bank cannot pull the rug from under you if circumstances (or the local manager) change.

Just over one-third of all term loans are for periods greater than 10 years, and a quarter are for three years or less.

Government small firm loan guarantee schemes

These are operated by banks at the instigation of governments in the United Kingdom, Australia, the United States and elsewhere. These schemes guarantee loans from banks and other financial institutions for small businesses with viable business proposals that have tried and failed to obtain a conventional loan because of a lack of security. Loans are available for periods between two and 10 years on sums from £5,000 to £2,500,000.

The government guarantees 70–90 per cent of the loan. In return for the guarantee, the borrower pays a premium of 1–2 per cent per year on the outstanding amount of the loan. The commercial aspects of the loan are matters between the borrower and the lender.

Securing a small firms loan

You can find out more about the Small Firms Loan Guarantee Scheme that operates in the United Kingdom on the Business Link website (www.businesslink.gov.uk>Finance and grants>Borrowing>Loans and overdrafts); and which banks operate the scheme on the Department for Business Enterprise and Regulatory Reform website (www.berr.gov. uk>Better Business Framework>Small Business>Information for Small Business Owners and Entrepreneurs>Access to Finance>Small Firms Loan Guarantee).

Money through credit unions

If you don't like the terms on offer from the high street banks, as the major banks are often known, you could consider forming your own bank. This is not quite as crazy an idea as it sounds. Credit unions formed by groups of small businesspeople, both in business and aspiring to start up, have been around for decades in the United States, the United Kingdom and elsewhere. They have been an attractive option for people on low incomes, providing a cheap and convenient alternative to banks. Some self-employed people such as taxi drivers have also formed credit unions. They can then apply for loans to meet unexpected capital expenditure for repairs, refurbishments or technical upgrading.

The popularity of credit unions varies from country to country. In the United Kingdom, for example, fewer than one in 300 people belong to one, compared with more than one in three in Canada, Ireland and Australia. Certainly, few could argue about the attractiveness of an annual interest rate 30 per cent below that of the high-street lenders, which is what credit unions aim for. Members have to save regularly to qualify for a loan, although there is no minimum deposit, and after 10 weeks, members with a good track record can borrow up to five times their savings, although they must continue to save while repaying the loan. There is no set interest rate, but dividends are distributed to members from any surplus, usually about 5 per cent a year. This too compares favourably with bank interest on deposit accounts.

Finding a credit union

You can find more about credit unions and details of those operating in your area from the Association of British Credit Unions Limited (www.abcul. org). For credit unions in the United States and in countries from Australia to the West Indies see Credit Unions Online (www.creditunionsonline. com).

Leasing and hiring equipment

Physical assets such as cars, vans, computers, office equipment and the like can usually be financed by leasing them, rather as a house or flat may be rented. Alternatively, they can be bought on hire purchase. This leaves other funds free to cover the less tangible elements in your cash-flow.

Leasing is a way of getting the use of vehicles, plant and equipment without paying the full cost all at once. Operating leases are taken out where you will use the equipment (for example a car, photocopier, vending machine or kitchen equipment) for less than its full economic life. The lessor takes the risk of the equipment becoming obsolete, and assumes responsibility for repairs, maintenance and insurance. As you, the lessee, are paying for this service, it is more expensive than a finance lease, where you lease the equipment for most of its economic life and maintain and insure it yourself. Leases can normally be extended, often for fairly nominal sums, in the latter years.

Hire purchase differs from leasing in that you have the option to eventually become the owner of the asset, after a series of payments.

Finding a leasing company

The Finance and Leasing Association (www.fla.org>For Businesses>Business Finance Directory) gives details of all UK-based businesses offering this type of finance. The website also has general information on terms of trade and code of conduct. Euromoney (www.euromoneybooks.com>Leasing & Asset Finance>Books) produce an annual *World Leasing Yearbook* with details on 4,250 leasing companies worldwide, price £170. You can, however, see a listing of most of the country leasing associations for free in the 'Contributors' listing on this site.

Discounting and factoring

Customers often take time to pay up. In the meantime you have to pay those who work for you and your less patient suppliers. So the more you grow, the more funds you need. It is often possible to 'factor' your creditworthy customers' bills to a financial institution, receiving some of the funds as your goods leave the door, hence speeding up cash-flow.

Factoring is generally only available to a business that invoices other business customers for its services, either in its home market or internationally. Factoring can be made available to new businesses, although its services are usually of most value during the early stages of growth. It is an arrangement that allows you to receive up to 80 per cent of the cash due from your customers more quickly than they would normally pay. The factoring company in effect buys your trade debts, and can also provide a debtor accounting and administration service. You will, of course, have to pay for factoring services. Having the cash before your customers pay will cost you a little more than normal overdraft rates. The factoring service will cost between 0.5 and 3.5 per cent of the turnover, depending on volume of work, the number of debtors, average invoice amount and other related factors. You can get up to 80 per cent of the value of your invoice in advance, with the remainder paid when your customer settles up, less the various charges just mentioned.

If you sell direct to the public, sell complex and expensive capital equipment, or expect progress payments on long-term projects, then factoring is not for you. If you are expanding more rapidly than other sources of finance will allow, this may be a useful service that is worth exploring.

Invoice discounting is a variation on the same theme, where you are responsible for collecting the money from debtors; this is not a service available to new or very small businesses.

Finding an invoice discounter or factor

The Asset Based Finance Association (www.thefda.org.uk/public/members List.asp) is the association representing the United Kingdom's 41 factoring and invoice discounting businesses. This link is to its directory of members. InFactor (www.infactor.co.uk) launched in April 2006 is on online service for comparing factoring services to select the best value for money for your need.

Supplier credit

Once you have established creditworthiness, it may be possible to take advantage of trade credit extended by suppliers. This usually takes the form of allowing you anything from seven days to three months from receiving the goods, before you have to pay for them. Even if you are allowed time to pay for goods and services, you will have to weigh carefully the benefit of taking this credit against the cost of losing any cash discounts offered. For example, if you are offered a 2.5 per cent discount for cash settlement, then this is a saving of £25 for every £1,000 of purchases. If the alternative is to take six weeks' credit, the saving is the cost of borrowing that sum from, say, your bank on overdraft. So, if your bank interest rate is 8 per cent per annum, that is equivalent to 0.15 per cent per week. Six weeks would save you 0.92 per cent. On £1,000 of purchases you would save only £9.20 of bank interest. This means that the cash discount is more attractive.

Checking your creditworthiness

Your suppliers will probably run a credit check on you before extending payment terms. You should run a credit check on your own business from time to time, just to see how others see you. You can check out your own credit rating before trying to get credit from a supplier by using a credit reference agency such as Snoop4 Companies (www.snoop4companies. co.uk) for businesses or Experian (www.experian.co.uk) for sole traders. Basic credit reports cost between £3 and £25 and may save you time and money if you have any reservations about a potential customer's ability to pay.

Family and friends

Those close to you might be willing to lend you money or invest in your business. This helps you avoid the problem of pleading your case to outsiders and enduring extra paperwork and bureaucratic delays. Help from friends, relatives and business associates can be especially valuable if you have been through bankruptcy or had other credit problems that would make borrowing from a commercial lender difficult or impossible. Their involvement brings a range of extra potential benefits, costs and risks that are not a feature of most other types of finance. You need to decide which of these are acceptable.

Some advantages of borrowing money from people you know well are that you may be charged a lower interest rate, may be able to delay paying back money until you are more established, and may be given more flexibility if you get into a jam. But once the loan terms are agreed, you have the same legal obligations as you would with a bank or any other source of finance.

In addition, borrowing money from relatives and friends can have a major disadvantage. If your business does poorly and those close to you end up losing money, you may well damage a good personal relationship. So, in dealing with friends, relatives and business associates, be extra careful not only to establish clearly the terms of the deal and put it in writing, but also to make an extra effort to explain the risks. In short, it is your job to make sure your helpful friend or relative will not suffer true hardship if you are unable to meet your financial commitments.

GETTING AN INVESTOR

If you are operating as a limited company or limited partnership you will have a potentially valuable opportunity to raise relatively risk-free money. It is risk-free to you – the business founder – that is, but risky, sometimes extremely so, to anyone advancing you money. Businesses such as these have shares that can be traded for money, so selling a share of your business is one way to raise capital to start up or grow your business. Shares also have the great additional attraction of having cost you nothing – nothing, that is, except blood, sweat, tears and inspiration.

Individual business angels, or corporates such as venture capital providers, share all the risks and vagaries of the business alongside you, the founder, and expect a proportionate share in the rewards if things go well. They are not especially concerned with a stream of dividends, which is just as well, as few small businesses ever pay them. Nor do they look for the security of buildings or other assets to underpin their investment. Instead they hope for a radical increase in the value of their investment. They expect to realize this value from other investors who want to take their place for the next stage in the firm's growth cycle, rather than from any repayment by the founder.

Business angels

One likely first source of equity or risk capital will be a private individual with his or her own funds, and perhaps some knowledge of your type of business. In return for a share in the business, such investors will put in money at their own risk. They have been christened 'business angels', a term first coined to describe private wealthy individuals who back a play on Broadway or in London's West End.

Most angels are determined upon some involvement beyond merely signing a cheque and hope to play a part in your business in some way. They are hoping for big rewards – one angel who backed Sage with £10,000 in its first round of £250,000 financing saw his stake rise to £40 million.

These angels frequently operate through managed networks, usually on the internet. In the United Kingdom and the United States there are hundreds of networks, with tens of thousands of business angels prepared to put up several billion pounds each year into new or small business.

Finding a business angel

The British Business Angels Association (www.bbaa.org.uk) has an online directory of UK business angels. The European Business Angels Network (eban) has directories of national business angel associations both inside and outside of Europe (at www.eban.org>Members) from which you can find individual business angels.

CASE STUDY

PPLParty.com

Calum Brannan was just 15 and taking his GCSEs when he started up PPLParty.com from his bedroom in Coventry. Brannon felt there was an unexploited niche proving a website to share pictures and information on clubbing. He invested £200 earned from his part-time job at Pizza Hut and through little more than word of mouth now has over 400,000 members. Next came a small amount of money from a business angel to help pay for his eight staff, and now he is looking for around £400,000 from a venture capital firm to enable him to move his business to the next stage.

Venture capital/private equity

Venture capital (VC) providers are investing other people's money, often from pension funds. They have a different agenda from that of business angels, and are more likely to be interested in investing more money for a larger stake.

VCs go through a process known as 'due diligence' before investing. This process involves a thorough examination of both the business and its owners. Past financial performance, the directors' track record and the business plan are all subjected to detailed scrutiny, usually by accountants and lawyers. Directors are then required to 'warrant' that they have provided all relevant information, under pain of financial penalties. The cost of this process will have to be borne by the firm raising the money, but it will be paid out of the money raised, if that is any consolation.

In general, VCs expect their investment to have paid off within seven years, but they are hardened realists. Two in every ten investments they make are total write-offs, and six perform averagely well at best. So the one star in every 10 investments they make has to cover a lot of duds. VCs have a target rate of return of 30 per cent plus, to cover this poor hit rate.

Raising venture capital is not a cheap option, and deals are not quick to arrange either. Six months is not unusual, and over a year has been known. Every VC has a deal done in six weeks in its portfolio, but that truly is the exception.

Finding a venture capital provider

The British Venture Capital Association (www.bvca.co.uk) and the European Venture Capital Association (www.evca.com) both have online directories giving details of hundreds of venture capital providers. The Australian government (www.austradeict.gov.au/Globl-VC-directory/default.aspx) has a global venture capital directory on this website and the National Venture Capital Association in the United States has directories of international venture capital associations both inside and outside the United States(www.nvca.org>Resources).

You can see how those negotiating with or receiving venture capital rate the firm in question at The Funded website (www.thefunded.com) in terms of the deal offered, the firm's apparent competence and how good it is at managing the relationship. There is also a link to the VCs website. The Funded has 2,500 members.

Valuing shares in your business

Selling anything for the best price is a matter of skilful negotiating, and selling shares in your business is no exception to that rule. There are, however, a couple of basic guidelines that will help you in starting to work out the value of your business to an outside investor.

One way to measure value is to work out what the various assets of the business would be worth on the open market. So vehicles, premises, equipment and any other assets could be professionally valued. From that sum you would take any outstanding liabilities to creditors, bank borrowings, tax authorities and redundancy payments due. This might make sense if the business is actually going to stop trading, but it is unlikely to produce the best value. This is also unlikely to be a useful approach if you have not even started your business yet.

Part, perhaps even all, of what a small business has to sell, in the final resort, is its capacity to make profit. If you are starting up, it is the future profits demonstrated in your business plan that will be the base for assessing value. If you have been trading for a while, your historic profits will influence how any investor will regard your projections.

The most commonly used formula to value a business is the price/earnings (P/E) ratio. This indicates the number of times annual profits at which a business is valued. If you look up any listed company's performance in the financial press, you will see a P/E ratio, calculated as the share price divided by the earnings per share. So, if the share price of the business in question is £10 and the earnings per share are 80p, the P/E ratio is 12.5. This is another way of saying the company is worth 12.5 years' profits. This is a reasonably typical figure, but a company in the internet sector, for example, might have a quite different multiple in force. Two hundred and thirty-five years times earnings is an all-time record in this sector. For less glamorous sectors with much lower growth prospects, the P/E ratio might be in single figures. While it may seem a pretty rarefied idea to someone starting out in business, the stock market is where the framework for values is set.

So if your business is in the food sector, and a typical P/E ratio in that sector is 12, that is where outsiders will start when they think about valuing your business. Then a few things get added and taken away. The first seriously negative event is the discount that will be applied because your business is not on the stock market. Private businesses are generally viewed as being worth at least a third less than a publicly quoted firm listed on a stock exchange. That is because shares in a public company are much more liquid. There are more shares and more buyers and sellers for a quoted than for an unquoted business's shares. Valuations are also affected by the numbers and skills of the founding team. A business run by one person is generally valued at around half the value of a comparable private company run by a team of three or more experienced managers. The reasoning here is that customers are probably loyal to the owner manager and may not come over to any new owner. That in turn means that the future value of the business will be lower, in the absence of extra sales effort.

One last factor that affects private business valuations is the economic cycle. At the bottom of the cycle (a downturn), on average small private firms sell on multiples of between 6 and 8. At the top of the cycle (a boom), the same firm may sell for between 10 and 12.

Finding your potential P/E ratio

You can check out the P/E for your business sector either by looking in the financial section of a paper such as the *Times*, *Daily Telegraph* or *Financial Times* or at a financial website. For example using ProShare's website (www.proshareclubs.co.uk) select click Research Centre, then Performance Tables, then Choose a Sector. There you can see the current P/E ratio for every company in your sector listed on the London Stock Exchange. Private companies don't trade on as high a P/E multiple as companies on the stock market. Typically if a public company in your sector has a P/E of 12, a private company would have a P/E of around 8, or a third less. The reason for the difference is that a stake in a private business is harder to dispose of, whilst you can sell or buy shares in a public company every business day by making a phone call to your broker. BDO Stoy Hayward's Private Company Price Index (PCPI) tracks the relationship between the current FTSE price/earnings ratio and the P/Es currently being paid on the sale of private companies. Go to www.bdo.co.uk, then select Publications, View by title, then Private Company Price Index.

Rules of thumb

Some business sectors have their own rules for valuing a business. Annual sales turnover, the number of customers, the number of outlets and in the case of businesses selling consumer goods, a formula based partly on their turnover and partly on the value of the stock they hold, are all common 'rules of thumb' for valuing a business. BizStats (www.bizstats. com/rulesofthumb.htm) has a table listing these rules.

How much equity should you sell?

The answer is as little as you can to raise the money you need now. If you are successful in business you will need to raise more money in the future. Also, as you grow and become profitable, your shares will be worth more. The more your shares are worth, the fewer you have to sell to raise a given amount of finance.

As a benchmark you should remember that retaining less than 76 per cent of the business will mean that you do not have absolute control. If outsiders have over 25 per cent of your shares they can challenge your decisions and slow you down, in much the same way as the House of Lords can hold back the Commons. If you end up with less than 50 per cent, then you have lost effective control. However, these figures represent the legal position, and may have little impact on the real position on the ground. If you are doing a great job and all is going to plan, it is unlikely that you will face any serious challenge to your decisions.

No outside investor in an early-stage venture will want to take so many shares away from you that it acts as a disincentive. Investors know they have to keep you motivated and feeling like the owner, rather than simply being the manager. So plan on selling no more than a third, and ideally less than 15 per cent, of your shares on any initial round of financing.

GOING PUBLIC

Stock markets are the place where serious businesses raise serious money. It's possible to raise anything from a few million to tens of billions; expect the costs and efforts in getting listed to match those stellar figures. The basic idea is that owners sell shares in their businesses, which in effect brings in a whole raft of new 'owners' who in turn have a stake in the business's future profits. When they want out, they sell their shares on to other investors. The share price moves up and down to ensure that there are as many buyers as sellers at any one time.

Going public also puts a stamp of respectability on you and your company. It will enhance the status and credibility of your business, and it will enable you to borrow more against the 'security' provided by your new shareholders, should you so wish. Your shares will also provide an attractive way to retain and motivate key staff. If they are given, or rather are allowed to earn, share options at discounted prices, they too can participate in the capital gains you are making. With a public share listing you can now join in the takeover and asset-stripping game. When your share price is high and things are going well you can look out for weaker firms to gobble up – and all you have to do is to offer them more of your shares in return for theirs. You do not even have to find real money. But of course this is a two-sided game and you also may now become the target of a hostile bid.

You may find that being in the public eye not only cramps your style but fills up your engagement diary too. Most CEOs of public companies find that they have to spend up to a quarter of their time 'in the City' explaining their strategies, in the months preceding and the first years following their going public. It is not unusual for so much management time to have been devoted to answering accountants' and stockbrokers' questions that there is not enough time to run the day-to-day business, and profits drop as a direct consequence. The City also creates its own 'pressure' both to seduce companies onto the market and then by expecting them to perform beyond any reasonable expectation.

Criteria for getting a listing

The rules vary from market to market, but these are the conditions that are likely to apply to get a company listed on an exchange:

- Getting listed on a major stock exchange calls for a track record of making substantial profits, with decent seven-figure sums being made in the year you plan to float, as this process is known. A listing also calls for a large proportion, usually at least 25 per cent, of the company's shares to be put up for sale at the outset. In addition, you would be expected to have 100 shareholders now and be able to demonstrate that 100 more will come on board as a result of the listing.

- As you draw up your flotation plan and timetable you should have the following matters in mind:

  - *Advisers*: You will need to be supported by a team which will include a sponsor, stockbroker, reporting accountant and solicitor. These should be respected firms, active in flotation work and familiar with the company's type of business. You and your company may be judged by the company you keep, so choose advisers of good repute and make sure that the personalities work effectively together. It is very unlikely that a small local firm of accountants, however satisfactory, will be up to this task.

  - *Sponsor*: You will need to appoint a financial institution, usually a merchant banker, to fill this important role. If you do not already have a merchant bank in mind, your accountant will offer guidance. The job of the sponsor is to coordinate and drive the project forward.

  - *Timetable*: It is essential to have a timetable for the final months during the run up to a float – and to adhere to it. The company's directors and senior staff will be fully occupied in providing information and attending meetings. They will have to delegate and there must be sufficient back-up support to ensure that the business does not suffer.

  - *Management team*: A potential investor will want to be satisfied that your company is well managed; at board level and below. It is important to ensure succession, perhaps by offering key directors and managers service agreements and share options. It is wise to draw on the experience of well-qualified non-executive directors.

- *Accounts*: The objective is to have a profit record which is rising, but in achieving this, you will need to take into account directors' remuneration, pension contributions and the elimination of any expenditure which might be acceptable in a privately owned company but would not be acceptable in a public company, namely excessive perks such as yachts, luxury cars, lavish expense accounts and holiday homes. Accounts must be consolidated and audited to appropriate accounting standards, and the audit reports must not contain any major qualifications. The auditors will need to be satisfied that there are proper stock records and a consistent basis of valuing stock during the years prior to flotation. Accounts for the last three years will need to be disclosed, and the date of the last accounts must be within six months of the issue.

Using AIM

London's Alternative Investment Market (AIM) was formed in 1995 specifically to provide risk capital for new rather than established ventures. AIM raised £15.7 billion last year – a 76 per cent leap from the previous year – and a record number of companies floated on the exchange, bringing the total to 1,634.

AIM is particularly attractive to any dynamic company of any size, age or business sector that has rapid growth in mind. The smallest firm on AIM entered at under £1 million capitalization and the largest at over £500 million. The formalities are minimal, but the costs of entry are high and you must have a nominated adviser, such as a major accountancy firm, stockbroker or banker. The survey showed that costs of floating on the junior market are around 6.5 per cent of all funds raised, and companies valued at less than £2 million can expect to shell out a quarter of funds raised in costs alone. The market is regulated by the London Stock Exchange (www.londonstockexchange.com>AIM).

You can check out all the world stock markets from Australia to Zagreb on Stock Exchanges World Wide Links (www.tdd.lt/slnews/Stock_Exchanges/Stock.Exchanges.htm) maintained by Aldas Kirvaitis of Lithuania, and at World Wide-Tax.com (www.worldwide-tax.com >World Stock Exchanges). Once in the stock exchange website – almost all stock exchanges have pages in English – look out for a term such as 'Listing Center', 'Listing' or 'Rules'. There you will find the latest criteria for floating a company on that particular exchange.

MONEY FOR FREE

Free money comes usually from the government, whose agenda is either to get businesses to locate in an area more full of sheep than customers, or to pioneer new technologies. Alternatively, businesses, newspapers and magazines run competitions offering prizes for achievements such as the best run, fastest growing, biggest exporting business and so forth. For the sponsor the reward is publicity and good stories, and for the business founders there is money, perhaps £50,000.

Gaining grants

Grants are constantly being introduced (and withdrawn), but there is no system that lets you know automatically what is available. You have to keep yourself informed.

Business Link (www.businesslink.gov.uk>Finance and grants>Grants and government support) has advice on how to apply for a grant as well as a directory of grants on offer. Microsoft Small Business Centre (www. microsoft.com/uk/businesscentral/euga/home.aspx) has a European Union grant advisor with a search facility to help you find which of the 6,000 grants on offer might suit your business needs. Grants.Gov (www.grants. gov) is a guide to how to apply for over 1,000 federal government grants in the United States.

Winning competitions

There are thousands of annual awards around the world aimed at new or small businesses. Most are based around a business plan or other presentation of your business ideas. For the most part, these are sponsored by banks, the major accountancy bodies, chambers of commerce, local or national newspapers, business magazines and the trade press. Government departments may also have their own competitions as a means of promoting their initiatives for exporting, innovation, job creation, and so forth. There is a Business Plan Competition Directory on the Small Business Notes website, run by Judith Kautz (www.smallbusinessnotes.com/planning/competitions.html).

CASE STUDY

Suffolk Farmhouse Cheeses

Jason and Katherine Salisbury started up their business, Suffolk Farmhouse Cheeses, in a renovated rundown cowshed next to their home. They bought secondhand equipment and despite having two young children put in 18-hour days since going it alone in 2004. Their annual turnover is now £275,000 which they have financed in part with an £80,000 bank loan from HSBC. Now they are entering business competitions to fund expansion. They narrowly missed out on a £30,000 government grant in their first year of operations but since then have won through to the regional heats of the HSBC's Start-up Stars Awards from which they could win up to £25,000.

WORKSHEET FOR ASSIGNMENT 21:
FINANCING REQUIREMENTS

Based on your financial projections, state how much cash you need to raise to set up your business, and how and when you propose to repay it. Use the questions below as the format for your worksheet:

1. Based on the maximum figure in your cash-flow forecast, how much money do you need and what do you need it for?
2. How does this compare with the sum that you and your partners or shareholders are putting in (ie level of gearing)?

$$\text{Gearing} = \frac{\text{Total funds required for business}}{\text{Money put in by you} + \text{shareholders}}$$

For example, if you already have £1,000 of assets and are looking for a loan of £5,000, the funds required are £6,000. If you have already invested £500 and plan to put in a further £2,500, then your gearing is:

$$\frac{6,000}{500 + 2,500} = \frac{6,000}{3,000} = 2{:}1$$

3. Where do you expect to raise the funds you need to finance your business?
4. Prepare a schedule showing when you need these funds.
5. How and when will any borrowing be repaid? Do a list like this:

   Source of repayment   *Amount £*   *Date*
   Total £

6. If you plan to issue shares, how will you value the business?
7. What percentage of your venture would you be prepared to sell to raise the required funds?
8. What exit route(s) could be open to potential investors?
9. What security, if any, is available as collateral for any loan?

   Security   *Value £*
   Total £

10. Will you be receiving any grants or loans to help to finance your business (other than from the organization to which you are now applying)?

    Source   *Date*   *Funds provided*   *Amount £*
    Total £

11. What further private cash, if any, is available to invest in the business?

    Source   *Date*   *Funds provided*   *Amount £*
    Total £

12. What are the key risks that could adversely affect your projections? (These could include technical, financial and marketing risks.)

    Risk area   *Financial impact on:*
    Sales   *Profits*

13. What contingency plans do you have to either manage or minimize the consequences of these risks?

    Risk area   *Plan*   *Effect*

SUGGESTED FURTHER READING

Barrow, C (2008) *Practical financial management: a guide to budgets, balance sheets and business finance*, 7th edn, Kogan Page, London

Barrow, C (2008) *Understanding business accounting for dummies*, 2nd edn, Wiley, New York

Phase 6

Business controls

INTRODUCTION

No one is likely to take any business proposition seriously unless the founder(s) can demonstrate at the outset that they can monitor and control the venture. Just as your business plan should include a statement of objectives and strategy, it must also contain a brief description of how you will monitor results. Every business needs to monitor financial, sales and market performance. Manufacturing businesses or those involved in research, development and fashion may have to observe results on a much wider scale.

In these assignments you should address the issues of importance to your type of business. If you do not have first-hand experience of working in a similar business, either find someone who has or find a professional adviser, such as an auditor, with that experience. As a minimum, potential financiers will want to see that you have made arrangements to keep the books and analyse and interpret key business ratios.

Financial controls

To survive and prosper in business, you need to know how much cash you have and what your profit or loss on sales is. For a business to survive, let alone grow, these facts are needed on a monthly, weekly or occasionally even a daily basis depending on the nature of the business.

While bad luck plays a part in some business failures, a lack of reliable financial information plays a part in most. However, all the information needed to manage well is close at hand. The bills to be paid, invoices raised, petty-cash slips and bank statements between them are enough to give a true picture of performance. All that needs to be done is for the information on them to be recorded and organized so that the financial picture becomes clear. The way financial information is recorded is known as 'bookkeeping'.

The basic data derived from the bookkeeping process is turned into the historic profit and loss account and balance sheet, subjects we examined in Assignments 18 and 19. Then those accounts are in turn analysed using ratios, the subject of the second part of this chapter.

It is not just the owner of a company who needs these financial facts. Bankers, shareholders and tax inspectors will be unsympathetic audiences to anyone without well-documented facts to back them up. If, for example, a tax authority presents a business with a tax demand, the onus then lies with the businessperson, using his or her records, to either agree with or dispute the sum claimed. If you are unable to adequately explain a bank deposit, the tax authority may treat it as taxable income. A bank manager faced with a request for an increased overdraft facility to help a small business grow needs financial facts to work with. Without them, the bank will generally have to say no, as it has a responsibility to the owners of the money it would be using.

KEEPING THE BOOKS

There are no rules about the format to be used for a bookkeeping system. Records can be on paper, in ledgers or on a computer. You must, however, be able to account for where all your business income came from and who you have paid and for what services. If you are registered for VAT (see Assignment 13) you will also need to keep a record of the VAT element of each invoice and bill and produce a summary for each accounting period covered by your VAT returns.

Starting simple

If you are doing books by hand and don't have a lot of transactions, the single-entry method is the easiest acceptable way to go. This involves writing down each transaction in your records once, preferably on a ledger sheet. Receipts and payments should be kept and summarized daily, weekly or monthly, in accordance with the needs of the business. At the end of the year, the 12 monthly summaries are totalled up – you are ready for tax time.

This simple record system is known as a 'cash book' – an example is given in Table 22.1.

In the left-hand four columns, the month's expenses are entered as they occur, together with some basic details and the amount. At the head of the first column is the amount of cash brought forward from the preceding month.

On the right, expenses are listed in the same way. The total of receipts for the month is £1,480.15 and that for expenses is £672.01. The difference between these two figures is the amount of cash now in the business. As the business shown in Table 22.1 has brought in more cash than it has spent, the figure is higher than the amount brought forward at the beginning of the month. The figure of £808.14 is the amount that is 'brought down' to be 'brought forward' to the next month. The total of the month's payments and the amount 'carried down' are equal to the sum of all the receipts in the left-hand columns.

Table 22.1   A simple cash-book system

Receipts				Payments			
Date	Name	Details	Amount £	Date	Name	Details	Amount £
1 June	Balance	Brought forward	450.55	4 June	Gibbs	Stock purchase	310.00
4 June	Anderson	Sales	175.00	8 June	Gibbs	Stock purchase	130.00
6 June	Brown	Sales	45.00	12 June	ABC Telecoms	Telephone charges	55.23
14 June	Smith & Co	Refund on returned stock	137.34	18 June	Colt Rentals	Vehicle hire	87.26
17 June	Jenkins	Sales	190.25	22 June	VV Mobiles	Mobile phone	53.24
20 June	Hollis	Sales	425.12	27 June	Gibbs	Stock purchase	36.28
23 June	Jenkins	Sales	56.89				
							672.01
				30 June	Balance	Carried down	808.14
			1,480.15				1,480.15
1 July	Balance	Brought down	808.14				

If there are a reasonably large number of transactions, it would be sensible to extend this simple cash book to include a basic analysis of the figures – this variation is called an 'analysed cash book'. An example of the payments side of an analysed cashbook is shown in Table 22.2 (the receipts side is similar, but with different categories). You can see at a glance the receipts and payments, both in total and by main category. This breakdown lets you see, for example, how much is being spent on each major area of your business, or who your most important customers are. The payments are the same as in Table 22.1 but now you can see how much the business has spent on stock, vehicles and telephone expenses. The sums total both down the amount columns and across the analysis section to arrive at the same amount: £672.01. This is both a useful bit of management information and essential for your tax return.

Table 22.2   Example of an analysed cash book

Payments				Analysis			
Date	Name	Details	Amount £	Stocks	Vehicles	Telephone	Other
4 June	Gibbs	Stock purchase	310	310			
8 June	Gibbs	Stock purchase	130	130			
12 June	ABC Telecoms	Telephone charges	55.23			55.23	
18 June	Colt Rentals	Vehicle hire	87.26		87.26		
22 June	VV Mobiles	Mobile phone	53.24			53.24	
27 June	Gibbs	Stock purchase	36.28	36.28			
Totals			672.01	476.28	87.26	108.47	

If you are taking or giving credit, you will need to keep more information than the cashbook, whether it is analysed or not. You will need to keep copies of paid and unpaid sales invoices and the same for purchases, as well as your bank statements. The bank statements should then be 'reconciled' to your cashbook to tie everything together. For example, the bank statement for the example given in Table 22.1 should show £808.14 in the account at the end of June. Figure 22.1 outlines how this works.

Building a system

If you operate a partnership, trade as a company or plan to get larger, then you will need a double-entry bookkeeping system. This calls for a series of day books, ledgers, a journal, a petty-cash book and a wages book, as well as a number of files for copies of invoices and receipts.

The double-entry system requires two entries for each transaction – this provides built-in checks and balances to ensure accuracy. Each transaction requires an entry as a debit and as a credit. This may sound a little complicated, but you only need to get a general idea.

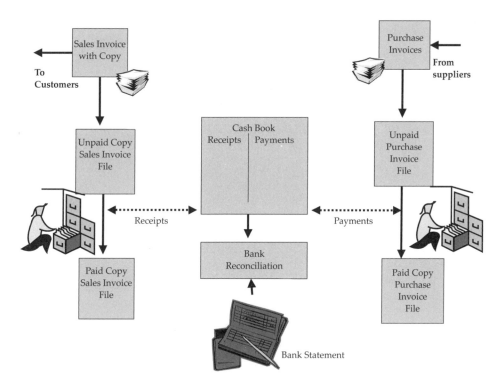

Figure 22.1   A simple system of business records

A double-entry system is more complicated and time-consuming if done by hand, since everything is recorded twice. If done manually, the method requires a formal set of books – journals and ledgers. All transactions would be first entered into a journal and then 'posted' (written) on a ledger sheet – the same amount would be written down in two different places. Typical ledger accounts include those for titled income, expenses, assets and liabilities (debts).

To give an example, a payment of rent in a double-entry system might result in two separate journal entries – a debit for an expense of, say, £250 and a corresponding credit of £250 – a double entry (see Table 22.3). The debits in a double-entry system must always equal the credits. If they don't, you know there is an error somewhere. So, double entry allows you to balance your books, which you can't do with the single-entry method.

Table 22.3   An example of a double-entry ledger

General Journal of Andrew's Bookshop			
Date	**Description of entry**	**Debit**	**Credit**
10th July	Rent expense Cash	£250	£250

Paper-based bookkeeping systems

If you expect to have fewer than 50 transactions each month, either buying or selling, then you can simply use analysis paper, either loose or in books that are available from any large stationers. These are sheets of paper A3 size, with a dozen or so lined columns already drawn so you can enter figures and extend your analysis as shown in Table 22.2 above. Alternatively you can buy a manual accounting system with a full set of ledgers and books for around £20 from Hingston Publishing Co (www.hingston-publishing. co.uk) or Collins Account Books available from most large stationers.

Getting some help

You don't have to do the bookkeeping yourself, though if you do for the first year or so you will get a good insight into how your business works from a financial perspective. There are a number of ways in which you can reduce or even eliminate the more tedious aspects of the task.

Bookkeeping and accounting software

With the cost of a basic computerized bookkeeping and accounting system starting at barely £50, and a reasonable package costing between £200 and £500, it makes good sense to plan to use such a system from the outset. Key advantages include having no more arithmetical errors, speedy preparation of VAT returns and preparing your accounts at the year end will be a whole lot simpler. There are dozens of perfectly satisfactory basic accounting and bookkeeping software packages on the market. The leading providers include:

- Dosh (www.dosh.co.uk);

- Microsoft Money (www.microsoft.co.uk);

- MYOB (My Own Business) (www.myob.co.uk);

- QuickBooks (www.intuit.co.uk/store/en/quickbooks/index.jsp);

- Sage (www.uk.sage.com);

- Simplex (www.simplex.net);

- TAS (www.tassoftware.co.uk).

Using a bookkeeping service

Two professional associations, the International Association of Book-keepers (IAB) (www.iab.org.uk; tel: 01732 458080) and the Institute of Certified Bookkeepers (www.book-keepers.org; tel: 0845 060 2345), offer free matching services to help small businesses find a bookkeeper to suit their particular needs. Expect to pay upwards of £20 an hour for services that can be as basic as simply recording the transactions in your books, through to producing accounts, preparing the VAT return or doing the payroll.

Hiring an accountant

If you plan to trade as a partnership or limited company, are approaching the VAT threshold of around £64,000 annual turnover or look as though you will be making over £20,000 net profit before tax you may be ready to hire an accountant to look after your books.

Personal recommendation from someone in your business network is the best staring point to find an accountant. Meet him/her and if you think you could work with him/her take up references as you would with anyone you employ and make sure the accountant is a qualified member of one of the professional bodies. The Association of Chartered Certified Accountants (www.accaglobal.com>PUBLIC INTEREST >FIND AN ACCOUNTANT) and the Institute of Chartered Accountants (www.icaewfirms.co.uk) have online directories of qualified accountants which you can search by name, location, the business sector you are in or any specific accountancy skills you are looking for.

BASIC BUSINESS RATIOS

Just keeping the books and accounts of a business is not of much use in itself if you can't analyse and interpret them. This involves measuring the relationship between various elements of performance to see whether you are getting better or worse. *Ratios* are the tools used here, and they are simply something expressed as a proportion of something else. So miles per gallon, for example, is a ratio showing a measure of the efficiency of fuel consumption.

Ratios are used to compare performance in one period, say last month or year, with another – this month or year. They can also be used to see how well your business is performing compared with another, say a competitor. You can also use ratios to compare how well you have done against your target or budget. In the financial field the opportunity for calculating ratios is great; for computing useful ratios, not quite so great. Here we shall concentrate on explaining the key ratios for a new venture.

Levels of profit

Look back to the profit and loss account and balance sheet for High Note, the example used in Assignments 18 and 19. These figures will be used in calculating the ratios that follow.

Gross profit

This is calculated by dividing the gross profit by sales and multiplying by 100. In this example the sum is 30,000/ 60,000 x 100 = 50 per cent. This is a measure of the value you are adding to the bought in materials and services you need to 'make' your product or service; the higher the figure the better.

Operating profit

This is calculated by dividing the operating profit by sales and multiplying by 100. In this example the sum is 8,700/ 60,000 × 100 = 14.5 per cent. This is a measure of how efficiently you are running the business, before taking account of financing costs and tax. These are excluded as interest and tax rates change periodically and are outside your direct control. Excluding them makes it easier to compare one period with another or with another business. Once again the rule here is the higher the figure the better.

Net profit before and after tax

These are calculated by dividing the net profit before and after tax by the sales and multiplying by 100. In this example the sums are 8,100/ 60,000 × 100 = 13.5 per cent and 6,723/60,000 × 100 = 11.21 per cent. This is a measure of how efficiently you are running the business, after taking account of financing costs and tax. The last figure shows how successful you are at creating additional money to either invest back in the business or distribute to the owner(s) as either drawings or dividends. Once again the rule here is the higher the figure the better.

Working capital relationships

The money tied up in day-to-day activities is known as working capital, the sum of which is arrived at by subtracting the current liabilities from the current assets. In the case of High Note there is £21,108 in current assets and £4,908 in current liabilities, so the working capital is £16,200.

Current ratio

As a figure the working capital doesn't tell us much. It is rather as if you knew your car had used 20 gallons of petrol but had no idea how far you had travelled. It would be more helpful to know how much larger the current assets are than the current liabilities. That would give you some idea of whether the funds will be available to pay bills for stock, the tax liability and any other short-term liabilities that may arise. The current ratio, which is arrived at by dividing the current assets by the current liabilities, is the measure used. For High Note this is 21,108/4,908 = 4.30. The convention is to express this as 4.30:1, and the aim here is to have a ratio of between 1.5:1 and 2:1. Any lower and bills can't be met easily; much higher and money is being tied up unnecessarily.

Average collection period

We can see that High Note's current ratio is high, which is an indication that some elements of working capital are being used inefficiently. The business has £12,000 owed by customers on sales of £60,000 over a six-month period. The average period it takes High Note to collect money owed is calculated by dividing the sales made on credit by the money owed and multiplying it by the time period, in days; in this case the sum is as follows: 12,000/ 60,000 × 182.5 = 36.5 days.

If the credit terms are cash with order or seven days, then something is going seriously wrong. If it is net 30 days then it is probably about right. In this example it has been assumed that all the sales were made on credit.

Days stock held

High Note is carrying £9,108 stock of sheet music, CDs etc and over the period it sold £30,000 of stock at cost. (The cost of sales is £30,000 to support £60,000 of invoiced sales as the mark-up in this case is 100 per cent.) Using a similar sum as with average collection period we can calculate that the stock being held is sufficient to support 55.41 days' sales (9,108/10,000 × 182.5). If High Note's suppliers can make weekly deliveries, this is almost certainly too high a stock figure to hold. Cutting stock back from nearly eight weeks (55.41 days) to one week (7 days) would trim 48.41 days or £7,957.38 worth of stock out of working capital. This in turn would bring the current ratio down to 2.68:1.

Return on investment

The fundamental financial purpose in business is to make a satisfactory return on the funds invested. Return on investment is calculated as a percentage in the same way as the interest you would get on any money on deposit in a bank would be. In High Note £28,700 has been put into the business from various sources including the bank, to generate an operating profit of £8,700 – that is, profit before paying the bank interest on money owed or tax. The return is calculated as 8,700/ 28,700 × 100 = 30.31 per cent.

Appreciating gearing

The return on investment ratio is arrived at taking into account all the sources of money used. However, High Note's owners only have £10,000 of their own money invested and the profit they make after paying bank interest of £600 is £8,100. So the return on the owner's investment is 8,100/10,000 × 100 = 81 per cent, which by any standards is acceptable.

If the owners had been able to get an overdraft of £15,000 rather than the £10,000 they secured and so only put in £5,000 of their own cash, the return on their investment would have been better still. Interest costs would increase to £900 so profit after interest would drop to £7,800, but the owners' investment being just £5,000 means that the return on their investment would rise to 156 per cent (7,800/5,000 × 100).

There is a limit to the amount of money banks will put up compared with the amount an owner puts in. Typically banks will look to no more than match £ for £ the owners' funding, and in any event they will want to secure their loan against some tangible asset such as a property.

RATIO ANALYSIS SPREADSHEETS

Bookkeeping and accounting software often have 'report generator' programs that crunch out ratios for you, sometimes with helpful suggestions on areas to be probed further. biz/ed (www.bized.co.uk>Company Information >Financial Ratio Analysis) and the Harvard Business School (http://harvard businessonline.hbsp.harvard.edu/b02/en/academic/edu_tk_acct_fin_ratio. jhtml) have free tools that calculate financial ratios from your financial data. They also provide useful introductions to ratio analysis as well as defining each ratio and the formula used to calculate it. You need to register on the Harvard website to be able to download their spreadsheet.

WORKSHEET FOR ASSIGNMENT 22: FINANCIAL CONTROLS

1. What bookkeeping and accounting system have you chosen and why?
2. What control information does it produce and with what frequency?
3. Who will keep the books and produce the accounts?
4. What will your basic business ratios be if you achieve your financial objectives?
5. How do those ratios compare with those of either a competitor or your current organization?
6. What would you consider changing as a result of carrying out your ratio analysis (for example, collect money in faster, carry less stock)?

SUGGESTED FURTHER READING

Barrow, C (2008) *Financial management for the small business*, 7th edn, Kogan Page, London
Barrow, C (2008) *Understanding business accounting for dummies*, 2nd edn, Wiley, New York

Assignment 23

Sales and marketing controls

In the early weeks and months of any new venture, large amounts of both effort and money will be expended without any visible signs of sales revenue, let alone profits. Even once the business has been trading for some time, the most reliable predictor of likely future results will be the sales and marketing efforts for the immediate past. Your business plan should explain how you intend to monitor and control this activity.

The Supreme Garden Furniture Company

Gordon Smith set up his business, the Supreme Garden Furniture Company, shortly after being made redundant. Using 800 square feet on the ground floor of an old Lancashire textile mill, he planned to produce a range of one- to four-seat garden benches in an authentic Victorian design, together with matching tables. Each item in the range was manufactured to a very high standard using top-quality materials, such as kiln-dried African Iroko hardwood.

With professional advice he drew up a business plan incorporating cash and profit forecasts, an assessment of the market and his likely competitors, the plant and machinery required and the start-up capital he would need.

His main customers would be garden centres, and he planned to spend a couple of days a week out on the road selling, initially in Lancashire, Yorkshire and Cheshire. He also produced a leaflet and price list which he intended to send to potential customers further afield. These he would follow up later.

Smith could incorporate the sales and marketing controls shown in Figure 22.1 (page 329) into his initial business plan to monitor his performance.

Once Smith had gained a number of customers, he found that future sales to existing customers were much easier than constantly seeking new customers. So, he kept records of existing customers, to monitor their purchases and plan follow-up visits.

From an analysis of his customer records Smith was subsequently able to discover that garden centres in the south-east placed average orders of £2,000 a time, while in his home area a £500 order was exceptional. In his business plan for his second year's trading he would be able to incorporate this information and alter his selling strategy accordingly.

Controlling your promotional costs and judging their cost-effectiveness is also an early, vital marketing control task.

CASE STUDY

Richer Sounds

Julian Richer opened his first Richer Sounds shop (www.richersounds.com) at London Bridge when he was 19. Today he has 50 outlets, and together with his online business generates sales of over £100 million a year. Performance measurement and control is based on a wide range of financial measures, such as profit, sales, and stock turn, enhanced by measures of customer satisfaction, employee involvement and employee satisfaction. In addition stores are assessed by 'mystery shoppers'. Employees are given performance information through weekly faxed reports and a monthly video from the chairman relaying facts about company performance on sales, margins, customer satisfaction and proposed changes.

Equally, advertising costs per sales lead generated and converted should be recorded, while tear-off coupons, discounts on production or special offer leaflets all help to measure the cost-effectiveness of your promotions.

CUSTOMER RELATIONSHIP MANAGEMENT (CRM) AND SALES FORCE MANAGEMENT SYSTEMS

CRM is the business strategy concerned with identifying, understanding and improving relationships with your customers to improve customer satisfaction and maximize profits. The myriad of facts and figures that need to be assembled have made the subject ideal for software applications.

For example, businesses can maintain a database of which customers buy and what type of product, and when, how often they make that purchase, what type of options they choose with their typical purchase, their colour preferences and whether the purchase needed financing. This information will advise the sales team on what products services or messages are likely to be the most effective and when would be a good time to target each customer.

While CRM systems put customers at the centre of the data flow, sales force management systems capture, track and manage sales enquiries in a central database that track leads throughout the sales cycle from lead generation to closed sale.

WORKSHEET FOR ASSIGNMENT 23: SALES AND MARKETING CONTROLS

1. Describe your records for monitoring sales activities.
2. Draw up a customer record card for your business, or show your existing one.
3. What other marketing records do you plan to keep, eg for advertising costs and results?

SUGGESTED FURTHER READING

Johnston, M and Marshall, G (2008) *Sales force management*, 8th edn, McGraw-Hill Higher Education, New York

Spiro, R, Stanton, W and Greg, G (2007) *Management of a sales force*, 12th edn, McGraw-Hill Higher Education, New York

Assignment 24

Other business controls

Depending on the nature of your venture, your business plan will have to show how you plan to control other aspects of the firm's performance. These could include:

- manufacturing and production;
- personnel records/accident reports;
- quality and complaints;
- new product development/design.

Stock cards for the different stages of your production process (raw materials, work-in-progress, finished goods) are particularly important to help you identify fast- and slow-moving items and to help you identify correct safety stock levels. Equally, to permit customers to complain (better than them voting with their feet, without telling you) you will need to provide customer suggestion boxes or explanations as to how to contact key managers, eg by giving a name and contact address on a restaurant menu.

WORKSHEET FOR ASSIGNMENT 24: OTHER BUSINESS CONTROLS

1. What other business controls do you plan to introduce into your business at the outset?
2. Why do you consider them important?

SUGGESTED FURTHER READING

Allen, M (2007) *How to develop and maintain quality*, Lotus Books, London

Gupta, P (2003) *Six sigma business scorecard: creating a comprehensive corporate measurement system*, McGraw-Hill, New York

Russel, R and Taylor, B (2007) *Operations management: creating value along the supply chain*, 6th edn, Wiley, New York

Phase 7

Writing up and presenting your business plan

INTRODUCTION

This section is in effect the culmination of your work to date. Inevitably everything you have been preparing should be seen as 'work in progress'. At each stage you may well have had to go back and review an earlier one. For example your mission may change in the light of market research uncovering different needs or unexpected competitors. Your marketing strategy or sales projections may in turn be modified as a result of concerns about the amount and type of money that you could realistically raise.

Now, however, all strands need to be pulled together into a coherent whole, perhaps using one of the many free business plan writer templates now available.

Writing up and presenting your business plan

Up to now, the workbook assignments have focused on gathering data needed to validate a business idea, to confirm the business team's capability to implement their chosen strategy and to quantify the resources needed in terms of 'men, machinery, money and management'. Now this information has to be assembled, collated and orchestrated into a coherent and complete written business plan aimed at a specific audience.

In this assignment we shall examine the five activities that can make this happen:

- packaging;
- layout and content;
- writing and editing;
- who to send it to;
- the oral presentation.

PACKAGING

Every product is enhanced by appropriate packaging, and a business plan is no exception. The panellists at Cranfield's enterprise programmes prefer a simple spiral binding with a plastic cover on the front and back. This makes it easy for the reader to move from section to section, and it ensures the plan will survive frequent handling. Stapled copies and leather-bound tomes are viewed as undesirable extremes.

A near-letter-quality (NLQ) printer will produce a satisfactory type finish, which, together with wide margins and double spacing, will result in a pleasing and easy-to-read document.

LAYOUT AND CONTENT

There is no such thing as a 'universal' business plan format. That being said, experience at Cranfield has taught us that certain layouts and contents have gone down better than others. These are our guidelines to producing an attractive business plan, from the investor's point of view. Not every subheading will be relevant to every type of business, but the general format should be followed, with emphasis laid as appropriate.

First, the cover should show the name of the company, its address and phone number and the date on which this version of the plan was prepared. It should confirm that this is the company's latest view on its position and financing needs. Remember that your business plan should be targeted at specific sources of finance. It's highly likely, therefore, that you will need to assemble slightly different business plans, highlighting areas of concern to lenders as opposed to investors, for example.

Second, the title page, immediately behind the front cover, should repeat the above information and also give the founder's name, address and phone number. He or she is likely to be the first point of contact and anyone reading the business plan may want to talk over some aspects of the proposal before arranging a meeting.

The executive summary

Ideally one but certainly no longer than two pages, this should follow immediately behind the title page. Writing up the executive summary is not easy but it is the most important single part of the business plan; it will probably do more to influence whether or not the plan is reviewed in its entirety than anything else you do. It can also make the reader favourably disposed towards a venture at the outset – which is no bad thing.

These two pages must explain:

- the current state of the company with respect to product/service readiness for market, trading position and past successes if already running, and key staff on board;

- the products or services to be sold and to whom they will be sold, including details on competitive advantage;

- the reasons customers need this product or service, together with some indication of market size and growth;

- the company's aims and objectives in both the short and the longer term, and an indication of the strategies to be employed in getting there;

- a summary of forecasts, sales, profits and cash-flow;

- how much money is needed, and how and when the investor or lender will benefit from providing the funds.

Obviously, the executive summary can only be written after the business plan itself has been completed. The summary below, for instance, accompanied a 20-page plan:

CASE STUDY

Pnu-clean

Pnu-clean will assemble and market an already prototyped design for a vacuum cleaner. The design work was carried out by myself and my codirector when we were at Loughborough University taking a BSc course in design and manufacture. The prototype was made during my postgraduate course in industrial design engineering at the Royal College of Art in London.

The vacuum cleaner is somewhat special. Its design, powered by compressed air, is aimed at the industrial market and fulfils a need overlooked by cleaning equipment manufacturers.

The vacuum cleaner offers to the customer an 'at-hand' machine that can be used by its employees to keep their workplace or machine clean and tidy during production. This produces a healthier and more productive environment in which to work.

It is cheaper than electrical vacuum cleaners and more versatile. It is also far less prone to blockage, which is especially important considering the types of material found in manufacturing industry.

The vacuum cleaner can be produced at low unit cost. This, together with the market price it can command for what it has to offer, will mean that only a small turnover is needed for the company to break even. However, with the prospect of a sizeable market both in this country and abroad, the company has the chance of making substantial profits.

The company will concentrate on this product for the first five years to ensure that it reaches all of its potential market and this will make a sound base from which we can either expand into other products or incorporate the manufacturing side of the product into our own capabilities.

The financial forecasts indicate that break-even will be achieved in the second year of operations, and in year 3 return on investment should be about 40 per cent. By then sales turnover will be a little over £1 million, gross profits about £400,000, and profit before tax but after financing charges around £200,000.

Our P/E ratio from year 3 will be 10 to 1, which should leave an attractive margin for any investor to exit, with comparable stock being quoted at 19 to 1.

We will need an investment of £300,000 to implement our strategy, with roughly half going into tangibles such as premises and stock, and the balance into marketing and development expenses. We are able and willing to put up £100,000. The balance we would like to fund from the sale of a share of the business – amounting to around 20 per cent.

The table of contents

After the executive summary follows a table of contents. This is the map that will guide the new reader through your business proposal and on to the 'inevitable' conclusion that they should put up the funds. If a map is obscure, muddled or even missing, then the chances are you will end up with lost or irritated readers unable to find their way around your proposal.

Each of the main sections of the business plan should be listed and the pages within that section indicated. There are two valid schools of thought on page numbering. One favours a straightforward sequential numbering of each page, 1, 2, 3 ... 9, 10 for example. This seems to us to be perfectly adequate for short, simple plans, dealing with uncomplicated issues and seeking modest levels of finance.

Most proposals should be numbered by section. In the example that follows, the section headed 'The Business and its Management' is Section 1, and the pages that follow are listed from 1.1 to 1.7 in the table of contents, so identifying each page as belonging within that specific section. This numbering method also allows you to insert new material without upsetting the entire pagination during preparation. Tables and figures should also be similarly numbered.

Individual paragraph numbering, much in favour with government and civil service departments, is considered something of an overkill in a business plan and is to be discouraged, except perhaps if you are looking for a large amount of government grant.

The table of contents in Table 25.2 shows both the layout and the content that in our experience are most in favour with financial institutions. Unsurprisingly, the terminology is similar to that used throughout the workbook. For a comprehensive explanation of what should be included under each heading, look back to the appropriate assignments, set out in Table 25.1.

Table 25.1   Using the workbook assignment data

Section in business plan	Relevant assignments
1	Assignments 1 and 2
2	Assignment 3
3	Assignments 4, 5 and 6
4	Assignments 7, 8 and 9
5	Assignment 10
6	Assignments 11, 12, 13, 14 and 15
7	Assignments 16–20
8	Assignments 21 and 22
9	Assignments 22–24

WRITING AND EDITING

You and your colleagues should write the first draft of the business plan yourselves. The niceties of grammar and style can be resolved later. Different people in your team will have been responsible for carrying out the various assignments in the workbook, and writing up the appropriate section(s) of the business plan. This information should be circulated to ensure that:

Table 25.2   Sample table of contents

5. Selling

Current Selling Method(s)	5.1
Proposed Selling Method(s)	5.2
Sales Team	5.3
In-house support	5.4

6. Manufacturing

Make or Buy Considerations	6.1
The Manufacturing Process	6.2
Facilities Needed	6.3
Equipment and Machinery Needed	6.4
Output Limitation, if any, and Scale-Up Possibilities	6.5
Engineering and Design Support	6.6
Quality Control Plans	6.7
Staffing Requirements	6.8
Sources of Supply of Key Materials	6.9

7. Forecasts and Financial Data

Summary of Performance Ratios, ROI, etc	7.1
Sales Forecasts	7.2
Assumptions Underpinning Financial Forecasts	7.3
Profit and Loss Accounts	7.4
Cash-flow Forecasts	7.5
Balance Sheets	7.6
Break-even Analysis	7.7
Sensitivity Analysis	7.8

8. Financing Requirements

Summary of Operations Prior to Financing	8.1
Current Shareholders, Loans Outstanding, etc	8.2
Funds Required and Timing	8.3
Use of Proceeds	8.4
The Deal on Offer	8.5
Anticipated Gearing and Interest Cover	8.6
Exit Routes for Investor	8.7

9. Business Controls

Financial	9.1
Sales and Marketing	9.2
Manufacturing	9.3
Other Controls	9.4

- everyone is still heading in the same direction;
- nothing important has been missed out.

A 'prospectus', such as a business plan seeking finance from investors, can have a legal status, turning any claims you may make for sales and profits (for example) into a 'contract'. Your accountant and legal adviser will be able to help you with the appropriate language that can convey your projections without giving them contractual status.

This would also be a good time to talk over the proposal with a 'friendly' banker or venture capital provider. They can give an insider's view as to the strengths and weaknesses of your proposal.

When your first draft has been revised, then comes the task of editing. Here the grammar, spelling and language must be carefully checked to ensure that your business plan is crisp, correct, clear and complete – and not too long. If writing is not your trade, once again this is an area in which to seek help. Your local college or librarian will know of someone who can produce 'attention-capturing' prose, if you yourself don't.

However much help you get with writing up your business plan, it is still just that – your plan. So, the responsibility for the final proof-reading before it goes out must rest with you. Spelling mistakes and typing errors can have a disproportionate influence on the way your business plan is received.

The other purpose of editing is to reduce the business plan to between 20 and 40 pages. However complex or sizeable the venture, outsiders won't have time to read it if it is longer – and insiders will only succeed in displaying their muddled thinking to full effect. If your plan includes volumes of data, tables, graphs, etc, refer to them in the text, but confine them to an appendix.

WHO TO SEND IT TO

Now you are ready to send out your business plan to a few carefully selected financial institutions that you know are interested in proposals such as yours.

This will involve some research into the particular interests, foibles and idiosyncrasies of the institutions themselves. If you are only interested in raising debt capital, the field is narrowed to the clearing banks for the main part. If you are looking for someone to share the risk with you, then you must review the much wider field of venture capital. Here, some institutions will only look at proposals over a certain capital sum, such as £250,000, or will only invest in certain technologies.

It is a good idea to carry out this research before the final editing of your business plan, as you should incorporate something of this knowledge into the way your business plan is presented. You may find that slightly different versions of Section 8.5, 'The deal on offer', have to be made for each different source of finance to which you send your business plan.

Do not be disheartened if the first batch of financiers you contact don't sign you up. One Cranfield enterprise programme participant had to approach 26 lending institutions, 10 of them different branches of the same organization, before getting the funds she wanted. One important piece of information she brought back from every interview was the reason for the refusal. This eventually led to a refined proposal that won through.

It is as well to remember that financial institutions are far from infallible, so you may have to widen your audience to other contacts.

Anita Roddick

Anita Roddick, the Body Shop founder, was turned down flat by the banks when she was starting up and had to raise £4,000 from a local Sussex garage owner. This, together with £4,000 of her own funds, allowed the first shop to open in Brighton. Today, there are hundreds of Body Shop outlets throughout the world. The company has a full listing on the Stock Exchange and Ms Roddick was a millionaire many times over. Before her untimely death in 2007 her personal wealth was £30 million and she controlled 1,800 shops – and one Sussex bank manager must still be feeling a little silly!

Finally, how long will it all take? This also depends on whether you are raising debt or equity, the institution you approach and the complexity of the deal on offer. A secured bank loan, for example, can take from a few days to a few weeks to arrange.

Investment from a venture capital house will rarely take less than three months to arrange, and will more usually take six or even up to nine months. Although the deal itself may be struck early on, the lawyers will pore over the detail for weeks. Every exchange of letters can add a fortnight to the wait. The 'due diligence' process in which every detail of your business plan is checked out will also take time – so this will have to be allowed for in your projections.

THE ORAL PRESENTATION

If getting someone interested in your business plan is half the battle in raising funds, the other half is the oral presentation. Any organization financing a venture will insist on seeing the team involved presenting and defending their plans – in person. They know that they are backing people every bit as much as the idea. You can be sure that any financiers you are presenting to will be well prepared. Remember that they see hundreds of proposals every year, and either have or know of investments in many different sectors of the economy. If this is not your first business venture, they may even have taken the trouble to find out something of your past financial history.

Keep these points in mind when preparing for the presentation of your business plan:

- Find out how much time you have, then rehearse your presentation beforehand. Allow at least as much time for questions as for your talk.

- Use visual aids and if possible bring and demonstrate your product or service. A video or computer-generated model is better than nothing.

- Explain your strategy in a businesslike manner, demonstrating your grasp of the competitive market forces at work. Listen to comments and criticisms carefully, avoiding a defensive attitude when you respond.

- Make your replies to questions brief and to the point. If members of the audience want more information, they can ask. This approach allows time for the many different questions that must be asked, either now or later, before an investment can proceed.

- Your goal is to create empathy between yourself and your listeners. While you may not be able to change your personality, you could take a few tips on presentation skills. Eye contact, tone of speech, enthusiasm and body language all have a part to play in making a presentation successful.

- Wearing a suit is never likely to upset anyone. Shorts and sandals could just set the wrong tone! Serious money calls for serious people.

- Be prepared. You need to have every aspect of your business plan in your head and know your way around the plan forwards, backwards and sideways! You never know when the chance to present may occur. It's as well to have a 5, 10 and 20 minute presentation ready to run at a moment's notice.

SOME FINAL MATTERS

Four other topics to consider are:

- how to prepare for spontaneous opportunities to discuss your business ideas, when a written document or a full-scale presentation is neither possible or appropriate;

- how to ensure the security of your business concept once in the hands of outsiders;

- what outside advisers to take on board;

- to what extent business plan software can help you write your plan.

The elevator pitch

Often the person you are pitching your proposal to is short of time. As a rough rule of thumb, the closer you get to an individual with the power to make decisions, the less time you will get to make your pitch. So you need to have a short presentation to hand that can be made in any circumstance – in a plane, at an airport or between floors in a lift, hence the name 'elevator pitch'.

CASE STUDY

Lara Morgan

Lara Morgan, founder of Pacific Direct, the hotel toiletries supplier, had come a long way from the garage in Bedford, England, where she started up her business, when she had the opportunity to pitch for a strategic alliance with one of the most influential players in her market. The scene was set for her to make a relaxed pitch over coffee at the Dorchester Hotel in Park Lane, when at a moment's notice the situation changed dramatically. Lara was told that due to a diary change she had 15 minutes in a chauffeur-driven limousine en route to Harrods to make her proposition.

She was prepared, made her presentation and secured a deal that was instrumental in creating Pacific's unique 5* hotel strategy. Pacific now has Penhaligons, Elemis, Ermenegildo Zegna, Nina Campbell, Floris, The White Company and Natural Products in its world-class product portfolio.

Non-disclosure agreements (NDAs)

If you are going to show or discuss your business plan with business partners and it contains confidential information on your business or on the development of a unique idea, you should consider getting them to sign an NDA. NDAs are confidentiality agreements that bind recipients to maintain your 'secrets' and not to take any action that could damage the value of any 'secret'.

This means that they can't share the information with anyone else or act on the idea themselves, for a period of time at least. NDAs are a helpful way of getting advice and help while protecting you from someone using your information to compete against you. Business Link (www.businesslink. gov.uk>Exploit your ideas>Protecting your intellectual property>Non-disclosure agreements) provides more information on this subject as well as a weblink to a free sample NDA.

Taking professional advice

There is a tendency towards secrecy amongst innovators, and those starting new ventures are no exception to this rule. However with an NDA in place there is no reason not to take outside advice, and indeed every reason to do so. Anyone reading your business plan will draw comfort from the fact that they are not the first, and that your ideas have been honed on the wisdom and experience of others.

In fact the more qualified, experienced and prestigious your advisers, the more their input will enhance your business plan, in the eyes of the reader. After all, rather than being the untested ideas of one or two people, they have been validated by professionals. If an accountant has looked over the figures, a lawyer the intellectual property rights, an engineer your prototype design and a software consultant your website plans, then real value will have been added to your proposition.

If you know or have access to people with a successful track record in your area of business who have time on their hands, you can invite them to help. The Appendix lists organizations that may have people able and willing to help. If you plan to trade as a limited company (see Assignment 2) you can ask them to be a director, without specific executive responsibilities beyond being on hand to offer advice. Check out organizations such as Venture Investment Partners (www.ventureip.co.uk) and the Independent Director Initiative (www.independentdirector.co.uk), a joint venture between Ernst & Young and the Institute of Directors, for information on tracking down the right non-executive director for your business.

Using business planning software

There are a number of free software packages that will help you through the process of writing your business plan. The ones listed below include some useful resources, spreadsheets and tips that may speed up the process, but are not substitutes for finding out the basic facts about your market, customers and competitors.

- BizPlanit.Com (www.bizplanit.com/free.html) has free resources including free business plan information, advice, articles, links and resources, and a free monthly newsletter, the *Virtual Business Plan* to pinpoint information.

- Bplans.com (www.bplans.com) created by Palo Alto Software, offers thousands of pages of free sample plans, planning tools, and expert advice to help you start and run your business. Its site has 60 free sample business plans on it and its software package, Business Plan Pro, has these plans plus a further 140. The sample business plans are tailored for every type of business from aircraft rental to wedding gowns.

- Royal Bank of Canada (www.royalbank.com/sme/index.html) has a wide range of useful help for entrepreneurs as well as its business plan writer package and three sample business plans.

WORKSHEET FOR ASSIGNMENT 25: WRITING UP AND PRESENTING YOUR BUSINESS PLAN

1. Who do you propose to send your business plan to first, and why have you chosen them?
2. Write a first draft of your business plan along the lines recommended.
3. Who can help you to edit and rewrite the final version of your plan?
4. Prepare and rehearse a presentation of your business plan.
5. Who aside from your team can you enlist to advise on your business plan?

SUGGESTED FURTHER READING

Ciampa, D (2006) *Taking advice*, Harvard Business School Press, Boston, Mass

Harvard Business School Press (2007) *Giving presentations*, Harvard Business School, Boston, Mass

Harvard Business School Press (2007) *Writing for business*, Harvard Business School, Boston, Mass

Appendix

Sources of business help information and advice – UK and international

These are the principal sources of help and advice for anyone starting a new venture. Other important sources have been provided directly in the relevant chapters throughout the book.

UNITED KINGDOM

ACCA (www.accaglobal.com>Public Interest>Technical Activities>Subject Areas>Small Business>Start-Ups>Start-up factsheets) is a link to this major accounting bodies' free factsheets, all 34 of them, on every aspect of starting a business including recruiting, advertising, grants, setting up an office, researching your market and effective selling.

The Asian Business Association (www.abauk.org; tel: 0161 615 5034) is a membership association costing £100 a year to join. Its 700 members sponsor training, lobby government and act as a networking resource for their community.

Black Business Association (www.bbassoc.org.uk; tel: 0121 260 0515) focuses on the issues of business and entrepreneurship in the African Caribbean community. Annual fees are £150.

British Association of Women Entrepreneurs (www.bawe-uk.org>Net working>Organisation Links; tel: 01786 446044) costs £175 for the joining fee and one year's membership. This link is to a free directory of international women's entrepreneurs' associations.

The British Library Business Information Service (www.bl.uk/services/ information/business.html) holds one of the most comprehensive collections of business information in the United Kingdom. Business information sources published in the United Kingdom are collected as comprehensively as possible; sources published elsewhere are taken selectively. It aims to cover the manufacturing, wholesale trading, retailing and distribution aspects of major industries and the following service sectors: financial services, energy, environment, transport, and food and drink.

BSI (www.bsi-global.com>Standards & Publications >How we can help you >Business>Small businesses) provide information and resources to help small business introduce quality standards such as ISO 9000.

Business Link (www.businesslink.gov.uk; tel: 0845 600 9 006) has a network of regional offices delivering tailored help, advice, training, grants, international trade and consultancy to small business. The website has hundreds of articles on every aspect of starting, growing and selling a business, dozens of online tools for such activities as writing business plans, benchmarking, carrying out market research, and links to thousands of other sources of information and advice. Scottish Enterprise (www.scottish-enterprise.com; tel: 0141 228 2000), The Business Eye (www.businesseye. org.uk; tel: 08457 96 97 98) and Invest Northern Ireland (www.investni.com) deliver similar services in the other countries of the United Kingdom.

Cobweb (www.cobwebinfo.com) is a specialist provider of information services for businesses, their advisers and other professional intermediaries. Its content is of particular benefit to new-start and small/medium enterprises. The production team continually researches, creates, updates and publishes a practical and authoritative range of business titles, subjects and products.

The knowledge base provides a blend of when, how, where and why content subjects covering thousands of business topics and types, market sectors, regulations, sources of business funding, advice, expertise, contacts and much more.

Directory of British Associations (www.cbdresearch.com/DBA.htm) lists over 7,000 associations, pressure groups, unions, institutes, societies and more, which are profiled, representing every interest area from abrasives through to zoos, from industrial, professional and business sectors to government, charities and the consumer, price £215.

e-Business Clubs (www.ebusinessclubs.co.uk) is a free service delivered through British Chambers of Commerce aimed at small businesses, offering access to a range of activities including events, ICT support and information from business experts. The start line 'How Technology can Improve Business performance' explains the central purpose of the clubs.

Enterprisenation.com (www.enterprisenation.com) founded in 2006 aimed primarily at homework ventures: the site has dozens of podcasts and links to help would-be business starters get underway.

Every Woman (www.everywoman.co.uk>Your Business; tel: 0870 746 1800) is a free service, registration required, giving access to over 30,000 like-minded women who are serious about business. The site has plenty of advice, tips, factsheets and online tools to help business starters.

The Federation of Small Businesses (www.fsb.org.uk; tel: 01253 336000) offers legal, environmental, fire and premises tips, as well as many other issues that the small businessperson may have to address as he/she grows. The Federation has the resources to take major test cases of importance to small businesses through the expensive legal process, and has been particularly effective in dealing with taxation and employment matters. Amongst the benefits on offer are access to in-house solicitors, barristers and tax experts and providing legal and taxation advice lines, including litigation and representation services. Membership is on a sliding scale dependent on number of employees, starting at c.£150.

First Tuesday (www.firsttuesday.co.uk) has 38,000 members with 10 branches across Europe, and hosts networking meetings on the first Tuesday of every month. The idea is to bring entrepreneurs, investors and service providers such as accountants, lawyers and bankers, together to create a 'circle of friends' that can help technology entrepreneurs get started or grow. It costs £30 to attend an event (£10 for early booking) or £190 to attend four seminars and four receptions.

The Forum of Private Business (www.fpb.org; tel:01565 634467) is a membership organization costing c.£150 to join, giving you information on tap when you need and management tools to help your business stay within the law – as you complete, you comply, covering employment, health and safety, bank finance and credit control.

Gateway 2 investment (www.g2i.org>About us>In this website>The Signposting Wizard) is a service provided by a consortium including Grant Thornton, which helps innovative companies find specific resources, including finance.

Homeworking.com (www.homeworking.com), started in 1999, is a resource rather than a job directory, and is full of useful tips and helpful warnings about the thousands of scam businesses on offer to would be homeworkers.

The Institute of Directors (www.iod.com; tel: 020 7766 8888) is the club for directors, membership of which costs £285 a year. For that you get access to a prestigious central London office and other offices around the United Kingdom and on the Continent, business information and research provided for you by the IoD's expert researchers and bespoke business advice on tax and law. It is also considered one of the best networking associations for entrepreneurs.

Lexis-Nexis (www.lexis-nexis.com) has literally dozens of databases covering every sector you can think of, but most useful for entrepreneurs researching competitors is Company Analyzer, which creates comprehensive company reports drawn from 36 separate sources, with up to 250 documents per source. So when you get tired of scouring different databases to find out all there is to know about a competitor, customer or supplier, you could consider using Company Analyzer to access legal, business, financial and public records sources with a single search. Company Analyzer provides access to accurate information about parent and subsidiary companies and their directors, to highlight potential conflicts of interest.

LibrarySpot.com (www.libraryspot.com)is a free virtual library resource centre for just about anyone exploring the web for valuable research information. Forbes.com selected LibrarySpot.com as the Best Reference Site on the web and *USA Today* described it as 'an awesome online library'.

The Market Research Society (www.mrs.org.uk) is the world's largest professional body for individuals employed in market research or with an interest in it. Founded in 1946, it has over 8,000 members working in most organizations currently undertaking market research in the United Kingdom and overseas.

National Federation of Enterprise Agencies (www.nfea.com; tel: 01234 345055). There are some 250 enterprise agencies in the United Kingdom which deliver business support services and directly or indirectly provide advice and information, counselling and training on a comprehensive range of business issues, to all types of owner-managed businesses including pre-starts, start-up, sole traders, partnerships, cooperatives and limited companies. NFA maintains a directory of English agencies on its website and links to enterprise agency networks in Northern Ireland, Scotland and Wales.

The National Statistics (www.statistics.gov.uk) website contains a vast range of official UK statistics and information about statistics, which can be accessed and downloaded free. There are 13 separate themes. Each one deals with a distinct and easily recognizable area of national life. So whether you are looking to access the very latest statistics on the UK economy, or research and survey information released by the government, or want to study popular trends and facts, click on one of these themes and explore!

NewsDirectory (www.newsd.com) is a guide to all online English-language media. This free directory of newspapers, magazines, television stations, colleges, visitor bureaux, governmental agencies and more can help you get to where you want to go, or find sites you didn't know about. It is a simple and fast site that can be used to access all the news and information that you can handle.

123 World.com (www.123world.com/libraries) claims to be the ultimate source of authentic and reliable information about the library resources of the world on the Net. Using 123world.com you can find out about all the libraries in your vicinity or anywhere else in the world. Its list of libraries includes public libraries, research libraries, state libraries, national archives, libraries of different educational institutions, agricultural and technical libraries, business libraries, science libraries and many other specialist libraries. The listing also provides helpful information about various libraries. The links in this directory will guide you to the official sites of the libraries that you are looking for, in alphabetical order.

The PRIME Initiative (www.primeinitiative.org.uk; tel: 0208 765 7833) claims to be the only national organization dedicated to helping people aged over 50 to set up in business. It has all the usual material on starting a business on its site, but has an emphasis on the issues older people will face such as dealing with tax credits and pensions.

The Princes Trust (www.princes-trust.org.uk; tel: 0800 842 842) runs business programmes and provides low interest loans for people aged 18–30 who want to start a business.

The Telework Association (www.tca.org.uk; tel: 0800 616008) costs from £34 a year to join its 7,000 other members who either work or are running a business from home. You get a bi-monthly magazine, a teleworking handbook with ideas for telebusinesses, and access to its help line covering all aspects of working from home.

UK Trade & Investment (www.uktradeinvest.gov.uk) is the government agency charged with helping UK-based businesses succeed in 'an increasingly global world'. It provides information on doing business with every country and every business sector from aerospace to water.

OVERSEAS AGENCIES

Australia: Invest Australia (www.investaustralia.gov.au) is the central information source for foreign investors. business.gov.au (www.business.gov.au>How-to guides) provides information, advice and contact points for all aspects of thinking about starting, starting, or setting up a business.

Canada: Canadian Federation of Independent Business (www.cfib.ca) represents the interests of over 105,000 owner managers across the whole of Canada. Industry Canada (www.ic.gc.ca>Resources For>Businesses>Start-up, Incorporation and Support) is the Canadian government's support agency responsible for all aspects of business and local support. Its Business Start-Up Assistant (http://bsa.canadabusiness.ca) is a one-stop source for all the information needed to start a business in Canada.

China: Invest in China (www.fdi.gov.cn>Opportunities>Intent for Inbound Investment) is an interesting subsite on this government website giving you the opportunity to state your interests and also to see who else is currently planning to come into China. BIZMATCHING (www.bizmatching.mofcom. gov.cn) is a site that sets out to put in contact sellers and customers for various products and services.

Cyprus: Ministry of Commerce Industry and Tourism (www.mcit.gov. cy>English>Industrial Development Service>One Stop Shop for Setting up a Business) has all the information on starting, running and accessing finance for a new or small business.

Developing Countries: the International Finance Corporation (www. ifc.org), a member of the World Bank Group, provides advice, loans and equity to help foster entrepreneurship in the developing countries.

Europe: European Commission Portal for SMEs (www.ec.europa. eu>Enterprise and Industry>Promoting Entrepreneurship>SME Portal) is the entry point to access all the European Union's schemes to help small businesses and to a range of business tools and advice. There are direct links to a network of over 300 Euro Info Centres, 236 Innovation Relay Centres, 160 Business Incubation Centres and Your Europe – Business, a site with practical information on doing business in another country within the European Union.

France: Agence Pour la Création d'Entreprise (www.apce.com>To set up a business; tel: 01 42 18 58 58) is the French small business service. The website is in English with advice and pointers on every aspect of starting and running a business.

Hong Kong: Hong Kong Trade Development Council (www.tdctrade. com>Small Business Resources) is a comprehensive resource for information, tips, seminars, events and online forums aimed at the small business community. Its customized business matching service (Premier Connect) extends its services into mainland China.

India: Indian Government National Portal (http://india.gov.in>Business> Starting a Business) covers all the regulatory issues about getting a business off the ground, hiring staff and raising money. The Ministry of Micro, Small and Medium Enterprises (http://msme.gov.in>Programmes and Schemes) takes you to the site with details of all the schemes operating in India to help and stimulate new business development.

Ireland: Irish Small and Medium Enterprise Association (www.isme. ie) offers a comprehensive range of advisory services and training and development for new and small businesses. The Department of Enterprise, Trade and Employment (www.entemp.ie>Start Your Own Business) is the government department responsible for initiative to help entrepreneurs start a business in Ireland.

Italy: the Italian Institute for Foreign Trade (www.italtrade.com) is the government agency that advises on information about the market, and gives help and advice with starting a business in Italy. By using the 'Your Business Proposals' facility you can search for a compatible Italian business partner.

New Zealand: Ministry of Economic Development (www.med.govt. nz>doing Business in New Zealand; tel: +64 4 472 0030) is the agency responsible for ensuring that New Zealand is one of the best places in the world to do business in.

Malta: Malta Enterprise (www.maltaenterprise.com) is a government site with information on inward investment, enterprise support and innovation and enterprise.

Portugal: Agencia de Inovaçao (www.adi.pt; tel: 351 21 721 09 10) is the agency that supports innovative businesses in Portugal. The 'Useful Links' section connects to other useful organizations including 'Invest in Portugal' and 'Portugal in Business'.

South Africa: the Small Enterprise Development Agency (www.seda. org.za) is the South African Department of Trade and Industry's agency for supporting small business. The site has all the information needed to start a business, find partners and access local regional support agencies throughout South Africa.

Spain: Invest in Spain (www.interes.org>Investor Services), created only in 2005 as part of the State Department for Tourism and Trade in the Ministry of Industry, Tourism and Trade, is the point of contact for all state, regional and local institutions helping businesses set up or expand into Spain.

Turkey: the Turkish British Chamber of Commerce and Industry (www. tbcci.org>Trade Services>Starting Your Business) has all the information on starting a business in Turkey. Use the 'Business Partner Search' link in the 'Trade Services' box where you can state the type of business and relationship you are looking for and so find a partner in Turkey.

United States: Small Business Administration (www.sba.gov; tel: 800 827 5722) provides financial, technical and management assistance to help Americans start, run, and grow their businesses. The website has a large quantity of information and business tools of value to businesses starters anywhere. Also BUY USA (www.buyusa.gov>Do you export U.S. products or services) is the website of the US Department of Commerce from which you can select any country you want to do business in. Though aimed at

US businesses the information is of value to anyone planning to start or grow a business anywhere in the world.

World: the World Intellectual Property Organization (www.wipo.int> Programme Activities>Small and Medium Sized Enterprises) has a range of advisory resources to help small businesses utilize intellectual property effectively anywhere in the world.

Overseas government statistics

Most countries have their own government sites for national statistics data. Below are listed some of the main sites, which in turn have links to other sources of general statistical data.

http://stats.bls.gov/. Site of the US Bureau of Labor Statistics, this contains lots of statistical material on the US economy and labour force.

http://www.insee.fr/va/keyfigur/index.htm. French National Statistics Organization.

http://www.statistik-bund.de/e_home.htm. German National Statistics Organization.

http://petra.istat.it/. Italian National Statistics Organization.

http://europa.eu.int/en/comm/eurostat/serven/part6/6theme.htm. Site of Eurostat, which is the statistical organization of the European Communities.

gopher://gopher.undp.org:70/11/ungophers/popin/wdtrends. United Nations world population figures.

Index